July 2000

For Julie — a small gift
from my garden bookshelf —
Hope you enjoy! These kinds of books
are fun to read in our gloomy winters)!

Joe Ingraham

THE COUNTRY GARDENER

THE COUNTRY GARDENER

PENELOPE HOBHOUSE

LITTLE, BROWN AND COMPANY · BOSTON TORONTO LONDON

This illustrated edition was edited and designed
by Frances Lincoln Limited, Apollo Works, 5 Charlton Kings Road,
London NW5 2SB.

Library of Congress Catalog Card Number 89-45618

1 3 5 7 9 8 6 4 2

Published simultaneously in Canada
by Little, Brown & Company (Canada) Limited

Printed and bound in Italy by Amilcare Pizzi

AUTHOR'S ACKNOWLEDGMENTS

I am very grateful to Frances Lincoln and her team – Erica Hunningher,
Penny David and Caroline Hillier – for their work on this book. The
photographers, particularly Steven Wooster and Andrew Lawson, have
contributed their skills to making it beautiful. After seven years of comparative neglect, in 1987 the garden at Hadspen was rescued by the
Canadian gardeners, Nori and Sandra Pope. Through their efforts, and
thanks to my son Neil who made it possible, Hadspen is a garden again and
flourishes under their care. I am indebted to Tony Lord for correcting and
bringing up to date all the plant names and for compiling the index.

PHOTOGRAPHIC ACKNOWLEDGMENTS

Linda Burgess/INSIGHT: 152; Geoff Dann: © FLL 41, 111; Derek Fell:
121; The Garden Picture Library/Clive Boursnell: 134; John Glover:
133; Jerry Harpur: 3 (Mirabel Osler); Marijke Heuff/Amsterdam: 11, 47,
52, 58 (Mr and Mrs Dekker); Jacqui Hurst: © FLL 7, 12, 15, 49, 60,
138, © FLL reproduced by permission of The National Trust and The
Knightshayes Garden Trust 10, 43, © JH 57, 69; Andrew Lawson: 17,
21, 26, 29, 33, 37, 39, 45, 65, 71, 92, 93, 98, 103, 117, 123, 125, 128,
131, 132, 141, 143, 145, 148, 151, 154, 157, 158, 163; Hazel le Rougetel/
Biofotos: 142; Georges Lévêque: 34, 96, © FLL 115; Tony Lord: 48, 95,
99, 161; S&O Mathews Photography: 1, 63, 67, 91, 107, 109, 146;
Natural Image/Liz Gibbons: 56, /Bob Gibbons: 68, 127, /Robin
Fletcher: 72, 76, 84, 155; Photos Horticultural/Michael Warren: 118,
136, 147; Steven Wooster: © FLL 9, 18, 25, 27, 30, 50, 55, 74, 77, 81,
82, 87, 100, 104, jacket front and back, © SW 78, 85, 112.

CONTENTS

PREFACE TO THE NEW EDITION

WHEN *The Country Gardener* was written, more than twelve years ago, it summed up and expressed most of my gardening experience and my philosophy on design and style. The book was written from the heart and I still fundamentally agree with what I felt then.

The approach I advocate was partly dictated by the practical situation in which I was then placed, with a neglected seven-acre garden to restore and afterwards manage with very little help. It was also determined by the fact that when you know less it is possible to see fundamental truths more clearly. In those days I felt more certain of which garden styles and even which plants I liked (or disliked); with increased knowledge in both spheres it is more difficult to see 'the wood for the trees'. In the process of learning one becomes more tolerant and more appreciative of different soil and climatic situations in other gardens. It was easy to dismiss or ignore certain types of plant because they had not come into one's own range of experience. I still cannot write authoritatively about many ericaceous plants but I have studied their culture and appreciate the garden styles which they evoke. I have been lucky to write books which have encouraged me to research general history and design. I have travelled more, and although I was already enriched by having seen the classical gardens of Italy and France, I have more recently had the opportunity to learn a great deal about the challenge of American gardening. In America a convincing 'national' style is emerging. Less obviously derived from classical European precedent, this new natural approach has a refreshing emphasis on regional native flora. It is readily adaptable to the wide range of climatic extremes throughout the country. Visits to America are very stimulating, and I learn about a whole new range of plant material as well as ways to use more traditional plants. This doesn't make *The Country Gardener* irrelevant today. In it I was feeling my way towards a very similar approach.

I have changed my practical point of view very little since I wrote the book, although I have had to learn and work in a much higher maintenance programme. At Tintinhull, where I have looked after a formal compartmental garden for the National Trust for the last eight years, all has to be immaculate. A great many shrubs and groundcover plants were grown to smother weeds at Hadspen, whereas the details of distinct colour schemes and effects are mostly achieved at Tintinhull by non-woody plants, which certainly need more individual attention. Nevertheless basic pruning, weeding and feeding are still the seasonal priorities; the extra tasks for which there was no time at Hadspen mostly involve division of perennials and growing and planting of annuals to enrich the flower beds in summer. At Hadspen it was possible to collect plants (and plant names) for their own sakes, but each plant at Tintinhull is chosen for its contribution to predetermined themes. This is an excellent discipline and applies to all types of gardening. On the other hand it is much more limiting and I do miss the romantic charm of the wilder garden and the opportunities to experiment with new plants. In *The Country Gardener* I was writing about a series of experiments both with plants new to me and with horticultural techniques; I was certainly feeling my way. Since then I have learned that formal gardening is easier than 'wild' gardening; success in the former depends on following and perfectly executing rules, in the latter it depends on aesthetic and horticultural judgements which give a constant and exciting challenge. I hope in *The Country Gardener* I convey some of this excitement.

Although Tintinhull is primarily a 'colour' orientated garden and flowers play an important part, I still believe, as I did at Hadspen, that leaf shapes, textures and colours have a more enduring role in overall garden effects. At Tintinhull the flower schemes are set off by yew and box hedges and green lawns; in winter the horizontal and vertical 'greens' hold the garden design together. At Hadspen with fewer evergreen hedges but many more trees the design was dependent on tree and shrub structure as well as foliage. I was very fortunate to garden first at Hadspen and initially to attempt writing about that experience. By having to concentrate on the less gaudy aspects of gardening I believe I became more aware of the importance of detail. At the end of the last century, nearly one hundred years ago, Gertrude Jekyll, with her strained myopic sight, learned to see and feel plants and then write about them with an awareness seldom reached by others. She remains an influence on all my garden thoughts.

Although I feel so much more experienced and am more tolerant about design and plants, I am hopelessly prejudiced about the definition of 'good' or 'bad' gardens. In this sense I fully endorse everything I say in *The Country Gardener* — some gardens work; others don't. Today I am probably better equipped to analyse my instinctive reactions but they remain much the same. In the 1970s I probably did not sufficiently appreciate the importance of what I now call 'appropriate' planting. I chose plants for situations in which I thought they would thrive but I was not completely aware of the nuances of plant association. Now I am more likely to see plants in terms of their natural habitats and this will strongly influence where I place them. Even in the 1970s I remember feeling that a garden should fit into its surrounding landscape: Gertrude Jekyll had made me aware of this aspect of gardening. She recommended planting indigenous trees and shrubs (in her case hollies and junipers of her native Surrey) near the perimeter of the garden so that it should seem to merge imperceptibly into the countryside.

The garden at Tintinhull is wonderful; if it has a fault it depends too much on self-conscious perfection. One day I hope to have a romantic garden again; it will be small and

At Tintinhull House a pair of junipers flanks the steps leading to the pool garden. The pink rose, 'Nathalie Nypels', is underplanted with catmint, Nepeta nervosa; both, if regularly dead-headed, flower from June until October.

practical and it must contain some structural elements such as walls and hedges, which both at Hadspen and at Tintinhull help give garden structure and are an essential part of my gardening philosophy. But my new garden must also stir the heart by its overflowing profusion of free planting, which by disguising the formal structure, approaches a conception of a personal paradise. *The Country Gardener* expressed my search for that particular vision and the garden at Hadspen was my interpretation of it.

For this new edition I have avoided making major revisions. Although I would now perhaps include different topics – and certainly some different plants – I have confined myself largely to correcting errors and to bringing the text up to date to take account of changes in horticultural techniques, recommended herbicides and plant nomenclature.

I would like to dedicate this new edition to those who now garden at Hadspen and to those who will garden there in the future.

Penelope Hobhouse
Tintinhull House December 1988

INTRODUCTION

THE THEME AND scheme of this book stress the importance of planning or re-planning a garden for future ease and economy of maintenance, without losing along the way too much of 'the plantsman's' interest in the more beautiful and rarer plants. Not only trees and shrubs, but also plenty of herbaceous perennials and biennials, can give value and quality to the garden by contributing exciting foliage colours and textures which associate well with each other.

Although many of the suggestions have been tried out in my own garden, I have made use of associations of plants which I have seen during my frequent visits to other gardens, both great and small. Often an outstandingly successful arrangement of plants, or of plants and stonework on grass, or even of plants used themselves as architectural features, cannot be exactly repeated owing to differences in soil, aspect and climate between districts. But a similar visual impression can be conveyed by the use of suitable alternative plant material.

Much of the book describes parts of the garden here at Hadspen and personal taste and preference dominate each section. Many plants equally suitable for a particular purpose and aspect have not been mentioned simply because they do not interest me. On the other hand, knowing the soil and climate limitations here in Somerset I have included suggestions for ranges of calcifuge plants which seek conditions with pH well below our range of 6.5 to 7. By intention, as the subject is so vast, no mention has been made of the *Rhododendron* or *Camellia* genera, not because I do not admire them but through lack of space in the book and a lack of personal experience of working with them.

My garden is on a south-facing slope, warm and sheltered from the north and east, and contains within it areas of real micro-climates, allowing a wide choice of plants. I have an opportunity to experiment with tender shrubs, particularly evergreens from the southern hemisphere, which makes it possible to have a garden with good all-the-year-round interest without having to use annuals and the sort of herbaceous perennials which need frequent dividing and cosseting, for which we do not have the necessary labour.

The garden is about seven acres, and when we came here in 1968 had been very much neglected since the outbreak of war in 1939. Chapter 2 describes how the scheme of reclamation was tackled. It was essential for us here literally to cover the ground to minimize the maintenance costs and to eliminate the need to mow difficult pockets of grass or make a frequent change of plants. Upkeep has now become a routine matter of checking for seedling weeds, cutting the grass, and pruning trees or shrubs when necessary. Chapter 3 describes how the planting schemes were developed to achieve this.

One of our greatest advantages has been the fact that the garden was remade in Edwardian times, by my husband's grandmother, who designed and planted with skill and wisdom, and whose basic arrangement has given us the architectural bones. And we now have mature trees which give form to the whole. She added a new landscape section to the earlier more formal garden and carved terraces and steps out of parkland, which at one time reached – in the eighteenth-century landscape garden tradition – up to the front windows. She took advantage of the exciting plant discoveries being made in the Far East during the period she was redesigning and many trees and some shrubs of her choice have survived. The greatest single difference today is that whereas she had six gardeners we now have one, and have had to rationalize management inside that context.

Texture and colour of foliage, and the varying ways in which light and shade affect individual leaves, have come to interest me basically more than flowers. At the same time, at certain periods of the year the flowers become focal points in the garden and are an additional bonus. Leaves, bark, and the skeleton form of deciduous trees and shrubs in winter, cover all the seasons and are therefore the permanent architectural features of the garden, while separate flowering plants dominate it, or sections of it, for shorter periods. Without doubt, taste and preference become adapted to existing circumstances. All my planning is done on a permanent basis, although naturally plenty of replacement cuttings and seed are taken annually, especially of the more tender plants.

As far as this book is concerned, it has been necessary to omit many plants or types of plants, and those sections of the garden which could be called specialist ones. Among the omissions rhododendrons and camellias have already been

The view from the Peach Walk at Hadspen looking across the lily pond to the new border below where moisture-loving plants are tightly packed to save weeding. Frost drains quickly down the slopes at this top end of the garden.

mentioned, but to them can be added alpines, bulbs, water-plants, grasses and bamboos. Alpines need care and conditions outside the scope of a book on general ornamental gardening. Bulbs I would have liked to include and in particular those which naturalize in grass, but having separate beds and positions for them is another specialist activity. Water-gardens, grasses and bamboos need a book to themselves, if this were possible, and although they do affect the overall design and character of any garden, they are not a necessary part of every one. Roses, as a genus, are described only when they are grown as shrubs, and contribute in foliage, fruit and structure, as well as in flowers and scent, and even then only my own favourites can be included, with particular emphasis on those which are relatively free of disease. The growing of the modern bedding rose seems to me to be another specialist activity, all too frequently attempted with less than satisfactory results by the more casual gardener.

Besides these there are obvious gaps; but some, such as heathers and brooms, are intentional since I derive no pleasure from them. Many herbaceous perennials which I love have been left out as they are not inside the theme of the book, although we do grow some here for extra enjoyment, even if they are time-consuming subjects.

The genus *Hosta* is treated briefly considering its general foliage and flower value for every size of garden. We are very fortunate to have Eric Smith, from the Plantsmen Nursery, working in the garden here now, and he has brought with him many interesting species and hybrids of *Hosta*. This will give me an opportunity to learn more about them.

Annuals have had to be ignored, in the book as in our garden, as there is no labour available for anything except permanent planting; although of course, in the early days of the reclaiming period they could be used to give colour and interest in areas where the ground was not sufficiently clean, and to fill in gaps of bare earth while we waited for the other plants to grow together.

It is hard to know to whom to be most grateful – the gardeners of the past who, by their creations and designs, have constantly stimulated interest, the writers of all books on garden design, or the many kind friends who originally gave me help and guidance in learning to garden, even in such a limited way, and more recently have listened to my constant queries and problems. My first instructors were John and Faith Raven, when I began to struggle with a terraced cottage garden, and they have been constant advisers ever since. When we moved here Margery Fish was still alive and gave me moral support and many stimulating ideas, and her

Above *In the woodland at Knightshayes Court in Devon white foxgloves (the ordinary purple* Digitalis purpurea *were eliminated by years of careful weeding) glow in the shade. They flower in midsummer when the rhododendrons and azaleas are over.*

Right *At Hadspen alliums, columbines, catmint, white-flowered* Cerastium tomentosum *and pink* Cistus *'Silver Pink' are clustered together in one of the sunny borders south of the upper pond.*

books have been an invaluable source of reference, particularly for herbaceous plants and how to use them. Our generation of gardeners has been influenced by the style of gardening at Hidcote and at Sissinghurst, but two other gardens have repeatedly given me new and exciting ideas, and plants and cuttings from them have helped me to make mine a more interesting garden too. John Hussey, the gardener at Abbotsbury in Dorset, had similar problems of reclamation in an old and botanically interesting coastal garden, and both the original planting there and his new schemes have

been a source of inspiration. The late Sir John Heathcote Amory and Lady Amory have made one of the great modern gardens of England at Knightshayes near Tiverton, and in their kindness and generosity to me have contributed more ideas than has any other single garden or gardeners.

As far as books are concerned, apart from those by Margery Fish, Alice Coats has written two delightful books on the history of flowers and shrubs, and much of what I have learnt of the individual history of plants has come from these and not from the original sources. Works by Christopher Lloyd, Graham Stuart Thomas and John Raven have become my bedside reading, and Hillier's *Manual of Trees and Shrubs* and the Royal Horticultural Society *Dictionary of Gardening* have been my books of reference. Beyond this I have become absorbed in books on garden history such as those by Miles Hadfield, and on garden design by such authors as Sylvia Crowe and John Claudius Loudon. Gertrude Jekyll produced ideas we use today quite unconsciously and without attribution, and it is only on reading her books

that I have come to appreciate the extent of her influence, especially on the planning of borders for flower and leaf colour harmonies, and to see how many of her favourite plants are popular today.

I would like to thank John Calmann, and his parents, who also garden in Somerset, and who have constantly encouraged me with the book and my garden. From them I have repeatedly asked and received advice. I can hardly forbear from mentioning my own family, who have suffered over many years from my obsessive gardening and, more recently, have patiently endured neglect for the sake of the book.

Finally I am greatly indebted to John Raven and Diana Phelan who have both spent many hours on the manuscript correcting botanical, grammatical and stylistic errors, and I can never express sufficiently strongly my appreciation to them for undertaking this task.

Penelope Hobhouse
Hadspen House 1976

Chapter 1
THE IDEAL GARDEN

Most of us, as gardeners, tend to develop some interest of a specialist nature. There are always certain types of plants, such as roses, alpines, trees, shrubs, perennials or annuals, which have for each of us a particular charm. The professional landscape architect, on the other hand, can sometimes seem to be preoccupied with the use of space and its relationship to the house and to the surrounding landscape, at the expense of any individuality of plant selection.

The complete gardener must reconcile these two approaches and create a picture which satisfies both the plantsman and the planner. Whatever our circumstances and whatever the size of our garden we want to effect the best disposition of all our resources and available space to produce what is, to each of us, the ideal.

Whether we are involved in designing and planting a cottage garden, or are attempting to landscape a park, we should try to decide what constitutes our aim. The garden must be as visually perfect as we can make it but we must not forget that it should also be a source of constant pleasure and its upkeep therefore must not become a struggle for survival. Achievement of beauty alone is not worth the overstraining of physical strength or financial resources and we should cut our cloth according to our means. Limited labour and limited income now make it necessary for us to practise less costly ways of gardening than those of some of our predecessors, even if we have the same area to maintain. Our planting schemes, after an initial period for establishment, should be designed to save maintenance costs and effort. Within that context we can please ourselves as to our specialist enthusiasms.

The ideal garden is one in which a collection of trees, shrubs and plants have been procured and allotted to the best space available and are so arranged and tended that they are seen to their advantage, each in relation to the other. Every plant, of whatever shape or size, should be chosen not only

for its individual merits but for its power to enhance the charms of neighbouring plants by contrast or combination in foliage or in flower colour. The style of gardening should be in keeping with the architecture of the house and the life style of its inhabitants as well as with the other purposes for which the garden is required.

A garden is to be enjoyed, and should satisfy the mind and not only the eye of the beholder. Sounds such as the rustle of bamboo and the dripping of water, scents and sensations such as grass or gravel or stone underfoot, appeal to the emotions and play a part in the total impression. The eighteenth-century view of the garden was that it should lead the observer to the enjoyment of the aesthetic sentiments of regularity and order, proportion, colour and utility, and, furthermore, be capable of arousing feelings of grandeur, gaiety, sadness, wildness, domesticity, surprise and secrecy. Today we gain additional pleasure from the nostalgia of the past which can be conjured up by some aspect of a garden.

For those of us faced with the task of designing or redesigning a garden it would be helpful to possess something of the eye of the landscape painter with regard to composition, something of the science of the architect in the use of forms, and sufficient botanical and horticultural knowledge to ensure the growth and cultivation of the chosen plants from their early life in the garden to their maturity. In the past it was possible, and indeed usual, to create the architectural outlines of a formal garden – as opposed to a landscape garden – with stone walls and steps. These materials formed the straight lines and rigid forms of the garden while the plants themselves, as the living material, provided the furniture and irregular shapes. An example of a partnership in architectural and garden design is that of Edwin Lutyens and Gertrude Jekyll. In her sense of colour harmonies and use of foliage plants Miss Jekyll paved the way for modern types of mixed border gardening, but the success of her plant associations depended on a structural framework. Although today a new garden can be dug and shaped in a matter of hours by a mechanical digger, the average owner cannot spend the huge sums required on skilled stonemasons. Therefore the plants themselves become an even more integral part of the structure of the design. Where stone walls would have been

At East Lambrook a winding stone path focused on a variegated dogwood (Cornus controversa 'Variegata') is edged with luxuriant mixed planting of roses and perennials to give an almost jungle effect. Even 'natural' gardens must provide evidence of the gardener's skill in plant arrangement.

built, now rigid frameworks can be created by hedging plants, and banks can be clothed by trailing evergreens. In old gardens faulty stonework can be covered up by the living material, which may prop up an old wall or at least blur the broken edges of walls and steps. Plants have always been used to break up rigid lines, now they can also conceal their absence or disintegration.

If we could choose the ideal situation for a garden in the British Isles, however great or small the site may be, the house and the garden would be sheltered from the north-west, north and north-east, if possible by a natural range of hills but alternatively by suitable plantations of wind-resistant trees. For good frost-drainage the garden should be on a slope, or in a series of descending terraces which adds interest to a design. A basin between two projecting arms on the side of a hill would be very snug. Gardens situated in valleys or on the lower edge of a slope are vulnerable to frost which always rolls downwards; late-spring frosts can be particularly damaging to young shoots.

Each part of the garden will have a micro-climate of its own, depending on its aspect and on shelter from prevailing winds.

The house, if on a slope, could have some form of platform connecting it architecturally to the garden plan. The vegetable garden can be to the north-east of the house and take the same advantages of aspect, without interfering with either the view from the house over the garden, or the view from the house or garden to the landscape beyond.

If there is a distant view from the house it can be framed by planting schemes, rather than interrupted by miscellaneous trees, shrubs or flower beds. In the past many expanses of lawn have been disfigured by beds, either placed wrongly or cut in shapes, thus spoiling a coherent plan for the garden. Properly conceived carpet beds in geometric or symmetric forms for flat areas are effective, and today, with modern methods of upkeep, are less labour-intensive than informal 'free' styles. Undulating surfaces and changes of direction can be incorporated in the more natural style of garden which also makes use of flowing plant lines and shapes.

Leaving aside for the moment the question of the labour required to clip hedges, there is no doubt that the lines imposed on the gardener by the existence of enclosed areas make experiments with colour and foliage schemes much easier. The actual plants used as furniture in these separate 'rooms' should have a style or theme in common. The method of planting, which can be what we call mixed borders of small trees, shrubs, herbaceous plants and bulbs, has an absence of rigidity in design.

There are three English gardens – the second two partly derived from the first – which have had more influence on modern gardening than the flowing lines of the traditional landscape gardens. Hidcote in Gloucestershire, Sissinghurst in Kent, and on a smaller scale Tintinhull in Somerset, all have compartments which are symmetrical and devoted to certain colour schemes, or types of plants. At the same time, and particularly at Hidcote, the landscape beyond, framed in various vistas, has become part of the garden, in a true eighteenth-century sense.

The area inside these separate compartments can be used for specialized plants, or can be designed for maximum ease of upkeep with plants that smother the ground and seldom need pruning, dividing or replacing. The formal outline of the surrounding hedge or wall must be kept immaculately, even if additional interest is given by using flowering shrubs for hedge material.

Similarly, grass edges which join on to a gravel path or bed need to be kept well-trimmed, and where possible stone flags or bricks should be set just below the grass level so that the mowing machine can come right to the edges. Low-growing woody shrubs can be allowed to overhang the edges if an air cushion type of mowing machine is used as this can be swung beneath without damage to the plant. Evergreen herbaceous perennials which are sufficiently vigorous not to mind being mown at the edges can also be used and the contrast of grass with the other material makes a definite line.

Formality can be maintained inside enclosed areas by a symmetry of border design in shape or colour, even while using plants in more modern and labour-saving arrangements to help cut down on unnecessary work. Stone flags or bricks can be used as edging to beds and borders instead of grass, which needs time-consuming trimming. We can use schemes of permanent mixed planting of trees, shrubs and herbaceous plants that give visual satisfaction all the year round and eliminate the need to bed out half-hardy annuals and biennials. In the less formal part of the garden it is possible to keep the essence of the English or Romantic landscape, but to underplant the trees and larger shrubs with vigorous small dense ground-smothering shrubs or perennials, which require little maintenance and seldom need

The Raworths' garden in Twickenham is divided by hedges into a series of garden rooms which linked together make the garden seem much larger than it is. Hedges of beech and Thuja plicata make a perfect background for mixed flower planting. Roses, tall Crambe cordifolia, penstemon, Nepeta 'Six Hills Giant' and Geranium 'Johnson's Blue' frame an elegant white seat.

either pruning or division. Patches of difficult grass can be replaced by evergreen perennials or shrubs. One can introduce variety as much by contrasting heights of mown grass as by elaborate planting schemes.

No garden, great or small, should be seen all at one glance; barriers of some kind can be maintained or introduced to give some elements of surprise and secrecy to a garden tour. Each part, however, should lead naturally to another and this can be done by the repetition of a planting scheme or simply by paths of gravel or stone, or better, by extending a narrow section of lawn into another area. It is most effective to leave a tightly mown lawn as uncluttered as possible, but if space permits the lawn can lead on towards smaller hidden glades at the side, where different types of planting arrangements may be used. In a large garden these glades could be set in light woodland and devoted to cool white or yellow flowers or, if one has acid soil, used for one genus such as rhododendrons or azaleas. The plants should be just hidden but in such a way that curiosity tempts the viewer to seek more elaborate and secret inner gardens. Often, because of various circumstances, it has to be the other way round. The areas of walls and terraces surrounding the house may be the most suitable places for detailed planting, and simplicity is then found in more distant spots. Visual contrasts can be provided without the need for beds and borders by cutting the grass at different levels. A pathway effect is achieved by close-mown lawn next to rougher grass, which not only reduces the amount of mowing throughout the year but eliminates the need for edging materials or edging work. Flat areas beside mown lawn can be filled with flat-growing evergreen plants instead of grass.

In the great 'bedding out' era of the nineteenth century the country house was occupied for only two months in the summer, so all gardening efforts were directed towards a great show of colour in July and August. This was achieved by using half-hardy annuals and biennials, and later by the herbaceous border. Although arranged in colour schemes and with great attention to heights and depths, the border was interesting only for a relatively short period of the year. Now planting schemes are for all-the-year-round effect. Winter-flowering species which are generally very fragrant are nice to have near the house and on corners, and beside paths which are frequented even in cold weather, but unfortunately many of these plants do not have interesting summer foliage so it is difficult to give them choice positions. Many early flowering spring shrubs, such as *Prunus*, *Forsythia* and *Chaenomeles*, are vulnerable to birds which damage their buds; in a country garden, we can compensate by growing trees and shrubs with exciting young foliage.

Some gardeners grow only one family of plants, or one genus, or even one species; others are interested only in scented flowers and aromatic leaves, or in flowers or leaves of one or two colours. Some great *Rhododendron* gardens are exciting in spring but contain few summer-flowering shrubs or plants, in spite of having admirable growing conditions to suit almost any genus except perhaps roses. At Anglesey Abbey, where there is a magnificent collection of trees, the original owner (it is now National Trust) devoted two gardens entirely to dahlias. One has a curving border of mixed colours, and the other, called 'The Hyacinth Garden', was surrounded until quite recently by a hedge of *Thuja* and entirely filled with the dahlia 'Bishop of Llandaff'. Elsewhere there is an attractive herbaceous garden planned with expert colour and foliage sense by the National Trust advisers. None of these separate parts of the garden really hangs together and there is no attempt to lead on from one to another. Those of us who are working in an old garden often have to reconcile, as does the National Trust, the requirements of aesthetic considerations with the planting traditions of one particular garden and its eccentric previous owner, and sometimes it is right to sacrifice perfection of detail in order to retain historical oddities.

I referred earlier to Hidcote and Sissinghurst. In these gardens formality has been maintained by the rigid lines of the enclosures, but the planting arrangements, using widely differing materials in each case, emphasize the modern idea that each plant has its own shape and has its own contribution to make to the whole scheme. Borders, either of harmonizing or single colours of leaf or flower, are used extensively. Straight lines have been softened by billowing and flowing individual plants or groups of plants. Shrub roses, shrubs, perennials and bulbs have been mixed to give maximum groundcover and to eliminate unnecessary weeding, while at the same time continual use is made of new varieties to fit into existing schemes. All the borders can be readily adapted to a scheme with fewer varieties of different perennials and more low-growing evergreen ones if for economic reasons cuts in labour should become necessary. If the original lines of a garden are correctly laid out the actual planting can be simplified without loss of much visual interest, although obviously the plantsman's enjoyment of variety is reduced.

The garden at Knightshayes in Devonshire has a woodland area of very different style (although of course the Hidcote enclosures are also extended into woodland glades). Here on a slope, in half-shade, all the best varieties of each

A garden scene at Vann in Surrey where marsh marigolds (Caltha palustris), Onoclea sensibilis, Iris pseudacorus bastardii, *rodgersias and wood anemone* (A. nemorosa) *grow in drifts and white cherry blossom is reflected in the water. This is the Robinsonian 'ideal'; in* The Wild Garden (*published in 1870*) *William Robinson advocated planting both native and exotic plants where they would thrive and naturalize on the edge of woodland or by the waterside.*

species have been assembled to delight the visitor in curved island beds and borders matching the contours. A perfect natural garden has been established using the greatest possible range of exotic plants. Although many rhododendrons and azaleas are present in groups, other worthwhile types of plants have not been omitted, and shrubs and woodland perennials have been massed together to create superb effects of flower and foliage combination and contrast. The plantsman's knowledge has here been combined with all the skills of the planner.

The present-day concept of permanent planting, far removed from the seasonal and ostentatious displays indulged in by the Victorians, has not been entirely dictated by financial limitation. Before the end of the nineteenth century both William Robinson and Gertrude Jekyll had become apostles of a more natural form of gardening, incorporating herbaceous plants which had been relegated to the cottage garden as more and more exotic and tender plants were introduced. Many rectory gardens, where vast displays of carpet-bedded annuals were not possible, grew new exotics beside many of the old tried favourites. Canon Ellacombe of Bitton, outside Bristol, is one of the best known of a strong team of churchmen who gardened with their own hands and with little hired help contributed considerably to the growth in knowledge and skill in horticultural matters.

Finally, just as the original Western conception of a garden was as a necessary haven from the wilderness beyond,

and resulted from a natural fear of the environment, so today we make use of the eighteenth-century idea of the garden as part of nature, but we also see it as a way of preserving nature from the depredations of an industrial society. Since the countryside is increasingly encroached upon and spoiled, the garden can become the setting for rare and exciting plants from other countries, which may be used to contrast with the indigenous ones in the landscape beyond the garden fence, and can also preserve this natural landscape by using native trees, shrubs and perennials inside the garden when they are in danger of being lost or destroyed by urban development or chemical sprays. Some gardeners have become so interested in the ecological side of horticulture that sometimes they feel it is inappropriate to use plant material that does not belong either naturally or historically to the district. Personally I do not agree with them and feel as entitled to benefit from the discovery of foreign plant material and of methods of using it as I do to make use of scientific discoveries. Our skill lies in interpreting and assessing the relative merits of the bewildering choice of garden plants and styles, and in acquiring the necessary experience to adapt the use of them to our own individual needs and possibilities.

A garden is not just a collection of plants; it is the planner's interpretation of their historical significance and their suitability, aided by the experience of the plantsman who understands the habits and requirements of the individual plant.

Chapter 2
PREPARING FOR PLANTING

NATURE SOON TAKES over if the gardener is absent. In a few years even a well-stocked garden can become a jungle of weeds and plants without shape and quality, merely a formless mass of intertwining branches. To repair the damage it is necessary to have a systematic scheme of clearance, and to keep in mind and on paper as precise an overall plan as is advisable when making a completely new garden.

In many cases existing plants can be saved, particularly mature trees which are already playing their role in giving form, light and shade, and those shrubs which either respond to pruning and shaping, or can be temporarily removed to a nursery bed. Herbaceous perennials or biennials which have become overrun with herbaceous or woody weeds must first have all soil cleaned from their roots and then be put aside for later use. Ornamental plants which have seeded or spread beyond desirable bounds should be treated as ruthlessly as are the generally accepted weeds; the only difficulty is in deciding if they are worth keeping for later use.

Whatever size the garden, whether it is old and neglected or a bare field, the initial clearance and preparation before planting, including consideration of the condition of the soil, is as important for the future as the design and plan. My own experience has been gained from working in a garden of some seven acres, where my purpose was to save existing ornamental plants, and to restock, using only plants and designs and schemes of planting which would make maintenance possible with a little help. Basic planning rules which *can* apply to all gardens *must* apply here. Short cuts and inadequate weed clearance only lead to much extra work later, and no amount of skill in design or in plantsmanship can compensate for inadequate initial preparation.

After ten years of learning to garden in a cottage atmosphere, where I was able to indulge a growing interest in tender wall plants and evergreen shrubs, often at the expense

of coherent design, in 1968 I moved to Hadspen where I was faced with the task of reclaiming and replanting an old and much neglected garden. It contained the vestiges of historical lines of demarcation between different inner gardens, which reflected the contemporary taste in design and plants and schemes of planting of their separate periods. It seemed that I would have to learn to rationalize and simplify, without destroying the original relationship between these parts of the garden and the house and its occupants.

I knew it was important to interpret the existing architectural features, whether in building or in plant material, in terms of what the original designer intended. Then, having established these criteria in my mind and on paper, I had somehow to adapt what I had learned and re-create balance and proportion where they had grown out of step after years of neglect. I had to be ruthless when untended plants had grown beyond a desirable size, and I had to conserve, by reshaping and pruning, wherever possible. Perennial weeds had multiplied to such an extent that anything herbaceous had been smothered, and even vigorous shrubs found it hard to survive the strangulation of bindweed and bryony. On top of this there was the problem of the shortage and high cost of labour; the certainty that in the future one man would have to maintain an area, after reclamation and replanting, which in the past had been looked after by six gardeners.

Much of the garden was overgrown, and brambles, ground elder, bindweed and bryony were rioting among the many valuable and interesting trees and shrubs. It was difficult at first to see the general layout and to decide which plants were worth preserving. Some had grown beyond their prime or through neglect had grown out of shape, or were so entangled in these weeds that they could not be saved. Others, particularly the remaining herbaceous perennials, could be dug up and planted in a clean corner for future use. There were many excellent hostas, *Acanthus, Epimedium* and periwinkles which could be saved in this way, but several beds and borders had become ill-kept extensions of the lawn.

We were very fortunate in having old photographs and records which could show us the changes made in Edwardian times. We were even more fortunate in that these had been made by someone interested in general garden design and in

From the Peach Walk at Hadspen, the view reaches out into the countryside beyond the garden. Planting in the foreground is framed by older trees and shrubs growing at a lower level. In the border are mauve-flowered Erysimum linifolium, Phlox *'Chattahoochee' and* Geranium sylvaticum *'Mayflower' with silver-leaved stachys.*

the new ideas of natural gardening as recommended by William Robinson and Gertrude Jekyll.

New plans were made closely following the original schemes of the Edwardian period, when much of the garden was made from pasture round the house, and taking care to minimize the need for time-consuming upkeep of neat edges.

In the initial stages of clearance chemicals were extensively used to extirpate perennial weeds without doing long-term damage to the soil, and the garden was gradually replanted and restocked. The policy was to clean and plant up each area separately, starting with the area nearest to the house before continuing to the next section. This method resulted in considerable economies in plant purchases, since plants already established could be divided and increased for use as each new area was ready for replanting. Cuttings could be taken and rooted from shrubs and trees which had been put in quite recently in the beds already cleared, or from the valuable and interesting shrubs and trees which already existed. Cuttings acquired from the gardens of friends had time to reach a sufficient size before planting out, and spreading herbaceous plants could be given temporary homes in a clean area and moved as the next section was cleared and prepared for planting.

The two overriding considerations were to re-create the correct proportions in the garden, and to reduce future maintenance costs and effort to a minimum. After these requirements were met I was able to indulge my preferences for different genera. It was important, however, to ensure that an excessive interest in individual plants did not mar the overall balance of the design, for insufficient massing of groups can destroy the coherence of the visual scheme.

By using flat evergreen shrubs or herbaceous plants in place of grass where mowing was difficult and edging essential, I considerably lessened the costs of upkeep. Weed-smothering plants are massed in beds under shrubs and trees using one species on a large scale to unite the planting area, just as a lawn can unite different parts of the garden, and as underplanting can link trees and shrubs. In the outer garden larger shrubs are used, massed in a similar way, where they not only suppress weeds but, since they are planted in great groups, also benefit the general form of the garden. We now keep a rectangular piece of rough grass, surrounded by neatly kept lawn, which is filled not only with spring bulbs, but also with the orchids and cowslips from the neighbouring fields and woods which are threatened with extinction because of agricultural or forestry spraying. We cannot mow until August, when the orchids have seeded, but by surrounding this area with straight lines we have made it look purposeful

and not just shaggy. After August we have to keep it very tightly mown to discourage the growth of vigorous grasses.

For the more formal beds, which are emphasized by straight lines, mixed plantings of trees, shrubs, herbaceous perennials and biennials give all-the-year-round interest by a concentration on foliage contrasts and textures rather than on the actual flowers. This does not mean that there is no colour; on the contrary it makes it possible to have borders of colour harmony which continue even beyond the desirable flowering periods, as the leaves also play their important role in colour combinations and contrasts. Each feature of the plant is considered: shape, hardiness, foliage colour and texture, flower and fruit, as well as its ability to enhance a planting scheme by association with its neighbour.

I have gained many ideas from planting schemes seen in other gardens. Even if, owing to difference in soil, aspect or temperature, these schemes cannot be exactly repeated in our own garden, it is possible to absorb the visual impression and to create a similar effect by the use of alternative plant materials. The keynote to success in planting is not just to put the plant in the right place in relation to every other plant, but to place it where it will thrive. Some knowledge of the needs of individual plants or their genera is necessary before deciding on a scheme which is visually acceptable.

The site itself needs to be studied and carefully considered: the type of soil and fertility, the aspect and temperature ranges, shelter, the incidence of frost pockets, and finally the amount of annual rainfall, drainage and the possibility of drought. We cannot grow calcifuge plants from the damp forests of America or Asia if we have a stiff clay soil and much lime content, or a garden on shallow chalk. It is possible to compensate for certain deficiencies in the soil by adding appropriate chemicals or fertilizers, but in the long term, and especially with deep-rooting plants, it is better to grow only those that thrive in the natural conditions which we can offer. This does not mean that we should leave unimproved a soil which has had its balance upset or is starved of basic necessities, but to grow plants unsuitable to the site is seldom a success.

The soil

Before preparing to plant, it is important to understand some very simple aspects of soil analysis, construction and needs, as plants vary widely in their reaction to different soils.

First, there is the question of measuring the relative acidity or alkalinity, or what is often referred to as the 'sourness' or 'sweetness' of the soil. This is determined by a rather obscure formula of measurement known as the pH factor. It

*The meadow area at Hadspen
where mown grass paths outline
the beds of wild flowers. Tulips
and fritillaries, cranesbill*

*geraniums and native spotted
and bee orchids thrive in the
grass which is never cut until
August.*

is a symbol of the measurement of relative acidity and alkalinity, rather than a straightforward arithmetic scale. A pH of 7 indicates a neutral soil and the acidity increases as the numbers decrease. In the British Isles the range is roughly from a pH of 4 to 8.5, but in other parts of the world there can be a range of from 3.5 in peaty swamps to as much as 10 in the desert soils of arid alkaline regions. For most plants the best pH is around 5 to 7 (we have 6 to 7 in the garden here, but with quite considerable variations in some parts).

Plants from a low pH area which will thrive only in a pH of 4.5 to 5.5 include nearly all rhododendrons and azaleas, others of the *Ericaceae* family, and camellias. Basically these are all bog-loving plants. In the course of thousands of years the rain has washed the alkaline chemical elements such as calcium, sodium and potassium away from these areas, leaving a residue of acidic elements. It is possible to increase the pH by adding limestone at a rate which depends not only on the pH, but also on the texture of the soil which controls the use, or conversion for use, of the limestone. It is much more difficult to change an alkaline soil permanently into the acid condition which suits these plants since there will be continual leaching from surrounding lime areas.

The soil is the living quarters of the roots of all plants, and its texture, or workability, as well as the actual food materials which it makes available to the plant, need to be considered. Soil itself consists of mineral elements, vegetable or organic matter – which is turned into humus by the action of teeming hordes of insects and earthworms, as well as fungi and bacteria – and of air and water. The roots of many plants do not penetrate beyond the area of topsoil where the microbes are busiest. If you make what is called a soil 'profile' you will discover successive horizontal layers of varying colour and texture. The topsoil is most likely to be acid in content as it receives the rainfall first, and the lime and other nutrients are washed away. It is therefore possible for a topsoil over chalk or limestone to have a fairly high acid content, or low pH scale. On steep slopes the topsoil is often thin, and on the site of a new garden the topsoil may be covered by excavated sub-soil or removed or destroyed. This sub-soil is generally paler in colour and contains more clay or fine particles which are compacted and almost impenetrable to plant roots. Further below these two layers is the original geological formation and its texture will affect the drainage of water. If the soil is shallow above impermeable rock, which does not allow free drainage, then the roots of some plants may be permanently resting in water.

In an old garden the soil has been cultivated for many years and, with the constant addition of humus-forming organic manure, has become friable and easily workable. The organic matter is of animal or vegetable origin and has many functions in the soil. The humus is a colloidal material which holds together particles of sand, clay or grit through its moisture-retaining properties; it is not a substance which can simply be added to the soil but is formed by the action of the microbe population in the topsoil on the organic material, including most materials which are used for mulches.

The soil texture created does not itself provide all the essential nutrients for plant survival, but it provides the conditions whereby plants can best take advantage of the minerals and the air and water which are needed in varying proportions. The texture of the soil can be divided into three main groups: coarse, medium and fine.

The coarse is mainly composed of sand and loamy soil which is easy to work with, easy to cultivate after rain and, because of its looseness in texture, quick to warm up in the spring. On the other hand, the plant nutrients are easily washed away, it dries out quickly and needs heavy manuring and mulching to prevent the evaporation of moisture and to provide the essential moisture-holding humus in the soil.

At the other extreme is the cold clay soil which is formed of tiny fine soil particles which compact badly and make working extremely difficult. In this garden clay predominates although we are fortunate in having beds where many years of garden cultivation have counteracted the worst features of these conditions. When clay soil is wet it becomes sticky like plasticine; when it is dry it is apt to turn into solid concrete-like blocks. If trodden on when sticky it can be so compressed that its structure can be damaged for a whole season. It is slow to drain and slow to warm up in the spring. Plenty of organic matter must be added, and in low-lying areas some sort of drainage should be provided.

The third category of soil texture is every gardener's dream. It contains a natural mixture of sand, silt and clay in well-balanced proportions which make it very easy to work with, and provide the perfect conditions in which plants can most readily absorb their essential foods.

In between these categories of soil conditions there is a widely varying range, and in each individual garden there will be some variations, depending on previous use, existence of trees, mortar from buildings, and so on.

Finally, and basically, soil contains mineral elements of which the principal three are nitrogen, phosphorus and potassium. Nitrogen stimulates vegetative growth; phosphorus stimulates root development and the formation of flowers and fruit; potassium has a balancing effect which helps to combat disease and is particularly good for stimulating flowering. If necessary they can be added to the soil as chemicals in crystalline, pellet or granular form. They are marked nitrogen (N), phosphorus (as the pentoxide P_2O_5) and potassium (as the oxide K_2O, which contains 48 per cent potassium). A simple test can be made which will give an exact indication of any deficiencies in the balance of these minerals in any part of the garden. Unfortunately, although the test will indicate the intensity of the nutrients it cannot measure the capacity of the soil to make them available to the plants, or the rate at which these nutrients are released or renewed.

In a balanced chemical fertilizer the ratio of these three basic elements is generally called the NPK ratio, and they can be added to the soil in small quantities, just at the start of the growing season in early spring. These are, of course, only the main nutrients; there are many others which are essential for plant growth but are needed in very small quantities. Their presence or absence can be detected by analysis, or by skilled observation of the plant foliage. For instance, chlorosis in leaves of plants on chalk soils is usually due to iron or magnesium deficiency, while a nitrogen deficiency causes leaves to turn a sickly and lustreless colour.

Before discussing the importance of organic matter, it should be said that many people prefer to use organic fertilizers instead of chemical ones; these are usually in the form of dried blood, hoof and horn, or bonemeal, and are all good sources of nitrogen. (Bonemeal also contains a high percentage of phosphorus, but does not contain potash or contribute to the improvement of the soil structure.) Their rate of release of the nitrogen is slower and more balanced, and they contain more of the other trace elements required.

Organic matter is most commonly provided in the form of decomposed animal and vegetable material. When this is broken down by the earthworms the nitrogen becomes available to the plants. At the same time, the worms leave aeration channels, which make it easier for the roots to penetrate the soil, and provide channels down which water can run and be absorbed. Much water would otherwise be lost by remaining on the surface or by being drained off by the inclination of the slope. There are, or should be, about one million earthworms in an acre of soil surface, all of which can tunnel at least 1.5-1.8m/5-6ft and bring about profound structural changes in the soil. Nitrogen supplied in this way comes in a steady supply rather than in a heavy dose, which stimulates excessive growth.

Organic matter comes in various forms: plant remains and leaves which fall on the soil; a compost of large quantities of plant refuse, which involves hard work and is necessary only where farmyard manure is not available; peat and leaf-mould, which are excellent moisture-retainers, although peat itself contains no nutrients, while the leaf-mould contains those of the original plant or trees from which it has been gathered; and farmyard manure, which if well-made not only adds the important organic matter to the soil but also contains a balanced amount of fertilizer. Well-made cow manure contains a nutrient ratio of approximately 5:1:5 in the NPK scale, which is close to the ratio in which these important nutrients are required by all plants. The other trace elements come through the food material of the animals, and pass through the digestive system. Well-rotted manure is easiest to use, but if left in a loose heap and uncovered much of the nutrient material will be washed away; on the other hand, when used as a mulch fresh manure can burn the growing plants and, by removing all available nitrogen from the soil, can also starve them.

Using a good organic mulch helps to improve the structure of the soil and to feed it. It also helps to prevent the soil drying out in hot weather; but the soil should contain plenty of moisture when the mulch is applied, and any extra chemical or organic fertilizers should be added earlier. A winter mulch, besides protecting tender plants by raising the temperature around them and keeping the soil warm as the cold weather arrives, also benefits and keeps warm the industrious earthworm, which is at its busiest in autumn and spring.

Generally, plants have adapted themselves and their nutrient requirements to their natural habitats, so one should be able to ascertain the needs of every individual tree, shrub or herbaceous plant by finding out what would have been available to them in their normal environment. This imposes certain restrictions on the gardener in the selection of plants but that, to most of us, is a welcome form of control in so far as it helps us to make an appropriate choice.

Before the structure of the garden is complete and the plants are in their permanent homes, remember to provide adequate water facilities. If you want really moist conditions in any particular area it is possible to bury a perforated hose, which will ensure an even supply. Similarly if you have an area of the garden permanently in a swamp-like condition, it is worth laying land drains, unless you wish to grow only those plants which are happy to have their roots standing in water. Trees like the swamp cypress, *Taxodium distichum*, and moisture-loving bamboos and non-woody perennials are suitable too, but some plants, such as the Japanese iris, *Iris ensata*, which need water during the growing period, resent standing in water during the winter months.

Weed control
Before clearing and preparing the ground, decide on the best system of weed control. There are four methods: hoeing, digging and cultivating; heavy mulches for weakening and controlling the perennial weeds; using a complete cover of black polythene for at least a whole growing season (two for ground elder, creeping buttercup and bindweed); and chemical weedkillers, which, if used correctly, do what is required of them with the minimum number of applications and with the minimum damage to the structure of the soil. In nearly every garden, old or new, none of these methods will be sufficient on its own, but if all are used judiciously and if the planting afterwards is wise and selective, the problems of future maintenance are much reduced.

The ground can be dug by hand or by mechanical digger, and as many weed-roots as possible removed as the work proceeds. Some weeds, unfortunately, multiply when their roots are broken so this method, besides being very costly, may also need to be repeated almost every year. A hoe can be used to cut off shoots of perennial weeds as they appear – which will seriously weaken them and will discourage germination of annual weed seedlings.

Thick mulches of farmyard manure (which itself contains many seeds of annual weeds which have passed through the digestive system of the animals), leaf-mould, sawdust or shavings, mushroom compost (after sterilization), spent hops, peat, and any kind of decayed vegetable matter which has been turned into garden compost can be used. Besides their nutrient value these different mulches all help either to smother emergent weeds or, when the weeds come to the soil surface, to make them easier to pull out by hand. The mulch, as well as controlling the weeds, also helps to keep the soil warm in winter and cool and moist in summer, and acts as a humus-forming conditioner as the earthworms pull it into the topsoil. Later, the leaves of growing plants will mass together to act as a mulch, and as the leaves fall they will feed the soil and return to it the nutrients they extracted in growth. By itself mulching is successful only in very lightly infested areas, but it is particularly useful under established shrubs and around the stems of trees.

Whole areas of the garden can be sheeted with black polythene, which prevents any growth and can be left for a period of six growing months or even a year. Woody shrubs can be planted in holes made in the polythene and the sheeting will act as a mulch to keep the soil warm and moist. It is not an attractive practice but is a useful alternative to chemical sprays, and can be cheaper. I used it with great success to cover a part of our garden entirely infested with ground elder, creeping buttercup and the large white-flowered bindweed. It was less effective when used to smother mare's tail in another area, possibly because it was left for only six months while the stems which form chlorophyll were above ground, and I had not realized that the strange cones which appear in the spring spread spores on the soil which develop into new plants later. At the same time, the running roots are at such a depth that they can emerge with new shoots the following season, or perhaps even later. A contact herbicide, paraquat, controls their increase, but I try not to hand weed as a broken root is stimulated to make more growth.

There are two kinds of chemical weedkiller. Contact herbicides destroy only the plants whose green leaves they actually touch, leaving the soil virtually uncontaminated. Systemic weedkillers work either through the system of the plant and are applied to the leaves, or they act in the soil to sterilize either a few centimetres/inches or a greater depth, and can do damage to the structure of the soil which will last for a few years but will do a total kill of all living and growing material. Nowadays, a complete 'kill' of deep-rooting weeds is most easily obtained by using glyphosate, a translocated herbicide which acts through contact with the leaf of a weed but passes to other parts of the plant. In Great Britain it is available as Tumbleweed (or Round-up for commercial use).

At Hadspen I used contact weedkiller in the form of paraquat or a paraquat-diquat mixture, which is effective for all plants except persistent woody-stemmed ones which need a systemic to destroy the plant finally and prevent more shoots. Some form of brushwood killer, such as 2,4-D, can be used for this, preferably one which is sufficiently selective to cope with seedlings or brambles and nettles in grass, but will not be absorbed by the smooth surface of the grass leaf. Elder bushes can be cut down, and if treated with a strong solution of 2,4-D, the stump will not shoot again. For large stumps of trees which have to be felled this is also effective,

but certain old stumps become the breeding ground of Honey Fungus, and should be removed if it is possible.

The weedkillers which are applied to the soil are best kept for sensible use on paths and drives, but one such as simazine, which prevents germination of annual weed seedlings only in the top few inches of the soil, can be used around established shrubs if there is no underplanting of herbaceous soft-stemmed plants with shallow roots. Personally I prefer to use paraquat more frequently rather than resort to a method of soil sterilization.

A sensible idea is to give paths and drives a mixture of paraquat, which will kill all the plants with broad green leaves which it touches, and simazine, which lasts for six months in the surface of the soil. If this is done in early spring it should be effective for the year.

When clearing badly infested areas at Hadspen I used these methods in the following order. After clearing the undergrowth to ground level I waited for the plants to shoot again, and then sprayed for a summer season using paraquat or a mixture of contact and systemic herbicides according to the type of weed present. I sprayed at three-weekly intervals (depending obviously on the amount of rain and heat stimulating growth that season); others find that waiting for greater leaf-growth before re-applying the herbicide is more effective, but I prefer my method as I dislike looking at the weeds. Next step is to dig the ground to a spade's depth, removing old weed roots which may still cause trouble in the future; then apply a thick mulch; and finally in the following spring more mulch, and spot-spraying with paraquat – use a spray with a fine nozzle so that no damage can be done to plants already in the bed and avoid windy days. The spraying deals with any perennial weed remaining and kills off the annual seedlings.

No herbaceous plants should be put in the first year, but shrubs with woody stems can be safely added to those already there. Some stems of young trees and shrubs are also susceptible to the contact spray so great care must be taken; it is also possible to damage overhead leaves by the strong fumes given off by weedkillers on very hot days.

Eventually, in a garden the size of ours, the plants act as weed-suppressing mulches, and the foliage plays the most important role in preventing weed germination. The leaves

The foliage of ferns and glossy-leaved acanthus (Acanthus mollis latifolius) grows together to discourage the germination of weed seedlings, much reducing the time spent on the routine tasks of garden maintenance. In the garden at Hadspen there is no bare earth.

having grown together, there is no room for mulches but balanced organic or chemical fertilizers can be added by hand in spring as maximum growth begins.

At whatever season of the year you start in a new garden, it is worth remembering that the time to attack unwanted plants is from spring to autumn. It is no use deluding yourself that by clearing and digging what looks like clean earth in the winter you will have solved the problems, and if you plant too soon, especially with herbaceous perennials, you cannot use the sprays, and you cannot unravel the weed roots from the new plants without digging them up again.

The giant knotweeds, *Reynoutria sachalinenis* and *R. japonica*, which are attractive in a rough outlying area, are hopelessly invasive and destructive in beds or borders. It has taken me six to seven years to conquer them. In retrospect I think this might have been an occasion for using a complete soil sterilizer such as sodium chlorate or atrazine, which will penetrate deep enough to kill the roots. I have used a hoe continually, as well as paraquat, and sometimes brushwood killer, on the shoots as they spring up, and in the end this has been satisfactory.

The ordinary bamboo *Arundinaria japonica* (now correctly *Pseudosasa japonica*) grew here in an area where it was not possible to use a mechanical digger, but after two seasons of cutting down, spraying the leaves with paraquat, and at intervals dropping a 2,4-D solution down the hollow stalk, it could be finally dug out.

Alchemilla mollis, *Eryngium giganteum* and *Tellima* can seed too freely while *Ajuga*, *Symphytum* and periwinkles spread by runners and have to be restrained like the most common of them, the creeping buttercup – but these are the problems which inevitably arise from growing plants in the conditions in which they thrive. Certainly the most time-consuming task in this garden now is curbing desirable but invasive plants rather than dealing with the common weeds.

Planning

I think it is worthwhile trying, from an amateur's point of view, to establish some of the guidelines along which a trained designer works. Even if we are fortunate enough to obtain the advice of a professional, it is still helpful to be able to interpret his ideas in simpler language.

A first step in planning is to make a two-dimensional drawing of the existing space, including within it all the trees, shrubs and other plants already there. Between each point is a measurable distance, but a third dimension is introduced, as much by the living plant material as by the architectural features of buildings, terraces, balustrading,

walls and steps. In a new garden there may be only the mass of the house itself to consider. The living material varies in colour, shape, depth and texture; it also grows each year in unequal proportions. The area of planting below the horizontal lines of a wall or of hedging plants is not part of the original three-dimensional plan for the overall design; later it becomes of importance as each bed, border or enclosure is given its furniture.

Specimen trees which may already be in existence help to ensure shade and shelter but should also balance with the architecture of the house and adjacent or distant buildings. Geometric and symmetric beds, sometimes in formal patterns, stress the important relationship between horizontal planting and other, man-made, horizontal materials which together balance with higher building masses, trees and hedges. Without this balance of form the garden may become just a series of disconnected planting arrangements.

Apart from their use for structural purposes, trees and shrubs are important in the plan of the garden as shade givers, as shelter from wind and even from noise. When preparing a planting scheme for a bed or border, remember that the area over which a tree will cast its shadow will influence the choice of plants. If an area is surrounded by a hedge or wall or cut off at the end by a shade-making screen or windbreak, then it may not be possible to use a theme which depends on each part having similar and regular amounts of light and sunshine. These will vary with the time of day if the shade-giving barrier is anywhere except on the north side of the garden or planting area. A large leafy deciduous broadheaded tree will have quite a different effect on the plants beneath it from that of an evergreen, or of a wall or thick

Left *The spreading silver leaves of the globe artichoke (Cynara scolymus) are a foil to the dark flowers of tulip 'Black Parrot'. Later in the summer 2m/6ft stems bear the edible thistle-like flower heads. Most silver-leaved plants thrive in full sun in well-drained soil.*

Right *A purple-leaved form of the smoke bush,* Cotinus coggygria, *grows in the Peach Walk at Hadspen and provides a background to the paler foliage of a variegated fuchsia. Most purple and bronze leaves best retain their colours when grown in full sun.*

solid hedge. Certain trees cast just the right amount of dappled shade to give excellent growing conditions for many plants. Full sun, even in a temperate climate, is not such a necessary or desirable asset as was once thought, and some protection from the hottest and brightest rays, besides giving visual delight by the constant movement of light and shadow, also changes the colours and textures of leaves.

The appearance of green leaves varies enormously depending on the amount of light they receive and golden and silver variegated foliage are at their best when grown in partial shade. Plants that come from a hot climate, or from above the tree line, have leathery or hairy surfaces to lessen the outgo of water. Those with thin hard leaves generally have extra protection from strong aromatic oils. The grey-leaved plants appear to look so intensely grey or silver because of their many tiny hairs which protect the surface of the leaf. All these hot-climate plants are naturally at their best in full sun. Similarly, plants whose natural habitat is the rainforest tend to have smooth drooping leaves for shedding excessive rain, and need a site with plenty of moisture.

Purple foliage is apt to turn bronze or green in shade, and is at its most effective and translucent in sunshine.

All plants in their native habitat are wild flowers and it is their respective merits as individual specimens as well as their value as plants in association with others of different foliage, flowers or habits, that earn them a place in any planned scheme. Native plants should be used as frequently as those we think of as more exotic foreigners, if they are the best choice for any particular site. A plant which tends to spread and multiply at such a rate that it overtakes and eventually harms the growth of other slower and more delicate growers could also be called a weed – even if it is an extremely desirable garden plant. Some of these desirable garden plants spread by underground roots or stems, or by forming mats or clumps on the surface of the soil or by producing roots along their stems. Others seed prolifically and can quickly take over large areas if the conditions suit them. The choice and use of the correct plant, or groups of one particular plant, and their disposition in the garden are of primary importance today when there is generally only one gardener – namely oneself – to do all the work.

The choice of plants now available to us is so large and bewildering that we can none of us, even in the largest gardens, hope to do justice to more than a carefully selected few. Experience will help guide us to a suitable choice but it is worth remembering that the massing and grouping of a few species, rather than concentrating on individual specimens, produces a much more satisfying result. These suggestions are also applicable to the making of a completely new garden, where one may be faced with the stark reality of creating something out of a bare and exposed field, or worse still out of the builders' rubble and the unpromising sub-soil from below the foundations of a new house. We must study the aspect of the site and the condition and needs of the soil besides the actual planting schemes. However great the problems, we all wish to make the optimum use of the skill and experience, both in design and in horticultural knowledge, of the great gardeners of the past, and to combine this with a modern approach to garden landscaping and a modern attitude to the shortage and high cost of labour. Even if we have the means, it is now difficult to find skilled help.

The larger the garden with which we each have to deal, the greater the expenditure of money and time needed to correct initial mistakes in planning, or in my case, replanning. In a small garden the errors can be more speedily corrected, and with less effort, but the placing and choice of each individual plant is even more important. In both large and small gardens it is essential to weigh the desire to make a collection of favourite plants against the expense of appropriate attention to their arrangement and the problems of their maintenance in the future. It is also important to bear in mind other uses which the area may have. The practical must be balanced against the impractical in every individual case and the garden must have a consistency in its design so that it can be appreciated as a whole and not just as a collection of unrelated parts.

There should be some features which connect areas of a garden, and help to lead from one part to another. It is worth making a study of plant forms and shapes; indeed one should keep at hand a list with diagrams. There needs to be unity of design without monotony; this may be achieved by correct placing of contrasting or harmonizing shapes, and later by repetition using similar plant forms but different genera or species.

Plants should be suited to the soil condition and climate; provision can be made for future increase in size by adequate pruning and thinning and one must remember that plants alter their relationship to each other as they grow, and can thus destroy the proportions of the whole design. The professional, as well as the amateur who usually lives with his garden from its earliest stages, has to bear in mind that a scheme which needs ten, twenty, or more years to mature, should, in the intervening period, be capable of giving visual satisfaction to the casual observer.

While waiting for trees and shrubs to grow, or to reach the desired and optimum state of growth in proportion to each other and to the whole, it may be helpful to have a short-term plan, in order to avoid bare patches and a general air of emptiness and lack of form in the interim. In a large garden these temporary gaps may be filled in by quick-growing but short-lived shrubs, and in a smaller area annuals and biennials might be used. As long as they are not too vigorous, young plants can be packed fairly closely together, so that they will not only give immediate interest, but will afford one another some measure of shade and shelter in their earliest stages. There is nothing simpler than transplanting, at a judicious moment, those plants which have outlived their original purpose. It is little work compared to weeding and mulching large empty areas, and the plants that remain, as the thinning-out process is completed, are all the better for the protection they received while settling-in.

There are many useful foliage plants which have a limited life in terms of value of form, but which give initial body to any planting scheme. It is exactly the same principle as that used in large-scale forestry, and all that is necessary is vigilance and knowing the correct moment for transplanting –

In general, at Hadspen, good foliage is considered more immediately important than seasonal flower decoration; trees, shrubs and perennials are initially chosen for the shape, colour and texture of their leaves. A row of old yew trees provides a sombre background to modern planting of trees and shrubs which grow so closely together that the leaves shade the ground and prevent weeds germinating.

that is before plants have begun to jostle each other and before the consequent risk of permanent damage to their ultimate shapes. If the plants being moved are for another site obviously only those with suitable roots or habits of growth capable of surviving disturbance can be planted. Those with long taper roots or fanged or fragile fleshy roots will not take kindly to this sort of rough treatment and should be given a permanent place at the outset. *Eucalyptus*, walnuts, *Ceanothus*, *Pittosporum* and most of the *Leguminosae* family come into this category.

It is very easy to make costly mistakes either through ignorance of the true habits and requirements of any plant or group of plants, or through lack of sufficient study of the shape and scheme of the whole garden. Visits to great gardens, or indeed any garden, can be of assistance in stimulating ideas of design and growing methods, but it is not always easy to translate into practical terms, in a specific site with different soil, aspect and climate, what one has seen and admired elsewhere.

Chapter 3

COVERING THE GROUND

IN A SENSE all plants are groundcover. Yet it is the way in which they are arranged which will determine how they contribute to making garden maintenance more or less onerous. Many gardeners think of groundcover plants as almost a breed apart. They forget that the best groundcover plants are often familiar perennials and deciduous and evergreen shrubs which merit inclusion in any garden scheme in their own right. My type of gardening is not, to my mind, untidy. It is a planned jungle, where plants interwine and support each other, by their very existence preventing the growth or germination of weeds – the unwanted plants – which spoil a garden scene. I try by careful planning to reduce maintenance jobs to a minimum, but at the same time I do not like paths with weeds nor edges that are unkempt and uneven. I believe that, by keeping on top of these jobs, by rationalizing the upkeep of lawn areas and by planting 'to cover the ground' with appropriate plant associations, the garden will appear spruce.

Grass, long or smoothly mown, is not always the most economical form of groundcover. Until recently owners believed that there would be considerable economies if beds and borders were emptied and put down to grass. I believe that there are greater savings in manpower (and possibly other costs including machinery, repairs and servicing) if instead these areas are planted with suitable alternative plants which keep down weeds and need little attention. Instead of growing trees and shrubs in lawn it is more labour-saving to underplant them so that the soil is covered with creeping or mat-forming perennials or low-growing shrubs which literally knit together and prevent weed seedlings. These plants do not need 'edging'; instead many of the best evergreen perennials and some shrubs look good next to stone, or if edged with grass can be kept in trim with the mowing machine. Ivies, hypericums, periwinkles and epimediums can all be used in this way. They are an ideal choice for mass-

ing on banks, beside driveways or in any odd garden corner; they are especially useful where shade makes it impossible to grow grass well. Grass has to be cut fairly regularly, nourished and treated with herbicide, and kept away from the base of woody plants. Grass cuttings have to be brushed up or disposed of and grass edges have to be cut. Alternative plants with attractive foliage and flowers in season, once established, may need very little attention over a period of years and, planted in contoured sweeps, may set off trees and shrubs as well as any manicured lawn. Of course I do not recommend having no lawn areas. Every country (or family) garden needs some grass; this may be made more attractive if it includes sharply defined sections where, with naturalized bulbs in spring, grass is cut at different contrasting heights to give the illusion of beds or borders.

To achieve the ideal situation, where there is no place for an unwanted weed and little chance of a weed seedling germinating, it is necessary to know and understand the habits of growth in height and density of every chosen plant, where it will thrive and where it will become too vigorous a spreader. Most important of all is each individual plant's relationship to neighbouring ones; their relative size and form, the foliage contrast or harmony given by colour, shape and texture and finally the blending or clash of flower colours.

A strong-growing species may be chosen to fulfil as many of the above conditions as possible in relation to the plants on either side or to the taller shrubs behind, but if it is too strong it may ultimately weaken and overlay more important plant material for which perhaps it was originally chosen as a foil or background. Low-growing plants smother the ground under free-standing shrubs or groups of shrubs which, in their turn, may act as low cover to larger shrubs or small trees or may be themselves the form-giving furniture of the overall plan. Bulbs may be planted to give spring groundcover under deciduous shrubs which later in the season make a dense foliage cover to complement higher or neighbouring plants.

It is important to consider not only ultimate height relationships but also the relative rates of growth of adjacent plants. While each plant will spread and develop at a different pace these essential relationships must be maintained. The most usual mistake is to plant too many different

Miss Willmott's ghost, the biennial Eryngium giganteum, *still looks attractive when the flower heads are going to seed. In a corner of the upper garden at Hadspen, this thistle seeds and* *spreads among other sun-lovers in the loose gravel; in spring pathways have to be weeded to allow reasonable access.*

varieties in too small an area. Instead, identical plants in a broad mass create a restful picture which gives the eye satisfaction. It is the old problem of reconciling the desire for many species and their varieties with a more long-lasting and satisfying design which can be achieved only by simplicity. The bigger the garden the easier it is to devote a large area to one variety of groundcover plant and the more important it is to use plant masses. Just as grass, whether mown closely or kept to a desired contrasting height with smooth lawn, unites different parts of the garden, so plant material can unify an island bed or border and allow the eye to appreciate fully the characteristics of the taller shrubs or plants.

Obviously the scale of the garden determines in part the type of groundcover most appropriate. In a small garden, and under roses and relatively low-growing shrubs, the cover will be mainly herbaceous plants. In the large garden there will be opportunity to use other evergreens in place of grass, and vigorous low-growing perennials and shrubs where low cover is essential. There will also be places where spreading shrubs become, when planted in masses, suitable under-planting for much larger bushes and small trees. In our earlier cottage type garden a *Cotinus*, a rose 'Paulii' and a horizontal *Viburnum, V. plicatum* 'Lanarth', were such an integral part of the furniture of the garden that they determined the actual form, and it was the plants underneath and next to these bushes which I considered as the soil-smotherers – plants such as *Hemerocallis, Alchemilla, Hebe pageana* (now *H.* 'Pagei') and many others. Now in the open, in what can be called the 'landscape' area of the garden, the *Cotinus* and the *Viburnum* are the groundcovers in a correct scale for larger trees and a correspondingly larger background. However, every old garden, and particularly one of more than two acres, divides itself into compartments of historical or horticultural significance, and among these divisions and subdivisions the problem of scale relationships in planting is really no more difficult than in a cottage garden.

As far as possible, after other requirements have been attended to, and personal preferences indulged, plants with leaves contrasting in colour and texture should be planted next to each other. The texture of the leaf – its smoothness or hairiness – determines the way in which it reflects light, and this is particularly true of grey leaves. The very hairy-leaved and aptly named *Dorycnium hirsutum* has small woolly grey-green leaves and pale insignificant pink flowers but makes an admirable contrast to the leaves of *Alchemilla mollis*. The pale green softly hairy leaves of this well-known plant have a glaucous bloom and collect dew or rain drops in their centre like an inverted umbrella. The flowers are lime-green and tiny but carried in great clusters. It is a most desirable plant for all gardens as it contrasts with or sets off leaves of almost every shape, size or texture. *Alchemilla* harmonizes well with shady woodland plants or with plants such as *Acanthus mollis* with large sculptural foliage.

Plants with sword-shaped leaves such as *Phormium, Yucca, Iris, Antholyza* (now *Crocosmia*) and the more grass-like *Hemerocallis* are invaluable for foliage contrasts as well as for their contribution in flower colour. In their case the texture is subordinate to shape, size and the different shades of green, or green with white or golden edges. The old *Hemerocallis fulva* 'Flore Pleno', with its summer-flowering orange flowers, dies right down in the winter but starts growth again in February and its young leaves are of an intense pale greeny-yellow; from a distance they look like flowers. Later the leaf becomes an ordinary green, its spring appearance an excellent contrast to dark evergreens or to the pale green leaf of Rugosa roses. I have it planted in groups next to the spring-flowering euphorbias *E. cyparissias, E. characias* and *E. characias wulfenii*, as it contrasts well with the small yellow-green flowers of the cypress spurge and with the blue-grey rounded clumps of the evergreen shrubby *Euphorbia*. In another part of the garden it is grown in shade under a massed planting of the shiny evergreen Mexican shrub, *Choisya ternata*. By midsummer, when it is flowering, a fountain of blossom from a huge *Rosa filipes* mingles with the orange flowers and scents the whole garden. All the *Hemerocallis*, among which are many good new hybrids, make dense spreading clumps and are useful as gateway or corner plants for a small garden or as undercover to larger shrubs or trees in greater areas.

When choosing plants it is important not only to understand their general habits and appearance but, when thinking in terms of plant associations, to consider how one can maintain or create visual interest through all the seasons.

To sum up, in most gardens there are opportunities to use identical plants in various ways. I see the garden here as a series of existing physical divisions where appropriate schemes are worked out; each individual plant may be suitable for more than one section of the garden but will be used in each place in a different way for a different purpose. The first division, the subject of Chapter 4, is made up of the basic horizontal growing material which is the foundation of a garden whatever its size. It is essentially informal in conception, with the overall result totally dependent on the use of the plants themselves. 'Wild' planting is an aspect of this relaxed gardening.

The second division covers plants best suited for more

Rich planting surrounds a white-painted bench in the sunny upper garden at Hadspen, where old greenhouses used to stand. Silvery-leaved artichokes, white *snow-in-summer (Cerastium tomentosum), osteospernums and other silver plants are suitable for this hot site at the top of a slope.*

symmetrical formal beds, and those with remarkable sculptural leaves which give emphasis and balance to appropriate corners and contrast with stone, flat surfaces and straight edges. Growing material for informal planting in formal settings is described in Chapter 5.

The third division for plants used to cover the ground, as opposed to those which give botanical interest, consists mainly of evergreen and deciduous shrubs which are useful as individual plants in a small garden but can also be used for massing in large groups in the outer or wilder edges of a garden large enough to contain within it many sections, each one of different horticultural importance. These are the subject of Chapter 6.

All these divisions and the plants within them are held together by the need to cover the ground economically while maintaining a strong overall control of design. Some plants belong to more than one of these rather arbitrary groups; no botanical rules are followed in classification for planting or for use in design. Some species inside a genus belong to one part of the garden and others are more suitable in a different context. All my choices and decisions are based on personal preference and on my own experience, gained not only from working here but also from frequent visits to other gardens, many of them in quite different climatic and soil conditions.

Chapter 4
VIGOROUS GROUNDCOVERING PLANTS

HE PLANTS THAT form the foundation of a garden can be those which take the place of grass or they can be part of a design where low-growing shrubs and perennials associate together and form the lines of the garden by their own flowing forms or bushy shapes, creating a suitable background to individual shrubs and trees.

During the first few years these useful plants need care and nourishment. They have to be planted out by hand at suitable distances, according to their capacity for horizontal spread, and they have to be kept weeded and healthy just like other plants. Until they grow together they need at least an annual mulch of humus-forming material. Here we use both animal manures which have lost most of their food value through being exposed to rain during the rotting down period, and leaf mould. Hand doses of balanced feeding can also be given. The mulch itself helps to keep the soil warm in winter and cool in summer; but once the plants have formed into a continuous mass they will do this job themselves. The heavy clay becomes more workable and later on the dead leaves from the plants will nourish the soil in the same way. Animal manure increases the weeding problems in these first years as it always contains a crop of annual seeds which have passed through the digestive system of the animal.

Many perennials flower less well as they thicken into clumps, so to avoid division every few years it is advisable to choose them primarily for their foliage value. If you are making a new garden or renovating an old one basic economic necessity will at first lead you to divide and sub-divide as quickly as the vigour of the plants will allow. The ground must be covered and the self-propagating of plants encouraged. Here at Hadspen the prolonged practice of destroying old established weeds in areas which spread outwards from the house has enabled us to make use of thinnings from the first plantings as each new part has been cleared, dug and fertilized. The time comes, however, when even the largest garden has no remaining bare earth and then you do not want to be constantly digging up and dividing the groundcover for the sole purpose of encouraging flowers.

Acanthus The forms commonly grown in English gardens are varieties of *A. mollis* and *A. spinosus*, both of which come from the Mediterranean area and are well known for their association with the detail on Corinthian capitals. *A. mollis* has been grown in Britain since the mid-sixteenth century – its more vigorous form *A. m. latifolius* is a much more recent importation from Portugal. They are semi-evergreens with magnificent shiny green leaves which brighten up a dark corner of woodland or make handsome arching contrasts against stone in a formal garden. The leaves vary in length from 60cm/2ft to 90cm/3ft and are pinnate, with lobes deeply divided almost to the mid-rib and with tiny spines on the ends of each division. The leaves of *A. spinosus* and its variety *A. s. spinosissimus* are more deeply cut and although attractive lack the glowing quality of the *mollis* forms. All have long taper roots so it is not easy to start a new colony but once established they will spread rapidly by underground runners. If grown in the open the leaves are often marked or cut back by frost; they are also susceptible to some scorching in the sun. They flower freely in sun or shade, sending up 1.2m/4ft foxglove-like pink spikes in late summer.

In Italy I have seen a field of *A. mollis* under olive trees and the same pleasing effect might be created by planting it as dense cover under the weeping pear, *Pyrus salicifolia* 'Pendula', or with the spiky upright sea buckthorn, *Hippophae rhamnoides*, although both these trees, unlike the olive, are deciduous. Any small tree with strong-coloured foliage

In a sunken garden area at Hadspen, planting is extremely dense, indeed so tightly packed that there is no space for weed germination. Infested with ground elder, the soil was cleaned by covering with black polythene for a growing season. In front of the architectural shrub Sorbaria arborea, *with pinnate leaves and cream feathery flower plumes, fine foliage plants almost smother a silver willow. Pale-flowered hostas, starry white* Clematis recta, *alchemillas,* Geranium endressii *and startling scarlet astilbes all flower together.*

makes an excellent contrast. I have *A. mollis* surrounding the base of a variegated Chinese angelica tree, *Aralia elata* 'Aureovariegata', in semi-woodland, and also in a more exposed position around a free-standing golden-leaved *Catalpa bignonioides* 'Aurea'. Another variegated tree with horizontal branches and delicate foliage is *Cornus controversa* 'Variegata', which creates light shade through which the flowering spikes of the *Acanthus* penetrate. All grey-leaved plants make an excellent foil to the glossy soft leaves, but except for vigorous shrubs such as *Senecio* 'Sunshine' or *S. monroi* it is best to use small trees. I also have *A. mollis* next to a group of the white-leaved *Olearia mollis*; it looks effective but the *Acanthus* is proving too pushing a neighbour.

Alchemilla The best known of these and the variety which no garden should be without is the herbaceous perennial *A. mollis* from the Caucasus, which is a relation of lady's mantle. Although the pale green velvety leaves die back in the winter this plant is so vigorous and seeds so abundantly that it effectively prevents the spread of perennial weeds or the germination of annual ones. In a small garden it is simplest to prevent it seeding, since it can become over-invasive. However, its subtlety of leaf and flower makes it indispensable, whatever the size of the garden; suggestions for its use have already been made on page 32.

One of the most beautiful plantings of *Alchemilla* I have seen was at Alderley Grange in Gloucestershire, where it was used to carpet the ground beneath Iceberg roses which in their turn surrounded the silver-variegated form of the Chinese angelica tree. *A. mollis* thrives in sun or shade, but the smaller *A. conjuncta* and the almost identical *A. alpina* need more care in a sunny bed. The undersides of the cut leaves are clothed with silver hairs, which gives them a white aspect; they grow to 15cm/6in with sprawling stems to 30cm/12in and have rather inconspicuous flowers, much less decorative than their larger relation. They seed less freely and are best increased by division. *A. mollis* will thrive in wood or full sun and makes a good foil to leaves with purple as well as dark green tones.

Astrantia The black masterwort, as Gerard called it, was introduced before 1597, probably from Switzerland. *A. major* has now become widely naturalized and has the typical five-lobed radical leaves of all the different varieties, except *A. maxima*, which has only three lobes. The flowers of *A. major* look greeny-white because of the combination of tiny white flowers and pale green bracts. *A. maxima* has a pale pink flower with green bracts veined with pink. *A. major* has a very strong variegated form, *A. m.* 'Sunningdale Variegated', with some leaves almost completely cream – cream with splotches of green rather than the other way round. It looks excellent under a not too vigorous purple-tinted leaf such as that of *Weigela florida* 'Foliis Purpureis', or in front of the purple-leaved and -stemmed *Clematis recta*. All astrantias are happy in sun or shade but do not like the soil to dry out, particularly when in flower.

Berberis There are so many plants in the barberry family that it makes one feel almost guilty that out of such a range so few find a place in most gardens. The mahonias used to be classified as *Berberis* but now those with pinnate leaves have been allotted to the former genus and those with entire leaves to the latter. The large evergreen varieties, which are mainly South American, are discussed in the chapter on the outer garden (Chapter 6). The deciduous *B. vulgaris*, which is of European origin (but naturalized in North America), was grown in Britain to make impenetrable hedges even in the fifteenth century, but during the nineteenth was discovered to be the host of a fungus which attacked corn, thus proving an old theory which as late as 1848 was denied by Loudon as 'totally unfounded'.

Its variety *B. v.* 'Purpurea' has leaves which are less purple in tone than those of the berberis most widely grown for their coloured foliage, *B. thunbergii atropurpurea* and its variety *B. t.* 'Atropurpurea Nana'. These are useful for low cover in full sun or shade. Another striking bush is *B. t.* 'Rose Glow', sometimes described as having purple leaves mottled with silver pink and bright rose, later turning to purple. However, I find they do just the opposite and emerge plain purple, taking on their pretty colouring later in the season. It makes a good compact bush and a pleasant picture planted next to the crinkly grey-leaved *Senecio monroi* and in front of a mass of the golden-variegated *Cornus alba* 'Spaethii'. The lime-green flowers and dark green whorled leaves of *Euphorbia amygdaloides robbiae* are in the foreground. Purple foliage is very difficult to use in a garden as it is often heavy and dull, but these members of the barberry family, including an upright variety, *B. t.* 'Red Pillar', are among the best, with almost translucent reddish leaves.

Bergenia This genus has been variously classified under saxifrages and megaseas. It is the giant version of London pride. The large leathery and shiny evergreen leaves, sometimes with purple tints, were used extensively by Gertrude Jekyll for contrast with stone edges over which they spill. *B. crassifolia* and *B. cordifolia* were first introduced from Siberia in the last half of the eighteenth century and *B. cordifolia* 'Purpurea' was the one most frequently planted by Miss Jekyll. They have pink flowers and dark green rounded leaves. The 'Ballawley' hybrid has similar leaves which turn bronze in the

Most campanulas need remarkably little maintenance through the seasons. The peach-leaved Campanula persicifolia, *with blue or white flowers (double forms also exist), makes a dense mat of evergreen leaves at ground level and will colonize a corner of a border. Tall rather untidy stems bear a succession of summer blooms.*

winter; the pink flowers are borne on reddish stalks. I obtained mine as seedlings so they are a little variable. Another good hybrid is *B. × schmidtii* 'Ernst Schmidt', which has very large leaves and toothed edges. *B. ciliata* from Nepal is more tender and flowers earlier in the spring, with blush-pink, almost white, small petals. They are happy in sun or shade but do not like to be crowded overhead, and should be planted on a slope for drainage.

Brunnera *B. macrophylla* also used to be known under another name, *Anchusa myosotidiflora*, and is like nothing so much as a giant forget-me-not. It has hairy, heart-shaped leaves which remain almost evergreen at the base. The leaves are pale green in the spring but turn a dull coarse colour later in the year. For this reason care must be taken to plant taller eye-catching plants nearby with good summer foliage and flowers. The blue of the flower is intense and dark and very suitable for massing. It seeds prolifically but is easily weeded from unwanted spots. It forms a dense weed-free mass and goes well with the ferny leaves and yellow flowers of the spring-flowering shrub roses, and with grey-leaved shrubs

and small trees such as the weeping pear, *Pyrus salicifolia* 'Pendula', and the sea buckthorn, *Hippophae rhamnoides*. There is a much less robust variegated version which, unless carefully watched, tends to revert to plain green leaves, and which can be increased only by division and not by seeds. There is now one in commerce called *B. m.* 'Hadspen Cream'. *Pulmonaria, Symphytum, Mertensia* and *Trachystemon* all have the same coarse hairy leaves and, except for *Pulmonaria*, which is European, come from the Caucasus district. All are members of the *Boraginaceae*.

Bupleurum This is the ancient Greek name for an umbelliferous plant, and *Bupleurum* is only one of many of the *Umbelliferae* family. The evergreen shrubby variety of the genus which I grow, *B. fruticosum*, has glabrous leaves; the new young shoots are bluey-grey and almost glaucous. It forms a great spreading mass and is happy in sun or shade provided that the site is protected from strong winds and has adequate frost-drainage. It has a reputation for being tender so is often planted in maritime districts but if given some protection when small it quickly grows into a spreading bush 1.8m/6ft high and 3m/10ft broad. The tiny greeny-yellow flowers are carried in a flat head and the translucent leaves make an admirable foil to other leaf colours or textures.

Campanula Some of this family are perfectly suitable for naturalizing in woodland, especially the taller sorts which seed freely and spread by clumps. Like honesty or foxgloves, they will rapidly colonize a rough corner and cheer up an area composed mainly of spring-flowering shrubs or woodland plants such as trilliums or erythroniums, by their summer deep blue or white flowers. They need attention only once a year when they are cut down after or before seeding.

C. glomerata, a plant native to Britain, has typical bell flowers and thrives in deep shade. *C. garganica* from southern Europe is hardy and more prostrate. *C. latiloba* and the larger *C. lactiflora*, nineteenth-century importations from Siberia and the Caucasus respectively, are also tolerant of some shade and have much paler blue flowers. *C. latiloba* flowers in early summer. The prostrate pair from southern Europe with the impossible names, *C. poscharskyana* and *C. portenschlagiana*, flower in midsummer; the former is evergreen, quite tolerant of shade and will grow at the base of a greedy hedge such as box, privet or yew. It has trailing shoots and charming blue star-like flowers and makes an excellent edging plant. *C. portenschlagiana* prefers full sun and carries blue bells on upright 20cm/8in stems. *C. × burghaltii*, a hardy hybrid of *C. punctata*, has a sprawling habit and unusual pendent grey-blue flowers. The old-fashioned Canterbury bells (*C. medium*) and *C. pyramidalis* are both biennials and both

European and were grown in Britain probably earlier than Gerard (1597). *C. takesimana* from Japan is superlative.

Chiastophyllum *C. oppositifolium* (syn. *Cotyledon simplicifolia*) is the only member of this genus and comes from the Caucasus. The leaves are pale green and succulent and the small golden-yellow flowers are carried in hanging racemes about 20cm/8in high, while the leaves are prostrate. It is stem-rooting. It seems equally happy in full sun or creeping under the shade of a shrub. It could be used for quite formal carpet bedding as well as in light woodland. It also makes an admirable edging plant.

Choisya *C. ternata*, another genus of a single species, will flourish in the wilder part of the garden and can be used for massing in light shade; but it is not always reliably hardy, and has such a charming fragrance that it deserves a place near the house. It prefers shelter and dislikes full sun. Known as the Mexican orange blossom, it has shiny trifoliate leaves, aromatic when crushed, and contrasts well with dull green leaves or any coloured foliage, particularly pale shades.

Cornus One of the most delightful of small shrubby plants is the miniature dogwood from North America, *C. canadensis*, which spreads rapidly by underground roots in woodland in lime-free soil. It makes a regular carpet of flat rosettes about 15cm/6in high and in early summer produces four white bracts, like petals, above the rounded plain green leaves. It is deciduous and turns wine-coloured in the autumn. I have seen great patches of it in the Savill Gardens. It prefers moisture and shade, but shade given from high trees rather than close-growing shrubs, and makes a pleasant association with foliage plants such as hostas, quite often bearing one red berry in autumn. *Houttuynia cordata*, and its double form 'Flore Pleno', from Asia, can be used in the same way and are more lime-tolerant.

Corydalis The little evergreen *C. cheilanthifolia* has fern-like foliage and as it seeds itself happily in almost any situation is useful for growing under shrubs, having much the same effect from a distance as the little *Dicentra* 'Bountiful', but with yellow flowers instead of pink. More suitable for woodland is *C. scouleri* from the north-west of America, which is deciduous but can be treated like the early-flowering anemones and grown under deciduous shrubs as the leaf dies down early. It has strange purplish-white flowers and spreads rapidly. I let the grey-leaved *C. lutea* grow against stone as it becomes too invasive for a bed.

Cotoneaster This is a vast and useful genus. *C. horizontalis*, the herring-bone cotoneaster, is always wonderful with its architectural form and startling autumn colour and berries. Less often planted is *C. conspicuus*, which is semi-evergreen

and has pretty pink buds with white flowers, followed by attractive red, but not vivid red, berries. I saw it first at the Savill Gardens and it makes a completely weed-free thicket.

Danae The little evergreen *D. racemosa*, the only species the genus contains, is named romantically after Danae, the daughter of King Acrisius of Argos. It is closely related to the genus *Ruscus*, the best known form of which is *R. aculeatus*, the butcher's broom, used to make attractive cover in woods. *Danae racemosa*, the Alexandrian laurel, has bright green tapering leaves and seldom grows to more than 45cm/18in in height or width. The flowers are insignificant but are sometimes followed by red fruits. The foliage is excellent in a dark corner or against a shady wall. I have grown it in deep shade in front of *Pileostegia viburnoides*, one of the best evergreen climbers for north or shady walls but with dull green leaves which are relieved by the glossy leaves of the little laurel at its feet.

Digitalis The ordinary foxgloves are to be treated like honesty (see page 49); let them seed and literally crop up in groups where they will. They are easily eradicated if they become too rampant, and you can always prevent seeding. There are some with green to yellow flowers which look suitable in light woodland where strong pink is not so appropriate. At Knightshayes white foxgloves have spread through the woodland garden, a beautiful sight in summer.

Epimedium This is one of the most desirable foliage plants and once established it forms a mass impenetrable to weeds. We were fortunate to find clumps of the evergreen Algerian *E. perralderianum* here when we came and we therefore had at least one area not infested with perennial weeds. This plant is the tallest of the group, with glossy green leaves with prickly edges which almost hide the sprays of yellow flowers in the spring. It can be used instead of grass in a part of the garden where you wish to avoid mowing, and does not seem to object if the mowing machine is taken right up to its edge. It is much too vigorous as a groundcover for most shrubs but philadelphus seedlings have established themselves among it in our garden. An excellent plant for corners, it goes well with almost any other leaf. In the autumn the leaves become tinted pink to purple. The lower-growing varieties are less

At Stancombe Park in Gloucestershire, biennial foxgloves (Digitalis purpurea) are allowed to seed and flower where they will. They are equally suitable for woodland or for a more formal border arrangement. It is easiest to allow them to seed freely, removing unwanted plants as leaves spread and take up too much space. Here, in a bed with roses, ferns and Tibetan poppies (Meconopsis betonicifolia), the gardening style is casual but controlled.

vigorous but mix well with leaves such as those of astilbes.
Euphorbia The spurge family includes many desirable garden plants, among them tender succulents from southern Europe and Africa, recognizable to a non-botanist by their typical flower. Some are quite large shrubs, some evergreen or deciduous perennials spreading by seed and underground runners. Nearly all our garden forms (who would guess that what we call poinsettia is really a tender shrub *Euphorbia, E. pulcherrima*, from Mexico, with distinctive coloured bracts?) have green or yellow bracts surrounding tiny green inflorescences, but *E. griffithii* and its even more vivid cultivar 'Fireglow' have orange-red bracts surrounding the yellow-green flowers, and the summer-flowering *E. sikkimensis* scarlet ones. I have decided to ignore botanical divisions and simply arrange the euphorbias in three groups for garden use, bearing in mind that in late spring and early summer at least ten varieties are flowering in the garden, all, except *E. griffithii*, with typical lime-yellow colouring, but with very varied types and colours of foliage. Most of them have a charming habit of bending over the flower stems while the buds are swelling.

The woodland group includes the native evergreen *E. amygdaloides* which is completely hardy but not particularly showy. *E. a. robbiae*, also evergreen, spreads by underground runners and makes a dense mass in any rough corner in woodland or on the edge of woodland. It has darker green leaves carried in rosettes up the stem, and flowers which become brighter in proportion to the amount of light they receive. It is much to be recommended in place of grass but of course the untidy flower stems do need cutting down after they are dead. All these spurges exude a sticky milky substance when cut, but this is much less in evidence if you can leave the annual tidy up until the autumn when the flower stalks have dried up.

For semi-shade conditions *EE. cyparissias, griffithii, pilosa, polychroma* and *E. p.* 'Major', and *E. sikkimensis* are all valuable and, in their different ways, excellent weed-suppressors. *E. cyparissias* with its deciduous foliage of an intense pale green resembles tiny conifer seedlings; it is a rampant spreader by underground runners. The flowers are a bright lime-yellow, again brightest in full sunlight. I have grown it next to a mass of *Hemerocallis* and in front of and under shrubs with plain dark green leaves. It is also suitable for growing under shrub roses as although invasive it is not a strangler. *E. griffithii* also spreads by underground shoots but has long almost oblanceolate pale green leaves with delicate pink to red veining. The young shoots are pink, as is the whole stalk when the plant pushes up its 60cm/2ft stems; the

top surface of the bracts surrounding the tiny yellow flowers is scarlet-orange. The whole effect from a distance is of pale scarlet-orange and the form 'Fireglow' is even more striking. It is admirably suited to growing next to grey foliage. I have it beside *Senecio reinoldii* and *Olearia cheesemanii*, both of which have distinctive grey undersides to their leaf, and I intend to plant it – to join *E. sikkimensis* – next to the deciduous *Elaeagnus commutata* (syn. *E. argentea*) but am not certain whether it can stand full sun; certainly it is very startling and effective in a dark woodland corner.

E. sikkimensis has the same running and thrusting habits, and its leaf is rather similar, but longer and thinner with a pronounced central pink vein, which makes it an outstanding plant for spring foliage. It grows up to 1.2m/4ft and does not flower until midsummer when it surrounds its tiny yellow-green flowers with scarlet bracts. It is an excellent foil to any plant but grows in rather a straggly way. I have it climbing up through the lower branches of *Cornus controversa* 'Variegata'; it seems equally happy in sun or shade, in dry or wet conditions. It grows through the sprawling branches of a grey-leaved willow, *Salix lapponum*, and its spring foliage is very striking next to the more mounded *S. lanata*, the intensely grey woolly willow.

In the same group for planting purposes I include euphorbias with a thick rootstock, which spread by seed or as the clump gets bigger. Although rather woody, they can also be increased by division and, of course, by cuttings. *E. pilosa* from Europe and Asia has pale foliage making a mound on the ground and sends up 45cm/18in stems with lime-green flower effect. *E. polychroma* (syn. *E. epithymoides*) also makes a rounded hump and has darker leaves and 30cm/12in high flowers. Its variety 'Major' has paler leaves. It is a prolific seeder and I have allowed it to grow unchecked among a group of the Rugosa rose, 'Souvenir de Philémon Cochet', and among the lenten roses, varieties of *Helleborus orientalis*. It also contrasts well with fluffy and silver leaves such as those of the grey santolinas, and the pale grey sculptural leaves of the ornamental globe artichoke, *Cynara scolymus* 'Glauca'. It is a good undercover to all shrub roses, particularly those with grey foliage such as the Alba group or *Rosa soulieana*. In the spring it also makes a background to groups of hydrangeas which are rather dreary in that season. *E. palustris* grows higher, to about 60cm/24in: although valuable in the spring, it is not so suitable for growing under shrubs.

E. characias and *E. c. wulfenii* are similar, making 1.2m/4ft high rounded clumps with linear-shaped bluish-green leaves; flower spikes are surrounded by pale bracts. *E. characias* has a black eye in its flower. These two apparently hybridize freely and it is difficult to be completely certain which is which. Both mine originate from Mrs Fish's nurseries and now seem to show few differences. The *characias* pair seed prolifically, which is just as well as they seem to last only about three or four years and then quietly die. They intensely dislike damp in winter and should be given a well-drained site. They make excellent grey foliage plants and being evergreen are useful in a winter garden. The dead flower heads must be cut as soon as possible after the end of the flowering period as they are very unsightly, but it is a sticky unpleasant task as they drip milky fluid which must not be rubbed in your eyes. The more tender *E. mellifera* is a woody shrub, with linear leaves and clustered flowers.

Galium G. *odoratum (Asperula odorata)*, the sweet woodruff, which is native to Britain, can be invasive in shady sites. It is not evergreen but its narrow green leaves and small white-starred flowers appear regularly after it has become established in any rough corner. The foliage has a delicious scent of new-mown hay. It attains a height of about 12cm/5in and the flowers above the whorled leaves reach to about 17cm/7in. I grow it around the white stems of *Rubus cockburnianus* which, as a member of the bramble family, spreads by suckers at as great a rate as the little woodruff.

Gaultheria This genus belongs to the *Ericaceae* family, many of which carry a drooping lily-of-the-valley sort of flower and are shrubs or small trees which thrive only in acid soils. Looking through the list of garden genera inside this family, which also includes *Andromeda, Arbutus, Enkianthus, Erica, Kalmia, Leucothoe, Pernettya, Pieris, Rhododendron, Vaccinium* and *Zenobia*, the only odd-man-out with regard to soil tolerance appears to be the *Arbutus* of which two species are quite content in lime conditions.

There are two members of the gaultherias, G. *shallon* and G. *procumbens*, both from North America, which, given correct soil and shade, are a valuable addition to the list of really ground-smothering plants. The taller one, G. *shallon*, grows to about 1.2m/4ft and has pale pink bells followed by blue fruits. Mrs Fish suggested that it has equivalent uses in acid conditions to *Hypericum calycinum* in lime. Although it is a rather strong grower for the small garden, it has attractive rough evergreen leaves and makes splendid thickets in real woodland. G. *procumbens* is only 15cm/6in high but makes a substantial clump about 45cm/18in broad. The leaves are glossier and the flowers white, followed by scarlet fruits.

Geranium There are so many of this genus, some of which are well-known native plants, that I propose to divide them

In a 'green' garden in Highgate, London, euphorbias have been allowed to seed and spread. Euphorbia characias wulfenii, with evergreen glaucous linear leaves and lemon yellow flower spikes (mainly composed of showy bracts), makes a wonderful show in early spring. These architectural plants are also of value for their winter appearance. Mediterranean in origin, they revel in hot dry situations; like many other grey-leaved plants they often die from having water-logged roots frozen in winter rather than from extremes of cold.

into those which grow in shade and prefer it, and those which are smaller, happy in sun and not sufficiently rampant for wilder conditions where they must fend for themselves.

In shade G. *endressii* and its taller variety 'Wargrave Pink' flower continuously from midsummer onwards, and have attractive clear green foliage and pink flowers. They make dense cover under shrub roses, and the pale leaves are an admirable foil to all the varying rose leaves. They also look nice under escallonias and sea buckthorn. I confine them to the flower-bed area and keep them out of woodland, as the pink is too clear a colour to harmonize with the greeny-yellow flowers I use so much, whereas it goes admirably well with every shade of mauve and red-rose. G. 'Claridge Druce' is similar but with more magenta flowers. G. *ibericum* has darker green leaves but it and G. *wallichianum*, particularly its form 'Buxton's Variety' with soft velvet green leaves, are the strongest blues, and very useful for a blue or silver border, for growing under big bushes of pale yellow roses such as 'Frühlingsgold' or among white-flowering shrubs. The white variety of G. *macrorrhizum* has almost blush petals with reddish calyces and a rather hairy leaf almost similar to the invasive weed, the creeping buttercup. G. *nodosum* is one of the smaller ones growing to about 30cm/12in in height but revelling in shade. Mrs Fish called the colour of its flowers 'lilac', Graham Stuart Thomas 'lilac-pink'. It has very shiny and attractive leaves and should be given a shady corner to itself as it spreads rapidly. G. *macrorrhizum* was cultivated as long ago as 1658 in the Oxford Botanic Garden and may be indigenous, while G. *pratense*, and G. *sanguineum* and its variety G. *s. striatum* definitely are. G. *pratense* has pale blue or white flowers, either double or single. The double forms are rarer and do not seed while the single ones seed almost too fast. The mourning widow, G. *phaeum*, has dark mahogany flowers and rather untidy growth.

Requiring more sun, G. *sanguineum* and its varieties, G. *renardii* and G. 'Russell Prichard', are included in Chapter 5, as well as G. *palmatum*, a tender species from Madeira. G. *psilostemon*, meaning 'with glabrous stems', was easier to remember when called G. *armenum*; it has striking magenta flowers, about 3cm/1½in across, with a black spot at the centre. Since it grows to a height of 90cm/36in and is not vigorous enough to withstand encroachment by tougher herbaceous plants, I have planted it in front of the heavy purple leaves of *Corylus maxima* 'Purpurea' and in close proximity to the rose 'Scarlet Fire' with a group of the variegated hydrangea, H. *macrophylla* 'Tricolor', in the foreground.

Hedera So many of the ivies in the garden here have been gifts that it is difficult to identify them, but the important thing is their use and merit as ground carpeters rather than as climbers. They look particularly attractive as a large area under tree trunks instead of grass and once the ivy has grown together it needs little or no upkeep. The best ivy for rough cover is the Irish ivy, *Hedera helix* 'Hibernica' (it can also be grown as a flowering shrub with an upright and woody stem). It has very large leaves 7-15cm/3-6in wide, and a good variegated variety. H. *colchica* is the only ivy with larger leaves and its variegated version, H. *c.* 'Dentata Variegata', although not so prettily marked, is considerably hardier than H. *canariensis* from the Canary Islands.

At the peak of the ivy popularity in the last half of the nineteenth century Shirley Hibberd wrote of two hundred varieties, but today it might not be possible to obtain more than ten or fifteen from commercial nurseries. The smaller-leaved ivies include H. *helix* 'Parsley Crested', H. *h.* 'Goldheart', and H. *h.* 'Luzii' with silver variegation. H. *canariensis* 'Gloire de Marengo' has large leaves and does best in hot sun hanging in festoons, as seen in southern France and Italy. H. *helix* 'Conglomerata' and H. *h.* 'Très Coupé' are small-leaved ivies suitable for sun or shade, the former with dark green rounded edges and the latter, as you would expect, with deeply fretted edges.

All ivies are carpet rooters, but strive to push their way towards the light; they do this effectively using their fibril roots which cling to any surface but do not give the plant nourishment. They can flower only if they get to the sun. Ivy rarely clings to evergreen trees such as conifers, possibly because the overhead canopy is too dense, but Hibberd suggests that the resinous bark contains 'something distasteful to its teeth'. Don't plant ivy under yew hedges; it will inhibit growth and damage health.

Helleborus The most effective weed smotherer of this genus, the evergreen H. *foetidus*, is a European native with finely cut foliage and small pale green bell-shaped flowers carried in clusters. On close examination the petals are seen to have delicate maroon edges. It seeds abundantly and likes a shady border. H. *niger*, the Christmas rose, is also evergreen, with white flowers (the variety 'Potter's Wheel' has larger white ones, slightly tinted pink). Both H. *niger* and the semi-

Lenten hellebores (Helleborus orientalis hybrids), from Greece and Asia Minor, grow under a spring-flowering magnolia in the woodland garden at Knightshayes Court in Devon. These hellebores, with dusky purple, speckled pink or white petals borne on stems above the distinguished foliage, prefer a shady site and like rich top dressings of organic manure. They are easily grown from seed but flower colour will be uncertain. Good forms can be increased by division.

evergreen varieties of *H. orientalis* like to remain undisturbed by fork or hoe and need plenty of feeding. They also will seed prolifically and as they hybridize freely it is difficult to be sure exactly which ones are in the garden. They all flower in the early spring and the flowers vary in colour from dark purple, pale purple with greenish base and speckling, to creamy white with green tinges. The old leaves die down as the new ones shoot so the plants never look bare. *H. torquatus* is of exceptional merit for its translucent purple flowers.

H. argutifolius (syn. *H. corsicus*) will flourish in sun or shade and is not such a hungry feeder. It is almost evergreen and has clusters of apple-green flowers and large toothed, shiny green leaves. It is heavy headed and liable to be broken by strong winds.

Hemerocallis Although day-lilies are deciduous herbaceous plants their dormant period in the year is so short that they can almost be classed as evergreens for design purposes. Once they have become established these spreaders form a tight mat and permit only the odd weed seedling. The old variety *H. fulva*, with its double-flowered form *H. f.* 'Flore Pleno', has already been discussed with particular reference to its early pale green, grass-like foliage.

Most of the species have funnel-shaped orange to reddish-orange flowers, but breeding between the species has extended the range from lemon-yellow to apricot and even maroon and white. They make an excellent edging plant next to grass as the mower just cuts off the spreading shoot, and no other attention is necessary. The early summer-flowering *H. lilio-asphodelus* (syn. *H. flava*) has darker green young shoots, which are thinner, more strap-like and less decorative than *H. fulva*, but its pale yellow flowers are carried much earlier in the season. It is also more tender so needs tidying twice a year: once in the autumn to cut down the dead flower stalks and wrap the dying leaves round the crowns; and then in the spring when the old dead leaves need scraping away. I grow an attractive hybrid 'Pink Damask' in front of and under a purple-leaved *Cotinus* and this is another strong grower. All these are happy in full sun or in partial shade, and you can extend the flowering season by the amount of light you give them in each selected position. The pale yellow *H. lilio-asphodelus* has made a good clump round the base of a *Magnolia wilsonii* and helped to give it spring protection while it was very small. Now the pendent saucer-shaped flowers hang down above the yellow flowers of the day-lily in early summer. *H. fulva* itself does not set seed but must be increased by division.

Heracleum The generic name of *H. mantegazzianum* is derived from the name of Hercules, that aggressive Greek hero. It is arguable that the plant should not be allowed in any part of the garden except on the extreme edge of an extended wild area. However it has such architectural value, with its gigantic 90cm/36in long leaves with deeply cut lobes and its fine white umbels of clustered flowers carried on 3.6m/12ft stalks, that a place should be found for it providing it is strictly controlled. It seeds so prolifically that when you cut down the dead heads fallen seeds will germinate on the path and can blow many yards.

H. mantegazzianum was introduced from the Caucasus in 1893. It prefers a damp situation and where the soil is dry will grow rather less tall. My original plants came from John and Faith Raven in the 1950s and have only once – when we had to leave our first garden unattended for a summer season – got out of hand. Small children, or those with delicate skins, should beware of cutting the stalks of the giant hogweed or brushing against its stems as unpleasant blisters can result. Now I grow it decorously in front of yew trees; the young leaf each year makes a pleasant contrast to the narrow dark leaves of the yew, and I cut down all the heads except perhaps one for seeding. At the back of the yew trees is an old rubbish heap surrounded by ground elder and I am letting the *Heracleum*, and the common yellow-flowered *Ligularia dentata* which also seeds prolifically, take over.

Hosta Preferring damp soil, hostas are as suitable for woodland groundcover as for underplanting shrub roses. If grown in full sun, the leaves may scorch and die down earlier in the year. Even a north-facing site under shade-giving walls will suit them and they are ideal for growing among taller shrubs. The leaves have infinite variations of colour and texture and no garden should be without at least a few of the genus.

Almost all species of hosta are natives of east Asia and there are many garden hybrids. The leaves are in general very broad-veined, dark or pale green, glaucous or margined with white or yellow. Some have undulating leaves with cream edges or cream centres. There is such confusion over the correct names that even if you order what you are fairly certain you mean, the nursery may well send you something different. Graham Stuart Thomas gives an alphabetical list

The giant hogweed (Heracleum mantegazzianum) is a biennial bearing its umbelliferous cow-parsley-like flowers on sturdy stems in summer. With large sculptured green leaves, it is a perfect plant for wilder areas, growing here with Primula florindae. It gives a tropical air to the tamest garden scene and thrives in sun or half-shade. Because the stems contain sap that can cause an unpleasant skin reaction, plant the hogweed well away from paths or where children play. It can be kept under control by allowing only one flower head to develop seed.

in *Plants for Groundcover*, with careful descriptions of heights and spread as well as flowers.

It should not be overlooked that this genus also contributes a variety of flower colouring from lilac-mauve to pure white; the flowers are carried on strong spikes above the foliage and are of great value in a colour scheme and for the house. The foliage alone has such variation in texture and colouring that the flowers are an added bonus. These plants are always most beautiful grown in a mass. Unfortunately their leaves shoot relatively late in spring and seem to be appetizing to slugs and snails so that care must be taken to protect them, particularly at the stage when they are mere spikes in the earth not yet unfurled. The glaucous blue-leaved variety, generally classified as *H. fortunei*, is admirable against the dark leaves of evergreens, while the cool pale glossy green of *H. undulata* 'Erromena' makes an admirable foil to shrub roses. *H. sieboldiana* combines a glaucous tinge with a corrugated surface. If you cannot obtain them from a friend it is worth your time to visit a nursery and choose from available stock rather than ordering by post, because of the difficulty over the correct naming.

Houttuynia The little deciduous herbaceous *H. cordata* is a great spreader once it takes to you, and has very attractive 38cm/15in high cone-shaped white flowers among dark green leaves with a remarkable purplish tinge which deepens towards the autumn. It prefers a moist site but is spreading happily here, making a dense mat. It does, however, need protection from prolific seeders like *Tellima*, which I have growing close by. Weed seedlings and others are apt to germinate in the spring before the *Houttuynia* has pushed up its leaf shoots, but if you do an early hand-weed over the area it should give no more trouble. The double-flowered variety, *H. c.* 'Flore Pleno', is even more attractive. It is really a plant for a moist water-garden among herbaceous neighbours.

Hypericum The common St John's wort, *H. calycinum*, also known as the rose of Sharon or Aaron's beard, came originally from Turkey in the seventeenth century, but has become naturalized in so many parts of Europe and the British Isles that it is often believed to be a native. Of all the shrubby hypericums *H. calycinum* is the one most suitable as a low evergreen grass substitute for flat areas or for banks, spreading rapidly by underground runners and behaving more like an evergreen herbaceous plant than a woody shrub. During the 1980s this species has developed a disease, and is no longer recommended.

Of the many native hypericums we grow only *H. androsaemum* and *H. perforatum*. The former is an attractive sub-shrub with small yellow flowers and a more upright form of growth. For centuries it has been valued for its medicinal properties and was once believed to provide protection against the evil eye. *H. perforatum* is really a common garden weed and the only truly herbaceous member of the family.

The Chinese species *H. patulum* and its two varieties, *H. p. henryi* and *H. p. forrestii* (now correctly *H. pseudohenryi* and *H. forrestii*), have been hybridized to produce *H. × moserianum*. This shrub is generally grown in its attractive variegated form *H. × m.* 'Tricolor', which has strange white and pink splashes on its broad green leaves and makes a tidy spreading bush about 60cm/24in in height and width. *H.* 'Hidcote' may be a wild or hybrid variety of *H. patulum* and has very vigorous qualities, making a bush at least 1.5m/5ft high and with an equivalent spread which controls weed germination. The flowers are just about the largest of any *Hypericum* and after a few years this plant can have its woody roots divided into a dozen or more new plants. It is very suitable for massing in the outer garden or for use as a hedge, but is more difficult to place in a border scheme as the flower is a harsh and difficult yellow for blending with other colours. However, it is good for picking as the buds continue to open in water. *H.* 'Rowallane' is rather similar but, being a hybrid with the tender *H. leschenaultii* as one parent, is more susceptible to frost. Although it can look untidy in the spring it is beautiful in flower and if the conditions suit it. *H. inodorum* 'Elstead' is a suckering woodland shrub, mainly valued for its clusters of bright red berries. The small sun-loving *H. olympicum* likes dry conditions and is included in Chapter 5.

Iris The stinking gladwyn, or roast beef plant, *Iris foetidissima*, is a common British native. The smell, pleasant or not, implied by its names is noticeable only if the leaves are bruised. It makes pleasant clumps of green sword-like leaves and the insignificant flowers produce attractive orange seed capsules, but even so, it is mainly for use in the wilder garden. Its variety *I. f.* 'Variegata' makes a pretty clump in a dark corner. I have it in front of a group of *Pachysandra terminalis* but I find it a much slower grower than the type and considerably less vigorous.

Iris douglasiana and *I. innominata* are both from the western states of America. They have grass-like leaves, dark green and superficially more like a hemerocallis than an iris, and they spread in clumps in woodland conditions. Both have delightful flowers with extremely variable colours, those of *I. douglasiana* being about 20-23cm/8-9in high and those of *I. innominata* somewhat smaller. Many new garden strains have been introduced, all with long flowering periods.

Iris pseudacorus, the native yellow flag iris and the original of the 'fleur de lis' of France, likes damp places and acid soil.

Iris pallida is similar to the German iris but has more interesting almost glaucous leaves and, generally, pale blue flowers, and is more suitable for a dry sunny bed. *Iris graminea* has rushy green leaves and small scented purple and crimson flowers; it prefers some shade but is easily lost among stronger growers. *Iris orientalis* makes a stout clump 90cm/36in high and spreads rapidly. It is a total weed excluder, unlike the fleshy rhizomes of the German irises. Sometimes called the butterfly iris because its white-flushed yellow flowers are held in layers one above the other on a 90cm/36in stem, it grows happily in sunny conditions and does not seem to be fussy about having damp soil, although this is usually recom-

At Tintinhull a pair of variegated dogwoods (Cornus controversa 'Variegata'), with wedding cake layers of spreading branches, shelter other foliage plants. A foreground group of hostas with white-edged green leaves is backed by Rodgersia, glaucous-leaved Hosta sieboldii, grey-leaved Senecio and Phlomis. Silvery thistles and white campanulas give vertical accents.

mended for it. I have it in front of the horizontal *Cornus controversa* 'Variegata' and its sword-like foliage makes a good contrast in colour, shape and texture. I also have put it with *Arbutus unedo* and with variegated hostas. It also associates well with the silky leaves of creeping willow, *Salix repens argentea*, providing contrast of form.

Iris sibirica is one of the hardiest of the irises with grassy foliage and, like *I. delavayi*, has a long hollow stem with small flower heads above the leaf clump. *I. delavayi* is a semi-aquatic species with glaucous leaves but not comparable in value to the acid-loving Japanese irises, *I. ensata* (*I. kaempferi*) and *I. laevigata*, which are fussy about conditions. *I. ensata* particularly likes to be in water in the growing season, but out of it in the winter months. The smaller irises and the little early-flowering bulbs can really be grown only in a special bed; the large German irises like a well-drained site.

Lamium Many gardeners prefer to have no member of the genus *Lamium* in evidence, and this is a wise decision if space is limited. Its relative *Lamiastrum galeobdolon* 'Variegatum', the marbled-leaved dead nettle, is one of the few plants which will grow under the low branches of yew trees and it also makes a very satisfactory evergreen alternative to grass, either in a rough corner or under tree trunks. One of the prettiest ways I have seen it used is in Mrs Fish's old garden, as a bed on its own with the silver trunks of birches rising out of it. Certainly it trespasses far beyond its allotted space at the speed of knots but it can easily be mown down if next to grass. It will not harm trees with one stem or trunk, but will wind itself into those trees and shrubs which branch from the base. Keep it out of an ordinary flower bed if you want to have other herbaceous plants.

Lamium maculatum grows in much more of a tight clump and is a difficult colour of mauvy-pink, although the leaves are attractive with a white central stripe on dark green. The varieties of this plant with pale pink or white flowers are much less invasive. The white one is used in the White Garden at Sissinghurst and looks well with grey foliage, while the pink one, *L. m. roseum*, makes a tight groundcover under shrub roses. Two recent cultivars of *L. maculatum*, 'Beacon Silver' and 'White Nancy', glow in a dark corner and are not invasive.

Leucothoe This is another of the *Andromeda* type *Ericaceae* and is only for acid woodland. There are both deciduous and evergreen varieties. One of the evergreens, *L. fontanesiana*, is very charming, its arching branches eventually rising to a height of about 1.2-1.5m/4-5ft, with shining pointed leaves and white bell flowers carried in clusters. I was given it, or its smaller-leaved variety, *L. f.* 'Rollissonii', and it flourished for a few years in our limy soil before succumbing. I grew it between the strangely coloured New Zealand shrub *Pseudowintera colorata*, which has aromatic oval leathery leaves with every mixture of pale yellow, green and pink, edged and blotched with darker crimson, and the remarkable foliage of *Symphytum* × *uplandicum* 'Variegatum' (see page 54).

Above The Pacific Coast irises from western North America all flower in early summer. Iris innominata from Oregon bears cream, buff or yellow flowers all marked with rich brown veins. Preferring acid soil and some shade, these irises are more subtle than their German cousins.

Right The white-flowered form of Lamium maculatum is much less invasive than the type and is a perfect companion plant for self-seeders such as Bowles' black pansy. The green and white lamium leaves are attractive all year and can be cut back hard in spring.

Ligularia This herbaceous plant seeds abundantly and is most desirable in its forms with bronze leaves and deep orange flowers, namely *L. dentata* 'Desdemona' and *L. d.* 'Othello'. It prefers a damp corner, and makes a good foil to plants with sword-like leaves such as *Iris* and the New Zealand flax, *Phormium tenax*, and its variegated variety.

Lithodora This is another member of the borage family. The most commonly grown is the acid-loving evergreen sub-shrub *L. diffusa* (formerly *Lithospermum diffusum*) and its varieties 'Heavenly Blue' and 'Grace Ward'. The leaves are linear-shaped, with rigid hairs, and the flowers intense blue in small clusters. It makes a carpet in rich soil but does not welcome the close shade given by shrubs, so is best grown in a mass by itself. It will make a sprawling mound 30cm/12in by 90cm/36in wide. The more invasive and lime-tolerant

Buglossoides purpurocaerulea (syn. *Lithospermum purpureo-caeruleum*) is a wonderful groundcover in woodland.

Lunaria Honesty is best known for its transparent seed pods, but I find it a welcome addition when it is in flower in the spring garden. There are various colour strains around, from the muddy mauve often seen, to one of much clearer magenta colour, as well as plain white. As a foliage plant the variegated *L. annua variegata* is very decorative, but unfortunately the seedlings, although coming quite true in colouring, start their lives plain green, so it is important not to weed them out in error at this early stage. Otherwise this biennial seeds mostly in the vicinity of the parent plants and is no trouble. It makes a good, if rather high, cover under horizontal plants like *Viburnum plicatum* 'Mariesii', and the flowers just overlap in season. I have seen it with *Euphorbia amygdaloides robbiae* but do not really like the lime-green and magenta colour combination. At the end of April it is one of the few plants here, besides *Primula sieboldii* and *P. pulverulenta*, which has mauve tints, so it makes a welcome splash of colour. The maroon *Geranium phaeum*, which is in flower by April, does not show up from a distance, but there are a few purplish lenten lilies still giving a good colour, as well as the little *Pulsatilla vulgaris rubra*. The perennial *Lunaria rediviva* with lavender-white flowers is first-class for shade.

Mahonia These handsome evergreens have a place in different forms in all parts of the garden. The three suckering species, all of which make dense cover in shade, are M. *aquifolium*, M. *nervosa* and M. *repens*. All three are from the western United States and have shining green leaves, burnished in winter, and yellow clustered flowers. As was said earlier the mahonias have pinnate leaves but of very varying sizes. They all bear blue-black fruits. M. 'Undulata' is a garden hybrid of the taller one of these three, M. *aquifolium*, and is a distinguished bush as opposed to rough cover.

The very fragrant Asian varieties are outstanding winter-flowering shrubs and make dense large clumps. M. *bealei* and M. *japonica* are hardy and suitable for massing in the wilder garden, but also worthy of a place close to the house because of the scented lily-of-the-valley flowers. M. *lomariifolia* is more tender and has long thinner leaves and erect clusters of rich yellow flowers. M. 'Charity' is similar but hardier. The blue-green mahonias, M. *fremontii* and M. *haematocarpa*, from Texas, are suitable only for a warm sheltered wall site (see page 159).

Mentha I grow only two decorative forms of mint and both these should be placed where they can be kept within bounds. M. *suaveolens* 'Variegata' and M. × *gentilis* 'Aurea' are both strongly aromatic and vigorous growers. M. *suaveolens* 'Variegata' has very hairy leaves marked with splashes of white and sometimes almost completely white. It is pretty, especially when it appears in the spring, but it is too vigorous for all but the wilder areas of the garden. I planted it under the slightly bronze leaves of the Hybrid Musk rose 'Penelope' and they make an excellent foliage combination, but the persistent mint twines through the branches of the rose and makes too dense a mat of twisted roots to allow the rose freedom of growth. In another place the mint is better adapted and more restrained, contrasting with the purple foliage of a *Cotinus*. Any smooth-leaved plant contrasts well with its felted surface but a similar colour effect can be achieved by using other variegated plants of a less determined nature. The more golden mint, M. × *gentilis* 'Aurea', I have put between buddlejas in the outer garden, as although not evergreen it is so strong and persistent that it is an alternative to grass. Bowles' grey-leaved mint, M. *rotundifolia* 'Bowles', is a useful ornamental plant but equally invasive.

Omphalodes Blue-eyed Mary, O. *verna*, a native of southern Europe, has been grown in English gardens since 1633. It remained popular in cottage gardens all through the Victorian era, when it was considered too humble a flower for the grander garden. It is equally happy in sun or half-shade. The other garden variety O. *cappadocica* prefers full sun and is taller, 20cm/8in rather than 10cm/4in, and later flowering. It seeds and spreads itself and is admirable at the edge of borders or as a massed clump under shrubs which do not give heavy shade.

Origanum Oil extracted from wild marjoram *O. vulgare* was said to alleviate tooth-ache and the flower heads once yielded a form of purple dye. Its golden variety, *O.v. aureum*, makes a dense golden mound in the spring, the leaves turning a dull green later in the summer. The sweet marjoram was a favourite herb of the Greeks, who called it joy of the mountain and planted it on their graves in the belief that it enabled the dead to sleep in peace. *O. laevigatum* is a good form about 45cm/18in high with purplish flowers in early summer. Its dark leaves and flowers associate well with grey foliage and with plants such as *Viola labradorica purpurea*.

Pachysandra This little evergreen shrub from Japan, although an acid lover, has shallow-growing roots so it is possible to grow it even on lime as long as there is plenty of accumulated leaf-mould. It is an admirable plant for covering large areas and can be used in place of grass, although not for walking on. It has a shiny green toothed leaf and makes a regular low-growing bush, about 23cm/9in high and 90cm/36in wide. *P. terminalis*, the only variety I grow, has insignificant flowers but makes a good contrast with rougher foliage for large flat areas and under trees. There is a less vigorous variegated variety with which, however, I have had little success.

Pernettya This is a valuable shrub for the colours of its profusely borne berries, which range from white to pink and crimson. Unfortunately it will grow only on acid soil. Although an evergreen it does not make very dense cover, but if it grows untidily it can be cut down in the spring to encourage a regular and compact shape. The form *P. mucronata* 'Donard Pink' has rare pale pink berries, which it bears most freely in full sun. Probably it is seen at its best with a low-growing evergreen groundcover which will complement this 90cm/36in shrub without strangling it. It fits satisfactorily into a rhododendron garden, making a pleasant foreground planting and providing colour with its fruit in an alternative season to the flowering period of almost all the rhododendron and azalea family.

Phormium The New Zealand flax, both in its small form *P. cookianum* and in the larger and more tender species *P. tenax*, is an invaluable architectural and foliage plant. Both make

Shrubby potentillas, forms of Potentilla fruticosa, *flower for many summer weeks and although not evergreen have attractive brown twiggy stems in winter. At Hadspen a line of P. 'Elizabeth', with wide saucer-shaped primrose flowers, was planted on the border of a woodland bed. The lawn is lined with stone to simplify maintenance and plants are allowed to fall forward over the grass to soften the hard line. An air-cushion type mower can be swung under the overhanging foliage.*

excellent gateway plants or focal points and provide leaf contrast in colour, shape and texture, to virtually every other garden plant except irises and yuccas. Their leaves are stiff and sword-like; *P. cookianum* has yellowish flowers and *P. tenax* dark brown in panicles held as much as 3.6m/12ft high and 90-120cm/36-48in above the leaves. *P. cookianum* has a variegated variety with marginal bands of cream, while *P. tenax* has a variety with dusky purple leaves, as well as two variegated versions: *P. t.* 'Variegatum', striped with yellow and green, and *P. t.* 'Veitchii', which is bright green with broad creamy-white stripes.

You can use phormiums effectively at the end or beginning of a long path or vista, at corners of beds, as single specimens, or as large groups contrasting in shape or form with plants such as *Gunnera manicata*, or with a group of trees of rounded or branching shape. I have found that one of the best planting combinations is to use them with the different forms of *Rodgersia*; even to surround them by plants on a small scale, such as *Alchemilla mollis*, is worthwhile. Their severe shape is useful for finishing off an informal planting, in the same kind of way as pencil-thin or small rounded conifers are used. They complete a picture and do not leave the eye to wander away at the end of a planting scheme.

Phormiums do well in moist soil, but although they like moisture they are happiest at the top of a slope if there is any possibility of frost. Personally I have found them resistant to almost drought conditions, but I hesitate to contradict all the authorities who recommend damp situations.

Polygonatum The common Solomon's seal of gardens, *P. × hybridum*, does well in some shade and any sort of soil. Its large fleshy roots discourage weeds although the foliage is not dense. Traditionally the roots were thought to have healing properties for open sores and even broken bones; they are also edible. The young pale leaves, carried on arching stems, have a rich bloom and the flower stems bear greenish-white bells. There are several garden varieties, including variegated forms. Its hardiness, adaptability and form make it an outstanding spring plant, and its elegance is set off by any more clumpy bush with dark green leaves. It makes a perfect contrast with large glossy-leaved plants such as *Acanthus mollis*, but take care that the latter does not overwhelm the *Polygonatum* later on. An alternative might be to grow it in front of *Fatsia japonica* or the variegated variety of this magnificent shade-loving shrub.

Polygonum The knotweed, as a rule, thrives everywhere and the one we found in this garden, *P. cuspidatum* (syn. *P. sieboldii* but now correctly *Reynoutria japonica*), although in my mind entirely associated with eradication, is in many ways a

bold foliage plant with feathery white heads of great decorative appeal. If you wish to grow it, give it a bed to itself as you would bamboos and keep a close watch on any wandering shoots. The variegated *P. cuspidatum* is as tough and pushing as the type; if only it were less so, it would be a most desirable foliage plant. *P. affine* and *P. campanulatum* are less rampant and grow only to 60-90cm/24-36in, with green leaves and rosy-red or pink flower spikes. The former makes a mat and is tightly carpet-rooting, while the latter is of a more lax and branching habit. All except the strange wiry *P. equisetiforme*, which is tender and comes from the Mediterranean area, are from eastern Asia, and it is interesting to note that even *P. cuspidatum*, which has become a garden pest, was introduced from Japan as late as 1825.

Potentilla Both the shrubby and the herbaceous varieties of this genus are deciduous; the latter will be included in the next chapter as more suitable for flower-bed use. The shrub cinquefoil, *P. fruticosa*, is a native and has soft hairy small divided leaves of pale green or silver. They are low-growing shrubs for massing in a flat bed or between other taller growing plants; some are more sprawling than upright in habit and these are particularly suitable for foreground use. They vary in height from the 1.5m/5ft tall *P.* 'Vilmoriniana' with its intense silver leaves and primrose flowers and *P.* 'Katherine Dykes' with bright green leaves and yellow flowers, to the almost prostrate *P.* 'Manchu' which forms a mound 45cm/18in high and round and has silver leaves and white flowers. 'Elizabeth', 'Tangerine', and 'Primrose Beauty' all make regular-shaped bushes about 90 by 120cm/36 by 48in, with yellow, orange and cream flowers respectively, and 'Primrose Beauty' has silvery leaves.

Potentillas are very easy to strike from cuttings but often make their own layered roots and seed. They do not like being cut or shaped, and even the taller varieties are best pruned by cutting out the dead wood from the base, rather than by trying to encourage new bushy growth when they become leggy. On the whole they prefer sun. They have a long flowering season through the summer, and make delightful small hedges; they also look attractive in the winter with their brown stems and seedheads.

Prunus *P. laurocerasus*, the laurel itself, is well worth having in the outer garden and *P. lusitanica*, the evergreen Portugal laurel, which grows tall and branching, has a variegated form, *P. l.* 'Variegata', which deserves a place in a sheltered spot. Its leaves are margined white with a pink flush in the winter. There are two varieties of the common laurel which are nice to have in a woodland shrubbery. *P. laurocerasus* 'Zabeliana' has low horizontal branches and thin willow-like

long dark green leaves, paler beneath. It is a very free flowerer and useful for horizontal effect with upright growing shrubs and trees. I have it planted under yew trees along a path, and in spite of the dense shade it continues to flower and flourish. The other, *P. l.* 'Otto Luyken', is small and much more compact in form but has attractive erect stems and shiny dark leaves; it would be suitable for making dense clumps for flat beds as well as for low cover between deciduous shrubs and trees.

Rheum *Rheum, Rodgersia* and *Gunnera* all have magnificent foliage for contrast with sword-like leaves such as those of phormiums and irises or with other vertical and clumpy growers such as bamboo. In a small garden it is probably best to choose only varieties of rodgersias, in a medium garden rheums can be added, and in a large garden (with moisture and an acid soil) *Gunnera manicata* would be an obvious choice, using the two other genera inside planting schemes.

Rheum palmatum is from China and a relation of culinary rhubarb, *R. rhaponticum*. It has huge deeply lobed leaves, which are plain green in the type whereas the variety 'Atrosanguineum' has reddish stalks and a red underside to the leaf. The flowers are on huge feathery spikes 1.8m/6ft high. Like many plants which need moist conditions, they are susceptible to ground frosts, particularly if they have been encouraged into early growth by a mild spell. They prefer to be dry in winter but need moisture in the growing season.

Rodgersia All the rodgersias are Asiatics and prefer some shade and a rich moist soil. They will survive in quite dry positions but the leaves will shrivel up earlier in the year and shorten their seasonal value as ornamental plants.

The Chinese varieties, *R. aesculifolia* and *R. pinnata* have rough green leaves, one with the shape of the horse chestnut leaf and the other pinnate, as the names imply. They both grow 60-90cm/24-36in high and the same across, depending on growing conditions. The flowers of the former are white plumes, those of the latter pinkish, carried on 90cm/36in spikes. The rough surface of *R. aesculifolia* is heavily grooved or veined and covered with brownish hairs and the effect is bronze rather than green. It spreads rapidly and is most effective when planted in a mass, looking superb against light green or feathery foliage.

In the pond bed at Hadspen, rodgersias with corrugated leathery leaves and creamy flower plumes are tightly packed with alchemillas, geraniums and hostas. Although the circular stone-edged pool is quite formal, *the planting, extended in theme by the meadow of ox-eye daisies (Leucanthemum vulgare) in flowering profusion, is deliberately casual.*

There are also two smooth-leaved forms, *Rodgersia podophylla* and *R. tabularis* (now correctly *Astilboides tabularis*).

Sarcococca The Asiatic sweet box has charming form and fragrant flowers through the winter, and should be planted in a shady corner or in a mass under trees. None of the varieties grows more than about 38cm/15in high and wide and their shiny evergreen leaves make pleasant foliage for the tiny white flowers and for the coloured berries. *S. hookeriana digyna* has black fruits, and so does the slightly smaller *S. humilis*, while *S. ruscifolia* has red. They all have sufficiently dark foliage to make a strong contrast with golden-leaved shrubs such as *Philadelphus coronarius* 'Aureus' or the fretted golden leaf of *Sambucus racemosa* 'Plumosa Aurea', or with the grey-green leaves of herbaceous plants such as the ordinary *Alchemilla mollis*.

Senecio There are two shrubby evergreen senecios that are particularly suitable for foliage contrasts and are not as tender as the silver-leaved *Senecio bicolor cineraria*. *S.* 'Sunshine' and *S. monroi* both make bushy 1.2m/4ft shrubs with grey felted leaves. Both have bright yellow daisy flowers but if pruned and shaped in the spring new paler grey leaf growth is encouraged and flower buds will not be formed. They are splendid as specimen plants as well as massed in groups, and are suitable for all gardens as they respond to, and improve with, sharp pruning. *S. monroi*, which has smaller crinkly leaves with undulating edges, forms a more compact shape even if not cut back. They are not reliably hardy and can be pruned in the spring.

Skimmia These Asiatics prefer shade and are grown for their rich green shiny foliage and for their berries, which follow the dense creamy flower heads. Normally *S. japonica* will fruit only if a male plant is put in close association with one or more females, but there is now a variety which combines both the female and male on one bush. The leaves of this species are aromatic and indifferent to pollution, so it is often grown in towns. A variety 'Rubella' which I have seen in Cornwall is a male form of *S. japonica* and has attractive red buds which open out into cream flowers.

Skimmias are very useful shrubs for massing in heavy shade. They prefer an acid soil but do adequately in some lime, although sometimes suffer from chlorosis as a result of the calcium making the iron difficult to assimilate.

Smilacina There are two members of this genus that are commonly grown in the garden, both with a superficial resemblance to Solomon's seal. They are from North America and after they have become established make useful and ornamental groups. When introduced in the seventeenth century, they were classified as *Convallaria*, the genus that now contains the true lily-of-the-valley (*C. majalis*). The flowers of the *Smilacina* are much less fragrant. The leaves ascending the stalk are long and slender and the flowers are carried in terminal spikes of white starry clusters, more feathery and less elegant than those of Solomon's seal. *S. racemosa* attains a height of 90cm/36in and *S. stellata* about half that; they both flower in late spring, and the smaller one spreads by underground roots. Here *S. racemosa* grows in front of a flat clump of *Lonicera pileata* with *Euphorbia pilosa* in the foreground.

Soleirolia The curse of Corsica will never leave your garden once it has got a hold. *S. soleirolii* came to me uninvited in some soil but I have become attached to its tiny bright mat-forming green leaves and it is a useful alternative to grass for odd corners. It is only about 2.5cm/1in high and needs practically no soil to survive, but will peel away from earth or stone like sticking plaster when it has spread too far. In spite of its Corsican origin it likes shade and cool and will carpet under evergreen and deciduous shrubs although it may strangle herbaceous plants.

Sorbus *S. reducta* is a charming dwarf species of the Mountain Ash group (*S. aucuparia*) and although it makes only a small suckering shrub about 30cm/12in high it has typical aucuparia leaves which turn bronze to red in the autumn. I find it has been slow to spread here but I hope it will flower and bear its white fruits, quietly tinged with pink, when it has become better established.

Symphytum Many consider the evergreen comfrey too coarse a member of the borage family to include in the ornamental beds of a garden. I think they overlook the satisfactory denseness of its dark hairy foliage, which acts as a complete weed smotherer, and its early and long lasting flowers. I use it extensively in areas where I do not want to weed – mostly under vigorous but deciduous shrubs – and also for making flat beds in place of grass and at the base of tree trunks.

S. grandiflorum increases rapidly by long stems which spread out and anchor the plant securely in place. It has white bells or tubes with orange tips and in a mild winter will be covered in flowers. There are two varieties, 'Hidcote Pink' and 'Hidcote Blue', both of which are slightly taller than the type. An even taller variety with grey leaves and pale blue flowers is *S. × uplandicum* (syn. *S. peregrinum*); the buds are pale pink and it seeds abundantly but does not stem-root like *S. grandiflorum*. There is also a very beautiful variegated form of *S. × uplandicum*, the flowers of which are pale pink. It does not set seed and it is probably only possible to increase it by division or root cuttings. Another tall species, which has yellowish-white flowers, is *S. tauricum*.

Tellima This evergreen herbaceous plant from North America is invaluable for planting among shrubs. It has pleasant roundish heart-shaped leaves which in its variety *T. grandiflora rubra* become quite purplish in winter. *T. grandiflora* itself has creamy flowers while *T. g. rubra* has pale yellow, both carried on erect stems in the form of small bells.

Tiarella The foam flower, *T. cordifolia*, spreads into wide masses by means of runners and as it is evergreen it makes another useful plant for growing between shrubs, with attractive bronze-lobed foliage and small creamy-white flowers held in feathery spikes on 30cm/12in stems above the prostrate leaves. It is on a smaller scale than *Tellima* but otherwise rather similar and used in much the same way; both prefer cool shady sites to full sun. The more sun-loving *Heuchera* has formed an intergeneric cross with *Tiarella* to produce × *Heucherella tiarelloides* which has tiny pink flowers and soft green leaves without the typical *Heuchera* marbling.

Trachystemon *T. orientalis* is a Near East member of the hairy-leaved Borage family, and one of the plants reintroduced to gardens by William Robinson at the end of the Victorian era. It belongs to the outer fringes of the garden and should be used only under strong-growing trees and shrubs. It has large green leaves, the lower ones 30cm/12in long by 20cm/8in wide, and purplish-blue flowers carried in 45cm/18in high heads above the leaves. It is an excellent plant for poor soil and deep shade.

Veratrum These perfectly hardy foliage perennials have been grown in Britain since before 1596 but are comparatively rarely seen. Originally classified as a hellebore because of the similar purgative properties of its roots, it actually belongs to the lily family. It is one of the most effective and dramatic foliage plants when given rich and moist soil, but even in ideal situations it is very slow to form a satisfactory clump. It was planted by Miss Jekyll in her spring garden where the leaves proved an admirable foil to small flowering bulbs. The beautiful green pleated leaves are unfortunately popular with slugs and, like the hosta's leaves, appear rather late in the spring and die away early. They are borne around and up a stem which in the case of *V. nigrum* in midsummer carries strange almost brown star-shaped flowers in a terminal panicle. I have never been entirely successful with them, but the pleated sheath-like leaves make them plants well worth some perseverance. Possibly more feeding and slug pellets may be the simple answer.

Viburnum This genus covers winter- and spring-flowering tender shrubs, tender evergreen shrubs, and evergreen and deciduous shrubs of value for their foliage and also their

Viburnum davidii, *with evergreen corrugated leaves and shining turquoise fruits in late summer, is a fine weed-suppressor. It will grow in dense* *shade and is not at all fussy about soil conditions. The horizontal branches will eventually reach a diameter of at least 3m/10ft.*

Vinca The main forms of this genus, *Vinca major*, *V. minor* and *V. difformis*, are all from Europe. The periwinkle has been grown in Britain since the Roman occupation. Traditionally associated with funerals and wreaths for ceremonial occasions, it also had medicinal properties against toothache and cramp. All these forms produce long growths which root as they spread and only *V. difformis* from the Mediterranean area has a tendency to resent hard frosts.

V. major which grows to a height of 6ocm/24in is suitable only for the larger garden, as it is too rampant for growing alongside any but the taller shrubs or trees and is too tall for use in a flat surface instead of grass. Its variegated form is much less vigorous. Both have lavender-blue flowers. *V. minor* also has many forms, and again the variegated ones with white or pale blue flowers are much less strong growing. The double-flowered blues and purples are as suitable as the type for banks and large areas, especially if the ground is clean when the plants are first put in. The cream variegated form is most suitable for planting under low-growing shrubs and I find that it does no harm to suckering plants such as *Euphorbia griffithii* which flourish through the periwinkle. In fact it probably protects the young shoots. Martagon lilies will also thrive among densely planted periwinkle.

Wild garden planting

A logical extension to relaxed gardening, which involves massing plants together to save maintenance, is 'wild' gardening, where bulbs and other flowers are encouraged to naturalize in open grass, at the edge of woodland or by stream or pondside. There are two distinct styles.

The more sophisticated is a form of what has already been discussed: native and exotic plants are grown in natural-looking drifts which, in time, mat together and prevent most weed (including grass) seeds from germinating. This style, first advocated by William Robinson in 1870, has come to be called 'Robinsonian'. The secret of achieving success in this lies in grouping the right plants together and giving them situations in which they will thrive.

The second style, in which native flora compete as best they can with various perennial grasses, is the true 'meadow' gardening; there is no mowing until after the flowers have seeded. Most gardeners, as opposed to purists who are motivated by other complicated ecological requirements, do not restrict themselves to natives; they feel free to improve 'meadows' with any good bulbs, annuals, biennials and perennials which will survive. They are seeking definite effects; the results should be a brilliant tapestry with scattered colours seen in relief against a background of green

flowers and fruits. Two of the deciduous species, *V. lantana* and *V. opulus*, are native in Britain. The European species, *V. tinus* (laurustinus), is widely grown.

As is often the case, by far the most interesting viburnums come from Asia and many of them as recently as the first years of this century. For this chapter we need mention only the little evergreen *V. davidii* and the hybrid *V. × juddii*. Others are mentioned in Chapters 6, 7 and 10.

V. davidii is of dense compact growth, about 9ocm/36in high and wide, and has dark green corrugated leaves, pointed and slightly toothed. The white flowers are densely set in flat corymbs and the female form has vivid turquoise-blue berries. Several should be planted to ensure cross pollination. They make ideal corner plants and as well as being decorative are good weed smotherers. *V. × juddii* is a deciduous cross between the tender *V. carlesii* and the hardier *V. bitchiuense*. It thrives in an open shrubbery and produces its very sweetly scented pink-tinted flowers in spring.

grass. It is what we imagine a medieval flowery mead to have looked like, although, in fact, in the thirteenth and fourteenth centuries, the results are likely to have been quite dull. The longer grass, allowed to grow uncut until the flower seeds have matured and scattered, not only becomes an attractive 'flower bed' but is labour-saving. Most tidy lawns need regular weekly cuts all through the growing season; in meadow-gardening the grass must be tightly cut after the flower-seeding and again before the winter, but its treatment can be much more casual.

Soil types and differences in acidity and alkalinity determine which flowering plants are chosen; meadows can be in open sunny areas, on chalky downs or in fertile low-lying land, or can even be in shade where more woodland-type plants flourish. They can be made simply by adding bulbs and herbaceous plants to an existing orchard or any area of rough grass and then introducing an appropriate mowing timetable, starting by raising the blades of the mowing machine in order to allow wild flowers to develop leaves and flowering stems. Alternatively a meadow garden can be started from scratch; after the land has been cleaned and rotovated, sow a suitable grass and flower seed mixture, including perennials, biennials and annuals. A new meadow is most successful in poor soil; in rich soil even the less vigorous grasses tend to smother flowering plants. Usually the first seasons after the meadow is established will be the most colourful; after that annuals and biennials may get pushed out as grasses and other perennials get the upper hand. This is only a generalization, and much depends on the management.

Some meadows are designed only for spring-flowerers; bulbs such as aconites, snowdrops, narcissus, crocus, scillas,

Fritillaria meleagris, primroses (and cowslips) and spring-flowering anemones and even tulips (although their flowers will get attractively smaller each year) are naturalized to give colour through the winter and spring. Mowing can be started as soon as the leaves start to yellow (it is reckoned to be safe to cut daffodil leaves six weeks after flowering). Other areas include later-flowerers such as peonies, cranesbill geraniums and plenty of native flowers whose natural habitat is grassland. Orchids usually take about six or seven years to flower once they have seeded; their seed matures late, so mowing cannot be started until later in summer.

A well-managed meadow should never be dug again, after being established; this means that it is not possible to have wild poppies and cornflowers, which only surface and flower in disturbed soil, as they cannot compete with perennial roots. On the other hand it is possible to have several meadow areas, or to treat parts of one area in different ways. Some of the most beautiful 'wild' gardens are very simple – bluebells (*Hyacinthoides non-scripta*) in deciduous woodland, a waving carpet of white ox-eye daisies (*Leucanthemum vulgare*) on a grassy bank or, in a moister site, a sea of golden buttercups (the lesser celandine – *Ranunculus ficaria*).

Another advantage of this sort of relaxed gardening is the contrast between mown lawn, which is usually bright emerald, and the paler buff colours and rougher texture of the longer grasses. Any two grassy areas mown at different intervals produce an attractive dissimilarity which is not dependent on any flower colour. Personally if lawn and a meadow area are adjoining I like a crisp straight edge between them; a weekly mown path through a meadow or round its edge gives the best effects and requires the minimum of effort.

Left *White ox-eye daisies,* Leucanthemum vulgare, *flourish in rough meadow grass to make a flowering carpet in summer. Later wild native orchids, which have taken six or seven years to flower from seed, extend the season. The grass is finally cut after the orchids' seed has ripened. It is then mown regularly until winter frosts slow down growth.*

Right *Field poppies and corn cockles growing in a field in Suffolk. The seed of these beautiful plants can be broadcast* in tilled soil but they will not survive competition from grasses once the meadow is established. Papaver rhoeas, *a common weed in cornfields until selective herbicides were used, is a European native which still often flowers in waste areas or in disturbed soil. The annual corn cockle,* Agrostemma githago, *now rare, is a member of the pinks family; it has scentless pinky-mauve flowers and silky stems and is appreciated by butterflies.*

Chapter 5

PLANTS FOR BEDS
AND BORDERS

LANTS BEST SUITED for more symmetrical beds, and those which give emphasis and balance, establish the structure of this section of the garden as well as being furniture inside a frame. Many can be used deliberately to break up the straight lines of the design but still contribute to the relative formality of beds and borders. Architectural plants which have natural strength of form or which can be trimmed in a firm shape contribute to a formal setting. Plants with large sculptural leaves provide points of focus.

At Hadspen, even in the formal settings of beds and borders, the emphasis is on foliage association rather than flower colour as the primary purpose has been to cover the ground as quickly and attractively as possible. Once one becomes interested in foliage, and more particularly in foliage contrasts and the incidence of light and shade on different textures, it is possible to get as much excitement from leaves, in varying shapes and shades of green, grey, purple or more ostentatious markings, as from flowers which have a much shorter season. Leaf textures also vary between smooth, leathery, felted and rough and colours vary when plants are grown in sun or shade. These effects will vary according to the time of day as well as the weather conditions. Textures can be matt or glowing; leaf shapes can range from the sculptural to the insignificant. They all, in relationship to one another, play a part in creating a garden which has been planned to give satisfaction and delight throughout all the seasons of the year.

The section of the garden which is formal in outline but informal in planting is inevitably the part which needs the most care, not necessarily in weeding and renewing, but in terms of individual attention to the weaker species. At Hadspen difficult plants were at first excluded as rigorously as those which only have a seasonal flower contribution. Nevertheless, on the whole this division consists of rather less vigorous plants which make suitable undercover for roses and shrubs which cannot survive competition for space or soil. Sun-loving and grey-leaved plants are included here as they need warmth, sun and well-drained soil and even then are often short-lived and unreliably hardy. They do not thrive if shaded by larger plants and are happiest next to stone surfaces which reflect heat.

Some plants end up by strangling the shrubs with which they are associated. This is especially true of underplanting in rose beds and under delicate shrubs against a wall. Some of the herbaceous plants with large sculptural leaves, such as *Onopordum arabicum*, *Cynara cardunculus* or *Crambe cordifolia*, can be bad neighbours, easily smothering or damaging vulnerable young shrubs or other 'soft' plant material.

In this chapter the greatest difficulty is to know which plants to leave out. Shrubs suitable for massing together in a large garden or for growing as single specimens in the planned border of a smaller garden are not included as they belong to Chapter 6, and tender wall perennials, shrubs and climbers are also kept for the appropriate chapter.

Ajuga The little creeping evergreen bugle prefers sun, and the coloured leaf varieties such as *A. reptans* 'Atropurpurea' and 'Variegata' lose much of their interest when grown in shade. *A. r.* 'Variegata' can be seen at its best at Sissinghurst where it has been grown in full sun to fill in a patch of earth between stone; it also looks attractive under a deciduous shrub which makes light shade in the summer; the 'Rosemary Rose' and the purple-tinged *Weigela florida* 'Foliis Purpureis', are good examples. The bugles all have spikes of blue flowers in the early summer.

Alstroemeria These are herbaceous perennials of great value for their foliage in early spring. They make a tidy carpet of

Good foliage plants and flowers are packed together in borders where some formality is given by the firm outline of the clipped yew dome on the corner. Flowing plant shapes make labour-intensive edging minimal. Silver-leaved Elaeagnus angustifolia in the background is linked with grey-leaved Lychnis chalcedonica 'Alba' and Stachys byzantina along the front. Pink shrub roses ('Fantin Latour' and 'Félicité Parmentier') cascade over surrounding plants.

grey or green leaves with a regular lanceolate shape about 10cm/4in long and are excellent under deciduous shrubs. The more ordinary variety *A. aurantiaca* (now correctly *A. aurea*), with orange and yellow flowers carried on 90cm/36in stems, will thrive and flower in considerable shade. The colour of the flower makes it a suitable plant for mixing in woodland with shrubs such as *Potentilla fruticosa* and the large Frühlings rose hybrids, and strangely successful with a shrub such as *Vestia lycioides*. I had always thought this last needed full sun but, having run out of sunny sites for yellow flowering shrubs, I stuck a rooted cutting in the shade of a spring-flowering *Prunus* and find it seems to like this treatment.

The fleshy white roots of the *Alstroemeria* are difficult to establish; my most successful method is to dig out a trench about 30cm/12in deep and throw them in wrapped in cocoons of damp peat and cover them up with loose soil. Once they are established you cannot get rid of them, but the leaf is good and the flowers, particularly the pink shades of the Ligtu hybrids, are invaluable in a summer border; they are also ideal for picking since they last for days in water. I have them in front of *Abutilon vitifolium* and *Weigela* 'Florida Variegata'. I have also planted them quite recently among the cordoned apples around my pond, where their leaves make a pretty background to the flowering apple and their flowers mingle with those of the shrub roses in June and the various clematis which twine among the apples and the more vigorous roses. I did have *A. brasiliensis*, which is perfectly hardy and has attractive darkish red spotted flowers, but idiotically forgot it and it was smothered by a rampant *Hebe*, which shaded it in the early spring when light is essential.

Anaphalis These have grey downy leaves and ideally should be grown in full sun but, especially in the variety *A. yedoensis* (now correctly *A. cinnamomea*), are able to survive in half shade. *A. triplinervis* is less of a runner than *A. yedoensis* and grows to 60cm/24in to the latter's 90cm/36in or more. Both look attractive under the leaves of a purple *Rhus* (*Cotinus*) and also beside a strong shiny dark green, such as *Escallonia* 'Iveyi' or *Acanthus*. The white everlasting flowers need cutting down in the autumn and I find that it is worth pulling out some of the runners at the side at the same time as a form of annual control. In the autumn I leave the dead stalks to look untidy around a plant of the tender *Melianthus major* as they give it protection; its sea-green leaves of vast size make an admirable contrast to the silver-grey of the *Anaphalis*.

Angelica *A. archangelica* is a biennial grown for its foliage and attractive flowers. As well as being ornamental, angelica is grown for its stalks, which are candied for preserve. It has large compound leaves of fresh bright green and greenish-

Peruvian lilies, both the old orange-flowered Alstroemeria aurea (syn. A. aurantiaca) *and the more gently coloured Ligtu hybrids, lean over a path at Tintinhull. Difficult to establish (they are best grown from seed and planted out in peat pots), these South American plants will quickly spread and, with a dense root system, will suppress weeds.*

yellow umbels of flowers, 60-150cm/24-60in high. It is an ideal plant for filling up a new border quickly as last year's seedlings can be put among precious plants and then allowed to die off after flowering. I have used it in front of evergreen shrubs such as the apple-green *Griselinia littoralis* and it makes a good background plant to a grey border.

Anthemis *A. nobilis* (now *Chamaemelum nobile*), the common camomile, was used for centuries for medicinal purposes; sometimes it is grown instead of grass. It is prostrate with pale green, rather downy feathery leaves which are fragrant when crushed or walked upon. When grown into a dense mat for use as a lawn it needs some weeding, and is more satisfactory made into a cushiony bench as in the Queen's Garden at Kew. *Anthemis cupaniana* has similar silver-grey feathery leaves which are even more aromatic. It also forms a dense carpet and bears large white daisy flowers in early summer. Being stem-rooting it is easily increased or replaced. If the summer is wet, it gets untidy and straggly but it can be cut back ruthlessly. It makes an ideal plant for growing over low walls and I have used it extensively to cover the unsightly edges of the base of an old greenhouse in full sun. It is an excellent plant for breaking the rigid lines of a straight-edged border. As long as it has good drainage it will flourish.

Artemisia This important genus contains shrubs, sub-shrubs and perennials, but, except for A. *lactiflora*, all are grown for their foliage, which ranges from pale grey to dark grey, and from light and feathery to the thicker felted leaves of A. *stelleriana*, reminiscent of those of a chrysanthemum. Taking them alphabetically, the following should be in every garden.

A. *abrotanum*, the southernwood or old man, has been grown for centuries and will make a compact shrub, with leaves on the green side of grey. Like the santolinas it benefits from hard pruning after the last frost in spring; otherwise it will get leggy. The leaves are thread-like and give off a strong aroma.

A. *absinthium* is a sub-shrub, though strictly speaking it has the habits of an herbaceous plant but with strong brittle woody stems. It seeds prolifically, but at least the variety 'Lambrook Silver' is desirable so there are always corners of the garden where the seedlings can be absorbed, or they can help stock a friend's new plot. It grows to about 90cm/36in and is happy having seeded itself either in a hot dry pavement or under the half shade given by the light-leaved foliage of shrub roses. It is invaluable for foliage as it makes a perfect foil not only to green and purple leaves but also to thick felty pale grey leaves such as those of *Phlomis italica*.

A. *arborescens* is a shrub which can be tender but Faith and John Raven have a hardy form which they collected on a mountain-top in Rhodes. It is one of the most beautiful of the genus with silvery-white very finely divided leaves and silvery stems. It is at its prettiest in a silver border rather than as a contrast to plants with heavier foliage. The new silvery shrubby A. 'Powis Castle', somewhere between A. *absinthium* and A. *arborescens* in appearance, is the hardiest and most useful of all the woody artemisias.

A. *lactiflora* is hardier and more truly perennial than most of the species, but has greener leaves and is grown mainly for its plumes of white flowers. I have recently abandoned it as just not quite worth including.

A. *ludoviciana* is herbaceous with a horizontal rootstock and is very invasive, but does not damage neighbouring plants. It has felty leaves with a silver-grey underside. I grow it between *Acanthus mollis* and, for its later summer grey colouring, *Anthemis cupaniana*. In the centre of the bed is a bush of the extremely slow-growing *Catalpa bignonioides*

'Aurea', its golden foliage contrasting well with the green shiny leaves of the *Acanthus* and the different greys.

Artemisia maritima does not seem to care for me but I think it has been overwhelmed by seedlings of *Eryngium giganteum*. A. 'Silver Queen' is an herbaceous runner which survives the elbowing of the *Eryngium* seedlings.

A. *pedemontana*, sometimes known as 'Schmidtii', is tiny, only 2.5-5cm/1-2in high, woody, with filigree silver leaves. It likes to have a well-drained site. Each successive season I think it is going to give up, but by midsummer it has once again made a densely covered silver carpet. Unfortunately it looks horrible in the winter.

A. *pontica* is a little, shrubby, suckering plant about 45cm/18in high which will spread invasively if given a chance. It is best under open-growing deciduous shrubs as it does not compete successfully with herbaceous plants.

A. *stelleriana* is another invasive herbaceous artemisia which is easy to grow and has silvery-white leaves. It is excellent sprawling under pink shrub roses but I dislike the small yellow flowers, and try to remember to cut off the shoots in time to prevent flowering. If the shrubby forms are given a light prune in the spring this problem is avoided.

Astilbe These plants are grown for their lovely arching plume-like flowers as well as for their ferny foliage, which can be light green or have pink and purplish tints. They need plenty of moisture and are able to survive some shade but do not like being jostled by strong-growing shrubs. I have grown mine next to little grey willows and next to hostas, both those with plain green and those with variegated leaves. Most nurseries have good stocks and there are too many forms to list here.

Atriplex For some reason I grow only A. *halimus*, the tree purslane from southern Europe, and not A. *canescens*, the hardier North American species. A. *halimus* has long wide pale grey leaves, rather egg-shaped compared to the thinner narrow-oblong leaves of A. *canescens*. Both make sprawling shrubs which can be cut back to the hard wood by severe frosts and in the spring can be shaped to encourage tidy growth. I grow mine next to a blue-flowering *Ceanothus*, whose dark green leaves show up the intense whiteness of the leaves of the *Atriplex*, and also in front of the straggling *Phygelius aequalis* and *Salvia involucrata* 'Bethellii', allowing the pink and mauvy-pink flowers to trail through the silver leaves. The pink-flowered *Ceanothus* 'Marie Simon' which I included in this scheme has proved insipid in colour.

Ballota B. *pseudodictamnus* is a small woolly-leaved shrub. Its young leaves are truly silver and very attractive, almost round and 2.5cm/1in across. They become quite dark green in the late summer and the soft growth can be cut back severely in spring to encourage more young shoots and a compact habit. I have grown it in a mixed bed of greys and greens. It likes full sun and good drainage.

Ceanothus There are two prostrate members of this genus which are useful for their small dark green glossy leaves as well as for their intense blue flowers. Most of the *Ceanothus* originate on the west coast of North America and the evergreen varieties are by far the most attractive. One of these, *C. thyrsiflorus*, has a creeping variety *C. t. repens* which is most effective if allowed to trail over stone paving, rather in the same way as *Cotoneaster dammeri*. *Ceanothus prostratus*, known in California as squaw carpet, is more tender with less leathery leaves and paler blue flowers. Both like to be in full sun and need excellent drainage. I have grown one next to the glaucous grey-green *Othonna cheirifolia* and close to a hedge of silvery *Santolina chamaecyparissus*.

Centaurea I grow only the shrubby *C. gymnocarpa* (now correctly *C. cineraria cineraria*) and none of the thistle-like herbaceous perennials. *C. gymnocarpa* has outstanding silver-grey lacy leaves and was extensively used in the nineteenth century as a bedding plant, and still is today in public parks. Place it in a warm corner where there is good frost-drainage, but it is best to look upon it as a filling-in plant, and not one that will be permanent.

Ceratostigma The herbaceous plumbago, *C. plumbaginoides* makes an excellent deciduous carpeter, especially as its leaves have fiery red tints in the autumn at the same moment as it carries its dark blue flowers. It is reasonably shade-tolerant. The shrubby variety, *C. willmottianum*, also deciduous, has purplish stems, grows to 60-90cm/24-36in and flowers in the late summer. Either fits well into a grey-leaved border with blue-flowered plants, but strictly speaking only the herbaceous variety counts as a foliage plant.

Cistus This genus could be accommodated in Chapter 4 as basic horizontal growing material, in Chapter 6 on massing or single specimen shrubs, or in Chapter 10 as tender wall-loving plants. I have chosen to include it here as a foliage and sun-loving smotherer. Most of the genus are tender; they make excellent cover for sunny banks and corners but it is just as well to take annual cuttings of favourite varieties. They are short-lived and ideal for quick in-fillers in new borders. Naming and classification of these plants is difficult as they hybridize freely in natural conditions. The best bet is to beg cuttings from friends, since they are the easiest of shrubs to propagate, or to try to identify the foliage you want in a nursery before ordering it.

All *Cistus* come from around the Mediterranean area and

many of them are some form of hybrid of *C. salviifolius* or *C. monspeliensis*, or a direct cross between these two such as *C. × florentinus*. The latter is one of the most prostrate with wide *Salvia*-like leaves and white flowers stained with yellow. Unfortunately it is tender. Another low-spreading variety is *C. × lusitanicus* 'Decumbens' which has white flowers with a crimson blotch in the centre. *C. populifolius* is a hardy upright bush which has hybridized with *C. salviifolius* to produce a relatively hardy and low-growing variety, *C. × corbariensis*, which combines the qualities of both parents. *C.* 'Silver Pink', a garden hybrid raised at Hilliers, is hardy and dense in growth.

The dark green leathery leaves of *C. laurifolius* make an excellent contrast to grey or variegated leaves. *C. × cyprius* has a strange leaden hue in its dark leaves and is a cross between *C. laurifolius* and the true gum cistus *C. ladanifer*; from the latter it gets its attractive large white flowers with dark purple spots at the centre. All these are useful evergreens, and although their individual flowers last only a day, they have a long flowering period in hot weather and make interesting winter foliage.

Convolvulus *C. cneorum* is one of the most charming of all small shrubs. Its leaves are silvery and silky, and its white funnel-shaped flowers flushed with pink. It grows to about 60 by 90cm/24 by 36in and is effective if put in a narrow well-drained border in full sun. It looks perfect next to the more tender herbaceous perennial *Convolvulus sabatius* (syn. *C. mauritanicus*), a sprawler with green leaves and bright blue flowers which open from strange and attractively twisted and furled buds. Both these desirable convolvulus need winter protection.

Coronilla *C. glauca* is a medium-sized evergreen shrub with glaucous blue leaves and yellow pea flowers produced in late winter and on through the spring. It can be grown either as a wall shrub or as a sprawling mass in full sun. The foliage is welcome all the year.

Crambe The giant *Crambe cordifolia* has huge dark green rough leaves from which, in midsummer, spring up long-branched stems with countless white flowers. Although when flowering the giant *Crambe* is at least 2.5-2.75m/8-9ft high it is a pity to place it at the back of a deep border where

At Jenkyn Place in Hampshire, a border of creamy-white and pink-flowered plants in summer: tall goat's beard, Aruncus dioicus, with feathery plumes and the statuesque giant kale (Crambe cordifolia) provide an architectural background to hardy herbaceous cranesbills, burning bush (Dictamnus albus and D.a. 'Purpureus' with flowers surrounded by a halo of volatile oil) and peonies.

the leaves will hardly be seen. If possible put it in a corner, or use it against a wall in the same way as acanthus. Early in the spring the young basal foliage has a purple tinge to the underside, which is another good reason for not hiding it away at the back.

Cynara *C. cardunculus*, the cardoon, has edible stems while *C. scolymus*, the globe artichoke, has edible flowers. Both also make beautiful border plants. *C. cardunculus* has larger, more deeply cut grey leaves and is marginally the more stately and therefore the better choice architecturally for a border. If you allow it to flower the heavy heads will need staking, but it can be grown just for its foliage. In the end I have compromised and grow only *C. scolymus* 'Glauca', which has very silvery foliage and violet-blue flower heads. The leaves are so strong that is is difficult to protect adequately the flowers or foliage of less vigorous plants, so I have put the *Cynara* at the back of a very flat border filled with shrubs and perennials with greyish-green leaves. The *Cynara* leaves tower at the back with *Eryngium giganteum*, which also has hard-wearing foliage and helps to hide the artichoke's leaves in early autumn when they fade.

Dicentra *D. eximia* and *D. formosa* seem so similar that I am still not certain which I have. My plants were a present from Knightshayes, and later were identified by a knowledgeable American as *D.* 'Bountiful', and I took it for granted that a white one given to me later by other friends was *D. formosa alba*. However, my examples certainly do not exceed 23cm/9in in height and I wonder if they can be *D. formosa oregana* from Oregon, which has more glaucous leaves. Anyway, mine have grey glaucous ferny leaves and spread quickly in shade or in full sun. They make excellent cover under deciduous shrubs and I now use them under shrub roses.

Dictamnus *D. albus* and *D. a. purpureus* are herbaceous perennials which, once established, seem strong and free-flowering and quite at home in a mixed border next to shrubs. I have them in both light shade and in full sun in rich soil. Their pinnate leaves are a fresh green and make an attractive shape when unfurling; they need no staking and the pink or white flowers in long terminal spikes are very decorative. The name burning bush comes from the highly volatile oil which can be ignited without damage to the plants. The leaves are also aromatic.

Dorycnium *D. hirsutum* is from southern Europe and in our garden remains evergreen each winter. It is a semi-herbaceous plant with soft stems springing from a woody base. But whether woody or herbaceous, it is certainly one of the most desirable plants here, with its grey glaucous leaves and tiny pale pink pea flowers. Later it has brown pods which also

look nice among the furry foliage. That particular pink and silver-grey is repeated, on a much larger and coarser scale, in *Phlomis italica* and *Buddleja crispa*. By chance I have a *Dorycnium* next to some *Alchemilla mollis* plants and the combination of the grey-velvet with the grey-green of the *Alchemilla* is most effective, and the lime-green flowers of the latter are not too bright or harsh for the pink of the *Dorycnium*. Elsewhere, it is tumbling over the little *Viola septentrionalis* with its white flowers and rich shining green leaves.

Eriophyllum I have just one of this genus, *E. lanatum*. I saw it at the Margery Fish Nurseries and tried it as it fulfilled my immediate need for a small grey creeping plant. It has deeply cut leaves which are white-grey and hairy and only about 23cm/9in high. The flowers are bright yellow. It is spreading quickly and seems perfectly hardy. A North American plant, sometimes called *E. caespitosum*, *E. lanatum* makes an ideal carpeting plant for formal beds in full sun, either with other greys such as *Artemisia pedemontana*, or with plants with dark foliage such as *Viola labradorica purpurea*.

Eryngium I have too few eryngiums in my garden, only three out of perhaps a dozen desirable species. One of those I have, *E. giganteum*, came as a present from the Ravens many years ago. It is a rampant biennial which spreads itself, or rather its seed, so prolifically that rather to my shame I now use a contact weedkiller on its leaves to keep at least walking space on a gravelled path. For some reason the Ravens and I seem to be the only ones who have this problem. Of course it would be easy to remove the dead flower heads before seeding but the advantage in allowing the plant to do all the work of reproduction and not to have the bother of seed-sowing, pricking out, etc., rules out this solution.

E. giganteum – known also as Miss Willmott's ghost after the amateur gardener and rose specialist Miss Ellen Willmott, who was a contemporary of Gertrude Jekyll – has a long tapering root, another good reason for letting it seed itself where it can stay, and beautiful green leaves, which turn to pale shimmering grey. The flower itself is a grey-blue colour, typical of a thistle.

E. variifolium is an evergreen herbaceous biennial which also seeds abundantly, but is more delicate, less spectacular, and easier to grow among shrubs and other herbaceous plants. It has small dark green leaves strongly veined with cream and makes a basal rosette from which it sends up 60cm/24in stems with small thistle flowers.

A Mexican species completes my group, *E. bromeliifolium* (now *E. agavifolium*), which has long thin toothed and spined leaves about 25cm/10in long and white flower heads carried on 1.2m/4ft stems in July. It seems quite hardy here,

Eryngium giganteum, *the seed of which Miss Willmott used to distribute in her friends' gardens, is a biennial with prickly stems and thistle flower heads. The bluish tone to the leaves becomes less conspicuous after flowering.*

It is useful in groups in the border (seen here in front of Salvia haematodes *at Tintinhull), shimmering among duller tones, or can be encouraged to seed informally in gravel.*

grown in shade in its first year, but then it needs sunlight to encourage the leaves to fade from green in the spring to the almost translucent grey of its flowering period.

Euphorbia The fleshy-leaved euphorbias are much more tender than their relations discussed in the previous chapter, but if a warm and well-drained site can be found for them they amply reward any gardener for his extra pains. I grow both *E. biglandulosa* (now *E. rigida*) and the smaller *E. myrsinites*, the former from Greece and the latter to be found over most of southern Europe. *E. biglandulosa* has glaucous foliage but an upright habit, while *E. myrsinites* sprawls and is happiest on the edge of a dry limestone wall. Both have yellowy flowers, but those of *E. biglandulosa* are reddish. *E. seguieriana niciciana* has glaucous narrow grey leaves more like those carried by the large bushes of *E. charasias*, but is only about 45cm/18in high; it continues to flower for many weeks with sulphur-yellow heads and is most attractive. I am treating it as if it were tender but this may be unnecessary.

Euryops *E. acraeus* is a small African shrub with very erect rather stiff stems with intense silvery-blue linear-shaped leaves, and daisy-like yellow flowers in spring. The flowers are the least attractive feature of this plant but can easily be removed. It makes a grey mound about 45cm/18in high and is a very useful foliage shrub for the front of borders in full sun; it needs good drainage.

Foeniculum *F. vulgare*, the common fennel naturalized from the Mediterranean, in its bronze-leaved variety at least, is sufficiently decorative to be used as a foliage plant. Originally cultivated for medicinal purposes, its leaves, seeds, juices and roots are still used for culinary flavourings. The leaves are finely cut, giving a feathery effect, and it has pale yellow umbelliferous flowers. It seeds abundantly.

Gentiana *G. asclepiadea* is the only member of the genus we can include in this section as most are alpine plants that need special conditions, or at least an acid soil. This species, the willow gentian, has leafy arching stems carrying deep blue or white trumpet flowers. It seems to need damp rather than shade in a bed, but surprisingly has seeded itself in the wall of an old reservoir in our garden and appears to thrive there although it must be impossible for the roots to reach much moisture. It is reputed to be calcifuge, but perhaps some clones are more tolerant of lime than others. It is a valuable late-flowering plant enhanced by its graceful foliage.

Geranium *G. sanguineum* can grow 30-60cm/12-24in with large 3cm/1½in magenta flowers, while its variety *G. s. striatum* is smaller with pale purple-veined flowers. *G. renardii* forms clumps less than 30cm/12in high of velvet grey-green leaves, and has white flowers with maroon veins in early

but we have not had a difficult winter since I acquired it. Another Mexican species, the very beautiful *E. proteiflorum*, which has been grown from seed in a Wiltshire garden near here and has larger and greyer spiny leaves and big flower heads, is one of the most striking and interesting. The Ravens also have *E. pandanifolium*, which has paler green basal rosettes, superficially a larger version of a plant such as *Morina longifolia*, but of course with typical thistle heads. It seems to be semi-evergreen and perennial. All these eryngiums are useful as foliage plants but they do prefer a well-drained and sheltered site in full sun. *E. giganteum* can be summer – a beautiful plant for flower and foliage association. G. 'Russell Prichard' has intense carmine flowers and a creeping habit. G. *palmatum*, which was first introduced from the Canaries in 1778 was once known as G. *anemonifolium* and has been confused with G. *maderense*, has large cleft leaves and purplish-red flowers in early summer. The foliage is always slightly tinged with colour, either pink or red, which makes it worth growing in spite of its reputation for tenderness. I have it close to a warm wall with *Salvia officinalis* to protect it from draughts and *Viola labradorica purpurea* seeding under it.

I have used G. *renardii*, G. *endressii* and G. *macrorrhizum* extensively under shrub roses as well as in the more informal conditions discussed in Chapter 4.

Glaucium G. *flavum*, the biennial horned poppy, which is a native of Britain as well as most of Europe, North Africa and west Asia, has extremely glaucous and decorative leaves and a bright yellow poppy flower. This plant was given to me as a seedling and now has seeded itself in some unexpected places. John Raven, who gave it to me, used seed obtained on the shingle beach in Norfolk. It is a particularly useful and beautiful foliage plant.

Hacquetia The little *H. epipactis* has bright green trifoliate leaves and greeny-yellow flowers surrounded by a frill. In our rather heavy soil it is spreading into larger clumps and the shining quality of its leaves makes it an admirable foil to grey or dull green foliage. I have it next to the variegated foliage of a large *Sambucus nigra* 'Marginata' but would prefer it with a less coarse plant. I doubt if it is quite vigorous enough to make a flat cover under a specimen tree, but that is where its leaves would be most appreciated. It is not evergreen but is decorative for many months.

Hebe This is the name now given to the shrubby varieties of *Veronica*. Unfortunately, despite this attempt at simplification, in the confusion surrounding the species and hybrids it is still difficult to be clear about identification. Many of my own hebes were given to me either as cuttings or as seedlings; in turn, my seedlings revert in many cases to one of the original parent species and complete my muddled attitude to the whole tribe. They are, nevertheless, invaluable garden shrubs for foliage, flower and cover. Many of mine have come from the garden in the Isle of Colonsay and I had expected them to suffer here from our more severe winters, but given a position in full sun and some shelter all seem to thrive. I imagine that the large bushes I found here when we came are either *H. brachysiphon* or a hardy hybrid of *H. salicifolia*. Others that I have been given are, I suspect, hybrids of *H. speciosa*, which is a small rounded bush with leathery

leaves and late-flowering reddish-purple flowers. Those I can identify positively are listed here in alphabetical order.

H. albicans has rounded glaucous leaves with short white spikes in spring and makes a dense dwarf shrub for low cover and the front of borders. *H.* × *andersonii* is a hybrid of *H. salicifolia* and *H. speciosa*, with long leaves and a lax habit. Its variegated version is much more tender, but the soft lavender-blue flowers make a pretty contrast with the green and white leaves. *H. armstrongii* has 'whipcord' leaves and a fan-like method of branching which makes it more easily identifiable than some. *H.* 'Autumn Glory' has late flowers of intense violet, and purplish-green rounded leaves. Like *H.* × *andersonii* it will continue to flower into the winter.

H. cupressoides has slender greeny-grey branches and thin leaves which make it resemble a miniature cypress. *H.* × *franciscana* 'Blue Gem' is widely grown, and I did wonder if I had the variegated form. Now I am sure this is the white-flowered *H. glaucophylla* 'Variegata' which is an outstanding foliage plant with grey-green leaves margined in creamy-white. I have another form of this plant with grey-green leaves, very slightly shorter with a creamy-yellow variegation so that on some leaves there is only a thin pale green stripe in the centre. Both shrubs are very beautiful when covered in white flowers and sometimes are preferable to *H.* × *andersonii* 'Variegata' where the contrast of pale leaf and bright flower can be distracting. *H. glaucophylla* itself I have grown in a mixed hedge with *Myrtus communis*.

H. hulkeana is the most beautiful of those in garden cultivation and has glossy green toothed ovate leaves completely different from other members of the genus. In early summer it has delicate lavender flowers in loose large panicles. It is a tender species but well worth growing for the shiny foliage as well as for the flower. Unfortunately *H. hulkeana* does not root easily from cuttings.

H. 'Pagei' is a prostrate shrub making a mat of blue-grey foliage which is useful for carpeting flat areas, for creeping over stone edges, and for foliage contrast with purple or green leaves. It is quite suitable for groundcover under roses or any shrub which does not make dense shade, and carries short white flower heads very freely. *H. subalpina* makes a higher groundcover with greener leaves but similar short

Successful companion planting of tall Geranium psilostemon, *with its magenta black-centred flower petals, planned to blend with the bluish tone of the rose foliage (the blue pigment is also found in magenta) and the paler pink flowers of* Rosa glauca. *The stems of the geranium should be cut down after flowering is over to encourage fresh foliage growth.*

white spiky flowers. *H. diosmifolia*, which I bought somewhere in Cornwall, has leaves similar to the grass-green of the last mentioned and is flowering now with loose panicles of pale mauve, more like the flowers of *H. hulkeana*. In fact, it is a paler and prettier version of one grown in Mrs Fish's garden as *H. catarractae* (now *Parahebe c.*).

Helichrysum All plants formerly considered to be *Ozothamnus* have now been transferred to *Helichrysum*. Apart from the more upright and hardier species such as *H. rosmarinifolium* (formerly classified as *Ozothamnus rosmarinifolius*), there are only the rather tender sub-shrubs to be included here. Even *H. angustifolium* (correctly *H. italicum*), the familiar curry plant, with narrow grey leaves and unattractive rather dirty yellow flowers, may pack up in a cold winter.

H. petiolatum (now *H. petiolare*), although the most desirable, with trailing or climbing felty rounded leaves and inconspicuous white flowers, is unfortunately rarely able to see the winter through. Give it a warm wall and encouragement to climb and then hope for the best. Cuttings are very easy or it is possible to dig up the whole plant and give it shelter in the winter. *H. plicatum* has long thin silver leaves and for foliage purposes has the same uses as *H. siculum* (correctly *H. stoechas barrelieri*) but is not too reliable. *H. splendidum*, in spite of its name, is to me the least attractive, with coarse shorter leaves and a harsh yellow flower.

H. rosmarinifolium, as you may have guessed, is an evergreen shrub not unlike a rosemary in appearance but with quite different white flowers in early summer. These open from a dense corymb of reddish buds which are themselves attractive, and last for many weeks. It is a much more upright shrub than the rosemary with white woolly stems and more leathery leaves. Like many good but tender plants it comes from Tasmania. I have found it nearly hardy here, both against a wall, where it had grown to 2.75m/9ft and has just been cut back to 60cm/24in but is shooting again, and more recently in the open with some protection from surrounding bushes. It is one of the best shrubs for its regular shape, excellent foliage and unusual but decorative flowers.

Heuchera This is a useful evergreen perennial with attractive grey-green marbled leaves which will flourish in sun or half shade and produce red, pink or white flowers in plumes in summer. Another ideal plant for growing under and among roses, it also makes a flat cover under shrubs but probably flowers less vigorously if in too dense shade.

Hypericum Most of the hypericums were included in the previous chapter but the little Greek heat-loving *H. olympicum*, although needing full sun, good drainage and, as you would expect, reasonable care, actually seeds itself with

great abandon on a sloping gravel path, where it produces its large yellow flowers above almost prostrate leaves. So many other sunlovers have seeded themselves in the gravel that I have given up the idea of labour-saving weedkillers, and am back to hand weeding. *H. o.* 'Citrinum' has delightfully cool lemon-yellow flowers.

Kerria There is only one *Kerria* allowed in my garden and that is the single primrose-yellow flowered variety with pale variegated leaves, *K. japonica* 'Picta'. This, like the undesirable double-flowered form *K. japonica* 'Pleniflora', suckers freely, but instead of growing upright makes a useful sprawling shape and is an ideal foliage plant for a pale border.

Lavandula The ordinary English lavender is too well known to need description. Probably a hybrid of two Mediterranean species, it now has innumerable forms, many of which are worth growing for different purposes. Being a shrub which in its native habitat has had all the advantage of hot sun and good drainage, English lavender is apt to be rather short-lived in our climate, particularly if it has poor drainage. It should never be placed in a frost pocket. I have grown *L. angustifolia* 'Hidcote', a compact low bush with grey-green leaves and stems and very dark violet flowers, in an open

Far left *The French lavender,* Lavandula stoechas, *from the Mediterranean region, has purple bracts above the tubular flowers. There is also a white-flowered form. If given a well-drained site in full sun, it will thrive for many years and seed freely.*

Left *Catmint is ideal for edging, its soft grey-green foliage and blue flowers making a fine foil to other colours. At Brook Cottage, Oxfordshire, Nepeta mussinii flowers in profusion with pink and white Floribunda roses, 'English Miss' and 'Margaret Merril', and the apricot Hybrid Tea 'Just Joey'. The Rambler rose, 'Albertine', and the vast creamy-flowered* R. filipes *'Kiftsgate' provide background colour.*

position as a hedge behind a high wall so that it has perfect drainage conditions. I also grow *L.* 'Loddon Pink' which has narrow grey-green leaves and very pale spikes. *L. lanata*, from Spain, has leaves densely covered with white wool which make it a beautiful foliage plant for a silver and grey border. It is a sub-shrub and may be cut right back in winter. It too has dark flowers.

L. stoechas from southern Europe has a rather different appearance. Its leaves, also linear-shaped, are intensely aromatic and carried in bunches all along the stem, and the flowers are borne in terminal heads rather than spikes. It never becomes a bush of more than about 30cm/12in high, and then is often sprawling. No country garden should be without some examples of this genus. They are valuable foliage plants both for appearance and for fragrance, and the perfect foil to the smooth-surfaced green leaves of plants from wetter countries.

Morina When I first acquired a plant of *M. longifolia*, it never occurred to me that I could eventually treat this Asian perennial as hardy groundcover. I bought it for its thistle-like spiky foliage which survives the winter undamaged and eventually makes tufted rosettes, each leaf about 30cm/12in

long and 3cm/1½in wide with wavy margins. I had intended to increase it gradually by division, but the strange pinkish flowers seed so abundantly in the flower bed that they have made a solid mass in three years. Its behaviour is somewhat like that of *Eryngium variifolium*. I placed my first plant in rather a haphazard fashion in front of a group of *Eremurus bungei* (now *E. stenophyllus stenophyllus*), which is sheltered by the striped grass *Spartina pectinata* 'Aureomarginata', which in turn makes a higher and more graceful setting for the tall yellow spikes of the *Eremurus*. I little expected that the whole group would become the success it has. Now I must take some extra seedlings and put them among the shrub roses and cordoned apples around the pond.

Nepeta Catmint, although in many ways a great nuisance as it needs a twice-yearly tidy, is an invaluable plant for quick covering. The *Nepeta* we grow in our gardens is not the native plant which cats love so much, *N. cataria*. It is a hybrid of *N. mussinii* which was introduced from the Caucasus in 1802. Mine, I think, may possibly be the true *mussinii* as it seeds itself freely while the hybrid *N.* × *faassenii* is sterile, but more probably it is *N. gigantea* or 'Six Hills Giant'. It has been a very useful plant for smothering small weeds and its pale grey-green leaves and lavender-coloured flowers are pleasant to look at and much sought after by bees. There are very few months of the year when it is without a cushion of attractive leaves. It makes a small hedge and can also be used as a flat mass about 45cm/18in high for underplanting trees and shrubs or for covering a bank.

Oenothera The annual evening primrose seeds itself all over the garden and is reasonably welcome. There are two prettier and much smaller ones, both with white flowers fading to pink which open from huge funnels to large flat saucers at dusk. This particular habit is called 'vespertine', a word also used to describe the kind of scent that becomes more pronounced at night; Cestrum parqui and tobacco plants spring to mind as well as the well known night-scented stocks.

The flowers of the two Oenothera species, O. acaulis and O. caespitosa, are very similar but the leaves of the latter are much more attractive, being glaucous with a broad mid-rib. The leaves of O. acaulis are plain pale green and much smaller, while the 15cm/6in high branches form a sort of zig-zag pattern. Another variety is O. missouriensis, which is a trailing untidy plant with large yellow flowers and long glossy leaves. By far the best variety for foliage is O. caespitosa, and especially the form of it called O. c. marginata, which has a pinkish glow to its slightly glaucous leaf.

Onopordum Both the large thistles O. acanthium and O. arabicum are biennial foliage plants with statuesque qualities. Their lower rosette of leaves attains at least 90cm/36in across on the ground in the spring of the year in which they flower. The whole plant is silver-grey and during the early summer it starts to send up long branching stems which carry dark purple flowers by midsummer. There are snags however: each part – leaf, stalk, flower and seedhead – is covered with spiny thorns which not only make weeding painful but also damage the more delicate soft leaves of plants in contact with it. As with so many of these plants with long tap-roots, it is best to allow Onopordum to seed in the garden and destroy those seedlings that will become a nuisance as they approach flowering. It is beautiful at the back of a border and useful for making a new bed almost immediately effective.

Osteospermum Only one species of this South African sub-shrub is reliably hardy here but it is well worth growing where a flat rich green carpeter is wanted, whether under tall shrubs which do not give deep shade, or for sunny edges. O. jucundum has mauve daisy flowers which keep appearing almost all summer. I have grown it under the semi-evergreen Buddleja colvilei where it makes a dense cover next to Ballota pseudo-dictamnus. The more tender O. ecklonis bears white flowers with a blue-violet centre and grows more untidily. It has sur-

vived in the open here for the last few winters. A more upright variety is O. 'Falmouth' with pale pink flowers.

Othonna The most frequently grown is O. cheirifolia (syn. Othonnopsis cheirifolia). I always thought that the difference between an herbaceous plant and a shrub was that the former does not form a persistent woody stem from which leaf shoots come the following year, and this invasive plant certainly seems to come into this category. However I am glad to see that although some authorities classify O. cheirifolia as a shrub, Graham Stuart Thomas lists it under herbaceous plants. It is an odd-looking sun-lover, with strange paddle-shaped glaucous grey-green leaves and vivid yellow daisy flowers. It spreads as a carpeter, seldom more than 23cm/9in high, and needs good drainage. The colour of the flower is harsh and difficult but the excellent colour and texture of the leaves, resembling those of some of the sedums, make it a valuable small plant for sunny spots.

Paeonia For the sake of simplicity and clarity, as well as for difference in use, it is easiest to divide the peonies into shrubs and herbaceous forms, although they all have considerable value as foliage plants, with much variation. Unfortunately, the shrub peonies, and particularly the magnificent P. suffruticosa, are subject to wilt disease (Botrytis paeoniae) and here I seem to have been unlucky with this desirable group – the leaves develop in the early spring and then suddenly the attractive young shoots die back. Spraying with a copper fungicide is supposed to help.

All tree peonies are best planted in a west-facing position as early morning sun after frost can damage the flower buds. P. delavayi lutea and its relative P. d. ludlowii seem to be untouched by the wilt, and make attractive foliage shrubs at least 2-2.5m/7-8ft high with pale green deeply cut leaves. The flowers are of a pleasant yellow, largest in the ludlowii variety, and seed happily in the garden. P. delavayi, with maroon flowers, is otherwise rather similar, but far surpassed in beauty by the P. d. Potaninii group. This last is a suckering shrub, with more interesting leaves and flowers which, though slightly smaller, are of a richer colour and carried very freely. So far it shows no sign of disease.

Among the herbaceous species I grow P. mascula, P. mlokosewitschii, P. veitchii, both the Chinese P. lactiflora hybrids

Peonies are grown for their foliage effects as well as for their seasonal flowers. In this spring border, the undeveloped bronze leaf-stalks of young peony shoots push through the carpeting leaves of small spring performers such as grape hyacinths. In the background the leaves of tree peonies unfurl in front of contrasting iris foliage. By early summer the peonies will be in full flower with dramatic effect.

and *P. officinalis* in many of its single and double forms. *P. mascula* is a European species with rose-red flowers and attractive glaucous leaves. It flowers early and seeds abundantly. My first plant was a seedling gift from the Ravens. *P. mlokosewitschii*, which, except for the difficulty of spelling and pronouncing its name, is one of the best, has bluish-green leaves, pale and glaucous beneath, with red stalk and veins and an almost pink edge to the underside of the leaf. The flower is 10cm/4in across and pale yellow. The only fault in the plant is its tendency to be a shy flowerer; it needs a few years to get established. *P. veitchii* has deeply cut leaves and the flowers are magenta; there is also a rare white form. *P. wittmanniana* has greener leaves and quite a few different flowering forms, from white to yellow, surrounding crimson filaments. *P. emodi* has rather similar leaves and white flowers with yellow centres.

The *P. lactiflora* varieties are numerous and many are desirable; all have attractive foliage unless attacked by disease, and flower well except on the odd occasion when they produce a run of buds which fail to swell and dry up. *P. officinalis*, the old-fashioned European peony, makes healthy plants with fresh green foliage which lasts well all through the summer, and is useful for growing under and with shrub roses. It flowers early, as do all its various forms, and adds valuable colour to our garden in May.

Perovskia This delightful late-flowering shrub has blue-grey leaves and pleasant blue flowers in the late summer. It has all the appearance of being tender but, being only semi-woody, it often dies right back to the ground like an herbaceous plant; after a severe winter it normally shoots from the base. It is a great suckerer and one might almost call it invasive, but it is generally welcome however far away from the main stem it shoots up. The leaves are coarsely toothed and not individually particularly attractive but the whole plant makes a contribution to any foliage border by the blueness of its grey leaves. I grow it where I used to have *Caryopteris × clandonensis*, which I consider less decorative.

Phlomis I grow the Jerusalem sage, *P. fruticosa*, and *P. chrysophylla* which is very similar but with yellower leaves, and also the tender but more beautiful *P. italica*. *P. fruticosa* is a sprawling shrub with grey-green very hairy foliage and

bright yellow flowers. It makes a well-shaped corner plant of the same type superficially as *Senecio* 'Sunshine'. The flowers are carried in whorls at the end of the branches and are not at all like the *Senecio* daisies.

The splendid *P. italica* is more of a sub-shrub, with intensely grey hairy leaves and pink whorls in a terminal spike. It is one of the 'musts' in my garden. It will sprawl widely and sucker, and unfortunately gets so brittle as it grows older that even a light fall of snow will snap off the branches. Usually, however, there will be suckers ready to replace the damage. It is a native of the Balearic Islands, but seems to be hardy once well established.

Phygelius The two varieties of sub-shrubs of this genus that I grow here are *P. capensis* and *P. aequalis*. They are South African and may die right back to their base in winter; equally, after a mild winter, they may flower earlier on shoots which have retained their sap. Other plants like *Cestrum*, *Perovskia*, *Indigofera* and *Atriplex* behave in a similar fashion. *P. capensis*, known as Cape figwort, has scarlet to orange tubular flowers rather resembling penstemons and spreads rapidly by suckers. It has quite attractive green leaves but is chiefly of value for its ability to come up through the branches of other shrubs in the late summer, just when they are getting overblown. The other species, *P. aequalis*, is less rampant, has much more attractive pink flowers, and grows happily between grey-leaved olearias and through the foliage of the purple *Cotinus*. For some reason it is rarely seen in this country. *P. aequalis* 'Yellow Trumpet', recently introduced from South Africa, is proving a hardy and desirable garden plant. It has clear yellow tubular flowers displayed among fresh green foliage.

Potentilla The herbaceous potentillas are low-creeping perennials and in the two best forms have deeply divided grey-green leaves. *P. alba* and *P. montana* are very similar, both having white flowers, those of the former with an orange eye. They both prefer full sun. Fortunately they are not so rampant as the native *P. reptans*, which is stem-rooting and one of the most difficult weeds to eradicate.

Primula We do not have the right conditions here for establishing these desirable plants, so I feel on rather shaky ground when recommending a selected few. The common primrose, *P. vulgaris*, and the cowslip, *P. veris*, are native to Europe and well worth preserving: I encourage colonies in the garden. The cowslip has orange-yellow forms as well as the ordinary deep yellow. *P.* 'Guinevere' is a primrose type hybrid with dark bronze leaves and pale mauve flowers. It will thrive in any soil, is happy in shade, not fussy about having damp conditions and seems almost indestructible. It

Late-flowering Primula florindae, *the giant cowslip from Tibet, has attractive mid-green leaves and fragrant umbels of scented yellow flowers held on drooping stalks. It thrives in a moist spot but unlike most of the Asiatic primulas is tolerant of alkaline soils. Here it makes an admirable companion plant for pink and red astilbes.*

forms thick clumps which are easily divided and is an excellent foliage plant.

The other primulas that I grow are the hybrid 'Red Hugh' of *Primula pulverulenta* and the more prostrate species, *P. sieboldii*. Both should have damp acid soil but seem to thrive, and in the case of the *pulverulenta* hybrid, to seed abundantly, in my semi-water garden, which is really limy clay constantly improved in texture, and in water-retaining capacity, by peat mulches. Possibly it is just the seedlings which survive each year to flower the next, before their roots have penetrated into the less hospitable clay below. *P. sieboldii* has fresh green downy leaves and my variety is pale pink in flower with a conspicuous white eye. Often the flowers are fringed and darker in colour. They all make excellent foliage and flower contrast with other moisture-loving plants such as astilbes and rodgersias and low-growing grey-leaved willows.

Rosmarinus The ordinary rosemary, *R. officinalis*, is an evergreen shrub, and one which is indispensable for culinary purposes. There are several improved forms of it. Both 'Benenden Blue' and 'Tuscan Blue' have much brighter blue flowers than the type, darker green leaves and a more compact habit. Unfortunately they are also less hardy. 'Miss Jessopp's Upright' (or *R. o.* 'Fastigiatus') is upright in growth and, given a position against a warm wall, will almost become a climber. The variety *R. o. roseus* has pale pink flowers and blends attractively with grey-leaved foliage and other pinks and reds. The prostrate rosemary, *R. lavandulaceus*, is tender but, given adequate drainage, is reliable on the top of a bank or scrambling over a wall. None of the different types of *R. officinalis* has such strongly aromatic leaves as the type itself. I think the right attitude is to treat them as short-lived plants and replace them from easily rooted cuttings.

Ruta The little aromatic evergreen shrub *R. graveolens* has glaucous much-divided fern-like leaves and unimportant small mustard-yellow flowers in late summer. Long cultivated for its medicinal properties, it was thought to be an antidote to the plague. Many people get a rash from handling the leaves. It makes a striking blue-green mound but rapidly grows out of shape and should be replaced every few years. It provides good colour contrast to felted grey leaves. 'Jackman's Blue' is the most effective colour form.

Salix There is a group of small grey-leaved willows, all of course preferring a moist soil, which are invaluable foliage shrubs for every garden but are not large and vigorous enough to be in the outer wilder garden. The best and densest of these is *S. lanata* and its hybrid *S.* 'Stuartii'. The pale grey woolly leaves of this shrub make a rounded shape in summer, rather twisted and gnarled in the winter months. The leaves

The shrubby salvias (sometimes sub-shrubs), with evergreen aromatic leaves, are useful corner or edging plants in well-drained soil in full sun. Salvia officinalis 'Purpurascens' makes a spreading bush 90cm/36in wide. It has green leaves suffused with purple and bluish-purple flowers, making an admirable foil to grey or silver-leaved plants at any time of year. It is also effective massed in a parterre surrounded by box or some other good foliage plant with contrasting colour.

are ovate and the proportionately enormous catkins are pale yellow, and even larger in 'Stuartii'. It is a native of Scotland, northern Europe and Asia.

S. hastata 'Wehrhahnii' also has a spreading habit, but the leaves are less felted and give a less grey appearance. The catkins are a delightful silver-grey. *S.* 'Boydii' is small but grows erect and has the grey downy leaves of one of its parents, *S. lapponum*, the Lapland willow. I have just pruned back the latter hard hoping to make it bush again from the base as after five years it had become leggy.

The straggly creeping willow, *S. repens argentea*, is suitable for the front of borders with stone or gravel edges, and is semi-prostrate with silky grey leaves. In our garden we have another form of *S. repens argentea*, which has pale green leaves with grey undersides, short early catkins and now, after seven years, long thin whippy branches of 1.8m/6ft spreading almost horizontally. The silvery willow, *S. helvetica*, can be grown as a mop-headed standard.

Salvia The various forms of the shrubby evergreen sage, *S. officinalis*, are very useful foliage plants. They can be used in mixed borders with other shrubs and perennials and are valuable as edging plants over grass where the air cushion type of mowing machine can sweep underneath and eliminate the need for edging. They also make sufficiently hardy shelter in a wall border to give protection to more tender plants when young and vulnerable. The following forms of *S. officinalis* quickly make low-growing bushy shrubs: *S. o.* 'Icterina' has leaves variegated in green and gold; *S. o.* 'Purpurascens' has purple-grey leaves – one form of it, *S. o.* 'Purpurascens Variegata', has purple leaves with pink and white blotches; and *S. o.* 'Tricolor' has distinctive smaller leaves and habit and is coloured grey-green, veined yellowish-white and pink. All except the last make low-growing bushes and are stem-rooting and therefore self-propagating. The flowers are bluish-purple although none of these forms with coloured foliage is a prolific flowerer.

The more tender woody salvias such as *S. grahamii* and *S. microphylla neurepia*, and the sub-shrubs *S. guaranitica* and *S. involucrata*, will come into the chapter on wall shrubs. *S. dichroa*, of which I was given the seed, has large flat hairy leaves and is perennial in habit, although not reliably hardy. It comes from the Atlas Mountains and is interesting perhaps only because of its relative rarity; the flowers are a mixture of dark blue and pale blue lobes which gives an anaemic effect. *S. haematodes* is similar but has dark blue flowers. The blue of *S. patens* is very bright in comparison, and the plant has grey furry leaves. Unfortunately, although it has survived here for the last six years without protection, no one could describe it as a strong plant.

The hardiest of all the perennials are varieties of *S.* × *superba*, of which the forms 'East Friesland' and 'Lubecca' have sturdy violet-purple spikes. The variety *S. sclarea turkestanica* is a grey-leaved biennial with pinkish flowers. The leaves have an unpleasant smell when touched or brushed against, so it should be kept away from path edges and corners. It seeds itself very freely and is a valuable foliage plant in any situation. *S. argentea*, another biennial, has the whitest leaves of all – large with crinkled and toothed edges. The flower is insignificant and if you cut off the stem before flowering the plant will acquire perennial qualities.

Santolina The cotton lavenders are indispensable small fragrant evergreen shrubs and reasonably hardy provided they are given full sun to ripen the wood and are not waterlogged in the winter. They can be planted in groups for flat cover (about 45cm/18in) or used as edging plants or for small hedges. They are all natives of southern Europe and the type, *S. chamaecyparissus*, was used even in Elizabethan times as an alternative to box for formal beds and knot gardens. They need an annual trim, if possible after the last frost, to keep them in shape. This also discourages the vivid yellow-button flowers which are borne on last year's shoots.

S. chamaecyparissus has feathery grey foliage and the more fragrant *S. pinnata neapolitana* is even whiter. *S. virens* (now *S. rosmarinifolia rosmarinifolia*) has pale green leaves and attractive sulphur-yellow flowers. It seems to be more tender, but blends better into some planting schemes where the extreme whiteness of the foliage of the other two creates too great a contrast.

Saxifraga This family is too much for the non-botanist. As with *Sedum* it is hard to know where to start; and yet, as I grow some by chance and some by intention, for their green rosettes and pretty sprays of pink and white flowers, it would be wrong to ignore their potential as cover under shrubs or as flat carpeting. I am very fond of the old fashioned mother of thousands, which likes shade and spreads its marbled greeny-grey leaves, wherever you give it a chance, by its rooting runners, hence its name *S. stolonifera* (syn. *S. sarmentosa*). *S. umbrosa*, of which there are several forms and hybrids including the well-known London pride and others with variegated leaves, was probably introduced from the Mediterranean area. It is possible that London pride acquired its name because it was extensively used by Mr George London in the 1690s, after his appointment as Royal Gardener to William III.

An even more attractive saxifrage is *S. cortusifolia fortunei*, a clump-forming deciduous species from Japan, introduced of course by Robert Fortune in the mid-nineteenth century, and suitable only for a cool spot in partial shade. It flowers very late, in October here, with white sprays, and the best form is *S. c. f.* 'Wada' which has bronzy-purple undersides to the glossy green leaves.

Scrophularia This figwort, *S. aquatica* 'Variegata', is an attractive perennial for any damp spot, but not sufficiently vigorous for use as rough cover. It has green and white mottled leaves and looks pretty next to the leaves of plain green hostas.

Sedum This is another vast genus, including many half-hardy succulents which do not concern the average gardener. There are some species, however, which include several different forms of excellent foliage and flowering plants. *S. spectabile* is an herbaceous perennial with fleshy glaucous leafy stems carrying small starry flowers in crowded flat heads. Its flowers can be pink or richer darker colours, and are particularly attractive to butterflies and bees. It flowers late, usually at summer's end, and although it makes a very compact plant during the early summer, the heavy flower heads bend outwards and leave the centre of the plant bare and unsightly. The effect is made even worse if rain increases the weight of the heads.

The species *Sedum telephium* superficially differs only in botanical detail from *S. spectabile* but it grows in less of a clump and has forms with coloured leaves and stems. One form has white splashes on the pale green leaf and another has red stems and purplish-grey leaves. The best for colour and one which has longer stems, up to 90cm/36in as opposed to the 45cm/18in of *S. spectabile* and *S. telephium*, is *S. telephium maximum* and its various forms, but you sacrifice compact habit for strong foliage shades. The smaller sedums are really for selected spots in rock gardens, but those mentioned here are strong plants for open sunny borders and are suitable for mixing among shrubs or other herbaceous plants. *S. telephium* has been grown in gardens since before Gerard and is probably a British native. *S. spectabile* was a nineteenth-century importation from China and became very popular at the expense of *S. telephium* until quite recently; the latter has now been rescued from the cottage garden.

Stachys The two forms of *Stachys lanata*, the type and *S. l.* 'Silver Carpet', both make attractive grey woolly low-growing clumps very suitable for any well-drained site. They look pretty under roses but are not happy with too rich a soil or if given too much feeding. The advantage of 'Silver Carpet' is that it does not need the annual cutting down of flower heads, simply because there are not any; but I rather miss the seedlings which *S. lanata* distributes generously in odd corners of my garden, particularly in gravel paths. And the flower is not unattractive with its odd pale mauve colour.

Tanacetum The Mediterranean plant commonly sold as *T.* (formerly *Chrysanthemum*) *haradjanii* is the only one of these small mountain sub-shrubby plants that I grow. It reaches a height of only 15cm/6in and with its silver fern-like leaves looks nicest as a flat carpet mixed with plants such as *Viola purpurea labradorica* and the smaller perennial cranesbills, as at Knightshayes. *T. argenteum* is even more feathery.

Teucrium The little wall germander *T. chamaedrys* has come back into fashion lately with the increasing interest in garden history. Like the more woody santolinas, this little plant was used in edging and patterned schemes in Tudor gardens.

Above *Flowering in summer,* Thalictrum delavayi *(syn. T. dipterocarpum) has angled wide branching flower stems holding lilac-coloured sepals with central yellow stamens. It and the form T.d. 'Hewitt's Double' are amongst the best perennial border plants, having an airy ethereal quality reminiscent of tall crambes or gypsophila.*

Right Viola cornuta *and its hybrids like to weave in and out between neighbouring plants. At Hadspen they grow among euphorbias (forms of E.characias and E.c.wulfenii) and Alchemilla mollis in a sunny position at the top of the garden. There is also a white form, and several improved cultivars are available.*

It has a creeping rootstock, pleasant dark small leaves and a pale pink-lipped rather inconspicuous flower. Once established it flowers all summer and, given sun and a well-drained soil, will need little attention and quickly make a dense mat about 60cm/24in square. You can see an excellent planting of it in the reproduction seventeenth-century Queen's Garden at Kew.

The tree germander, *T. fruticans*, from southern Europe, is a grey-leaved shrub which makes a good corner or wall plant. The upper side of the small leaf is green but the intensely hairy underside and the hairy stems make the overall picture grey. It is a shrub which can be treated as a bush and grown in

a mixed border or given extra shelter against a wall, when it may continue to flower all winter. It has small blue flowers and looks very pretty growing at the base of a *Magnolia grandiflora* whose smooth glossy green leaves make a perfect blend of colour with the *Teucrium*.

Thalictrum All the meadow rues have elegant leaves, but if they are to be used in a mixed border with shrubs they associate best with tall deciduous ones with rather bare bases. A shrub rose, such as *R. glauca* (syn. *R. rubrifolia*) with its purplish-grey foliage, looks pretty with any of the thalictrums and its relatively light shade allows them to grow to their full height; the mauve fluffy heads of the yellow-stamened flowers above the grey-green leaves make a pleasant picture around the leggy base of the rose.

The two native meadow rues, *T. minus* and *T. flavum*, both have excellent garden varieties. *T. minus adiantifolium*, as its name signifies, has attractive maidenhair fern-like foliage and unimportant flowers; *T. flavum glaucum* (syn. *T. speciosissimum*) is a Spanish variety of *T. flavum* with glaucous leaves and tall stems with fluffy yellow flowers, and is excellent in an herbaceous border or in carefully chosen clumps with other grey-green foliage, such as that of *Euphorbia characias wulfenii*. *T. aquilegifolium*, another gift from the

Ravens, prefers full sun and will speedily increase by seeding. Its leaves are green and remarkably similar to the columbine but the flowers are very feathery and usually mauve; a white form is most attractive. The most beautiful of the genus is *T. delavayi* which was collected by seed in 1908 by E. H. Wilson from west China and has deeply divided leaflets and lavender flowers, but it grows tall and is more difficult to place in a mixed planting.

Tricyrtis The toad-lilies seem to thrive in shade, and have exotic looking flowers, like upturned lilies, with purple spots. I have only *T. formosana* which is stoloniferous, spreading by underground roots. It has mauve flowers, speckled with purple and carried on 90cm/36in stems. The leaves are dark green and healthy looking.

Verbascum The tall *V.* 'Vernale', sometimes reaching 2.4-2.75m/8-9ft, is a very useful architectural plant in the garden. It is a prolific seeder and seems not to be attacked by caterpillars.

Veronica I grow only *V. spicata incana*, with its spreading rosettes of grey-green leaves, and *V. gentianoides* and its form *V. g.* 'Variegata'. Both make spreading clumps with powder-blue flowers in 45cm/18in spikes. The variegated form is less vigorous but has leaves prettily margined with cream. *V. spicata incana* has brighter blue flowers and I find it more difficult but worth attempting for a blue and grey border.

Vestia The little South American evergreen shrub *V. lycioides* is reputed to be tender but except for the occasional dying back of a branch it seems to flourish here and sends up healthy suckers at frequent intervals. It has glossy leaves and a strong smell, reminiscent of *Cestrum parqui* to which it is related. Its flowers are tubular and pendent and continue almost all through the summer. At first I gave it preferential treatment and a warm sheltered wall, but now am happy to use it to fill any gap where it looks well, particularly next to grey foliage.

Viola I am always mentioning the little bronze-leaved *V. labradorica purpurea*, either for growing next to grey foliage or for use in quite formal bedding patterns. It is only about 15cm/6in high, with bright dark lavender-blue flowers, which later distribute seed in odd corners all over the garden, where they are always welcome. *V. septentrionalis* has large shining green leaves, which seem to get larger still as the summer progresses, and look cool and refreshing near grey foliage. The flowers are large and white, and come in the spring; unfortunately they have no fragrance. The taller-growing violas such as *V. cornuta* have less notable foliage, but continue to flower almost all summer and make a delightful straggling carpet under roses.

Chapter 6

PLANTS FOR MASSING IN THE OUTER GARDEN

 HATEVER ITS SIZE, every garden has a place for evergreen and deciduous shrubs. In a small garden many of them are decorative enough to be useful as individual plants. In the open, in what can be described as the outer garden at Hadspen, shrubs are used as underplanting for much larger shrubs and small trees.

Obviously shrubs with woody stems cannot serve the same purpose as herbaceous evergreen perennials used as edging plants next to mown grass. Their ultimate shape and form may be seriously and permanently spoilt by haphazard mowing. It is possible to use many arching and overhanging shrubs on the edge of island beds or borders or of what we call woodland or rough garden, and still be able to swing a rotary type of mower underneath them without touching the woody growth. The real edge between soil and grass will never be seen since it will be hidden by suitable evergreens such as *Senecio* 'Sunshine' or *S. monroi*, or some of the shrubby salvias, or the larger sprawling shrubs such as *Cotinus coggygria* or *C. obovatus* (syn. *C. americanus*) – which, although deciduous, make a sufficiently dense growth.

Many bushes also thrive in the conditions created by the existence of a carpeting of more or less impenetrable cover underneath them. As long as suitable foliage and flower associations are chosen, and as long as one species of groundcover is used to unite groups of different species of shrubs, there will be no need to spend much time on jobs such as trimming. As I mentioned earlier, a border of paving set just below the edge of the lawn will have the same result; but when the areas to cover are very large, or if the garden fades away into woodland, as ours does, then it is best to choose suitable plants rather than rely on stone or brick.

For some reason the join between plants and grass can make or mar the whole appearance of a garden. On the whole, it is more economical of labour to groundcover island beds rather than to dot shrubs or groups of shrubs straight into the grass, which is so often done in the expectation of saving trouble. In the end the shrubs will not give of their best unless their lower branches and stems are kept clear of matted grass during the first formative years, and cutting out what must necessarily be a symmetrical shape around them and carefully trimming and weeding at least three times in a growing season, will make considerable demands on one's time. Of course some trees, grown especially for beauty of bark or shape, should be placed as specimens in grass, and nothing can be more beautiful and effective. All I am saying is that it is not necessarily the most labour-saving method, and often the essential tidying and mulching is neglected. Therefore, for shrubs and some small trees carpeted island beds are to be recommended.

For banks and wild areas it is also possible to make use of plants which can climb and twine. True climbers in their wild conditions do not of course have ready-made walls. When there is no need for the extra warmth and reflection of heat which walls give then not only are all climbers at their best twining and scrambling among other plants or over dead trees or outlying fences, but also, by forming a curtain of blossom or foliage, they can add considerably to the visual excitements of the garden. The species roses from Asia which do this so well have been left to the chapter specifically dealing with shrub roses (page 135), and the more tender climbers have been reserved for the section on wall shrubs (page 153).

Hydrangeas, many of them autumn-flowerers, are suitable for the edge of woodland and the larger, shrub-like types have a strong architectural quality. Hydrangea aspera villosa will grow in acid and alkaline soil; its flowers, leaves and stems are all hairy. The showy but infertile sepals, surrounding central smaller flowers, become bluer as acidity increases.

Acer Most of the maples are naturally classified as trees but there are some which branch from the base and are more like a shrub, and these are suitable for growing in groups or in a mixed border. *A. ginnala*, an Asian species, is a large spreading shrub – its bright green leaves with red veins turn a mixture of orange and crimson in the autumn.

The slow-growing Japanese maples, forms of A. *palmatum*, can also be classified as shrubs. A. *p. coreanum* has leaves which turn a rich crimson in autumn and hang on late. The form *dissectum* has exaggeratedly dissected leaves and makes dense mushroom-like and rather artificial growth; but it has pale green spring and summer foliage and good autumn colour. The most exciting of all is A. *p. heptalobum* 'Sango-kaku' (syn. 'Senkaki'), the coral bark maple, which not only has lovely fresh green leaves in summer turning a soft yellow in autumn, but carries them on coral pink branches which add to its winter attraction. This is a shrub which needs a dark background such as a yew to show it at its best. The leaves of A. *p. heptalobum* 'Osakazuki' have the most fiery colours in autumn, but it is one of the slowest growers.

Actinidia Both species, A. *chinensis* and A. *kolomikta*, are twining climbers which can be used to disguise unsightly building or old stumps. The former is very vigorous, perhaps too much so for growing through a precious tree, but ideal for covering something that has had its best years. It is a deciduous hardy plant, quick growing, with red hairy shoots and attractive heart-shaped leaves. The flowers are carried in midsummer and are followed by edible fruits, hence its name – the Chinese gooseberry. It is happy in sun or shade. A. *kolomikta* is an odd colour, its leaves being strangely marked in creamy white and pink. It is much less rampant and can be grown through the leaves of something dark green, like an old bush of *Garrya elliptica*. It needs full exposure to light to bring out the best colour from its variegated leaves.

Akebia A. *quinata* has five-lobed leaves and fragrant dark purplish flowers. It should be allowed to trail through bushes and small trees; it is not sufficiently vigorous to damage a valuable tree or bush. I have mine mingling with a *Clematis chrysocoma* and clambering up the trunk of an old palm, but it also scrambles through the lower shrubs at the base.

Arbutus It is possible to grow two European species of the strawberry tree in a calcareous soil: A. *unedo* and the more tender A. *andrachne*. A. *andrachne* is grown mainly for its cinnamon-coloured bark, which is smooth and peeling and similar to the Californian species A. *menziesii*, which is clearly acid-loving and difficult to establish.

The forms of A. *unedo* all make bushy evergreen shrubs, with glossy dark green leaves and dangling white pitcher-shaped flowers which are followed in the autumn by strawberry-like fruits. These hang on through the winter, so the bushes often carry the new season's flowers simultaneously with the previous year's fruits. As was said earlier, it is one of the few members of the *Ericaceae* family bearing the typical lily-of-the-valley flowers which thrives in lime. Being a hardy evergreen which also responds well to cutting back, it is a useful plant for winter foliage. I grow it here as a group in front of the pale green bamboo *Sinarundinaria nitida* and contrasting with the sword-like leaves of *Phormium tenax*, both underplanted with *Rodgersia aesculifolia*. A grey-leaved *Olearia avicenniifolia* and a small deciduous willow, *Salix repens argentea*, add leaves of different colour and texture to the planting scheme.

Azara This is a genus of evergreen shrubs or small trees from Chile, among which I find A. *dentata* and A. *lanceolata* quite hardy, while the more desirable A. *microphylla* and its variegated form are for a sheltered spot (see page 154). A. *dentata* has ovate to oval leaves which are toothed and shining, and harsh yellow fluffy flowers in early summer. It makes an excellent spreading shrub up to 3m/10ft, and provides new plants by suckering. A. *lanceolata* has prettier, more lanceolate leaves of a brighter green, and a more graceful arching habit. I have grown it next to the grey-leaved weeping pear and near to a group of the fern-leaved early-flowering small yellow *Rosa xanthina* 'Canary Bird', with an underplanting of the coarse-leaved *Brunnera macrophylla* to make a good contrast with the shiny leaves of the *Azara* and give early colour.

Buddleja The more tender buddlejas belong with wall plants in Chapter 10, but there are many species and hybrids worth growing in the outer garden or as individual specimens. B. *alternifolia* can be trained as a one-stemmed tree to make a weeping shape or allowed to branch from the base. It has dark grey-green thin leaves more lanceolate than most of the other buddlejas. It flowers on the previous year's growth so must not be cut back in the spring as is advisable for the more ordinary *davidii* and *fallowiana* types. The flowers are pale lilac and very fragrant. It is an excellent standard tree for a small garden and where there is adequate space looks magnificent planted in a group. A silver-leaved form, B.*a.* 'Argentea', is even more beautiful but less vigorous.

B. *colvilei* and its darker-flowered form B. *c.* 'Kewensis' are semi-evergreen and have red tubular flowers held in hanging clusters, with grey hairy oval-lanceolate leaves, the new growth being very pale. This shrub can reach 9m/30ft but is more normally a rounded bush of about 3m/10ft square. It is hardy in most parts of Britain and should not be pruned. I have underplanted it with the prostrate hybrid rose 'Max Graf' and the intensely glossy leaf of the rose makes a perfect contrast to the felted leaf above. It does not make the same curtain of blossom as B. *alternifolia* but is more unusual.

All the forms and hybrids of B. *davidii* flower in late summer, and their flowers attract butterflies and scent the garden. B. 'Lochinch', a *davidii* × *fallowiana* hybrid, has grey

Clematis twines into shrubs to
make a background show behind
lavatera (Lavatera thuringiaca
'Barnsley') and a group
of silver-leaved lychnis
(L.coronaria oculata).
Clematis viticella 'Purpurea
Plena Elegans' is one of the best
of these small-flowered types, its
sultry purple colouring
contributing to many late-
summer effects. It should be cut
down to two buds in early spring
each year.

woolly leaves and pale violet-blue flowers with orange
centres. *B. d.* 'Harlequin' has attractive variegated foliage
and needs to be planted in a group to be seen to advantage. I
prefer not to have the yellow *B. globosa* or *B. × weyeriana*,
but they are useful strong fast growers if their difficult yellow-
orange flowers can be fitted into a colour scheme.

Clematis Most of the small-flowered species *Clematis*, as distinct from the more artificial large-flowered hybrids, are at
their best when allowed to scramble through trees, shrubs
and over old walls. Those suitable for this purpose need no
regular pruning and are in general spring-flowering, and if
not too vigorous are most effective grown through evergreens which often look unsightly in the spring, with leaves
damaged and browned by late frosts or frost-laden winds. Of
course, if you prefer the small-flowered species to the exotic
larger-flowered varieties, then they can be equally satisfactory against a wall. One of the best combinations in the
garden here has been the mixture of flower and foliage. A

double yellow Banksian rose tumbles over the broken walls of an old orchid house together with *Clematis chrysocoma sericea* (syn. *C. spooneri*), an attractive form of *C. chrysocoma* with white flowers instead of pink; both are similar to *C. montana* but are distinguished by their downy foliage.

C. montana is a rampant grower with many different forms. *C. m. rubens* has bronze-coloured shoots and leaves and clear rose-pink flowers. *C. m.* 'Tetrarose' has larger blossoms. One of the most satisfactory is *C. × vedrariensis*, a cross between *C. montana* and *C. chrysocoma*, which has purplish leaves and bright yellow stamens in a rose-pink flower. Actually until you pick them for close examination, as I have just done, you can see very little difference in their appearance and habit when they are all in flower at the beginning of summer. All look splendid draped over evergreens and they can also be used to cover banks and walls. They need little attention but, if grown in semi-wild conditions, care must be taken not to cut through the young stem growing at the base of an established tree; it is surprising how easy it is to overlook it when clearing away untidy undergrowth.

The evergreen clematis, *C. armandii*, should be grown through the base of a forked shrub or tree as it seldom shoots from low down and the long stem is not attractive. One of E. H. Wilson's discoveries in China at the beginning of the century, it has long leathery and glossy leaves with creamy-white flowers, or, in *C. a.* 'Apple Blossom', very pale pink ones. I have planted it on the north side of a 3m/10ft wall where it climbs up into the branches of an old cotoneaster and makes a fragrant canopy over the south border in March. *C. cirrhosa balearica* is also evergreen, with ferny foliage and pale small flowers in late winter. It is more tender and less suitable for the wild garden.

The later-flowering species such as *CC. rehderiana, tangutica* and *viticella* are all worth growing through other plants, but as they need cutting back in early spring they are best kept in the more formal part of the garden where this task will not be overlooked. *C. flammula* needs cutting down each year but will reach 4.5m/15ft in a season and has tiny white almond-scented flowers in the autumn. Most suitable for twining around a gatepost or for the back of a border

against a dark hedge, it was used by Miss Jekyll in many of her planting designs.

Clerodendrum Both *C. bungei* and *C. trichotomum* were in the garden here when we came and both are valuable late-summer flowerers with attractive foliage. *C. bungei* has dark red suckering stems and *C. trichotomum* seeds, so there is no problem in replacement. *C. bungei* bears large corymbs of rose-red flowers in early autumn and usually dies back to the ground each winter. It is excellent for a suckering thicket in a rough corner. *C. trichotomum* grows as a strong woody shrub with deliciously fragrant white flowers with maroon calyces in late summer, followed by blue shining berries. They are very fast growers but do not live for many years. They are not really tender but unfortunately often come into leaf in mild spells in the winter and then get cut back by later frosts.

Cornus Although strictly speaking we should be concerned here only with the suckering dogwoods which make weed-proof thickets in island beds or at the edge of the garden, this is such an invaluable genus for foliage, flower, fruit, bark and form, that it is worth trying to sort out some of the different groups.

Cornus mas, with its golden and variegated forms, belongs to the cornelian cherry section and is a native of central and southern Europe. In classical times it was the source of an iron-hard wood for spear shafts and, some say, for building the Trojan Horse. It was first grown in Britain for its fruit, which to modern tastes is not appetizing and, in fact, seldom borne. Later it was appreciated for its tiny yellow flowers carried on leafless branches in early spring. It can be pretty when trained to grow on a single stem. The varieties *C. m.* 'Variegata' and *C. m.* 'Elegantissima' are both attractive. One has the habit of the type while the latter, with variegated leaves tinged with pink, makes a sprawling shrub.

The group called benthamidias includes small trees and shrubs from North America and Asia, which have beautiful ornamental bracts surrounding the true flowers and are described in Chapter 8. The low growing sub-shrub *C. canadensis* has already been mentioned as acid-loving woodland cover. *C. controversa* and *C. alternifolia* eventually make small trees and are the only ones with alternate rather than opposite leaves, which makes them easily recognizable, and are usually grown for their horizontal form (see page 113). The former is a recent importation from Asia while the latter is from North America. Both of them have attractive variegated forms.

The suckering shrubs which are suitable for massing or for individual planting in mixed borders generally improve with

At Hadspen, the scented Clerodendrum trichotomum flowers in front of a large smoke bush (Cotinus obovatus) during late summer. In time, both become small trees rather than shrubs. The white flowers of the clerodendron are enclosed in maroon calyces. In autumn the clerodendron has translucent turquoise blue berries which are spectacular beside the fiery colours of the foliage of the American smoke bush.

cutting back every few years in spring and so are useful for the smaller garden. They are grown for their remarkable coloured stems and for their gold and silver variegated foliage. *C. sanguinea* is to be found in our hedgerows; the leaves turn red in the autumn. *C. stolonifera*, introduced to Britain from North America in 1656, forms a dense thicket of dark red stems, while its variety *C. s.* 'Flaviramea' has yellow young shoots. The Russian cornus is the true red-barked dogwood, *C. alba*, so-called for its fruit, and its many splendid forms are useful in all parts of the garden. Its green-leaved type was first grown by Philip Miller in the Chelsea Physic Garden; its variety *C. a.* 'Sibirica', the Westonbirt dogwood, has the most scarlet winter stems of them all. For foliage effects alone, *C. a.* 'Elegantissima' with silver variegation and *C. a.* 'Spaethii' with gold, are the best of those listed here; they are often planted with purple-leaved shrubs but personally I prefer them with the contrast of smooth greens, and with underplantings of hostas or against a dark background. The golden variegated 'Spaethii' looks prettier and less vivid when in semi-shade.

All these shrubs are suitable for planting in groups with other strong growers chosen either for flower, like the large spiraeas and deutzias, or for their attactive foliage in the case of *Olearia macrodonta* or *Elaeagnus* × *ebbingei* or the almost weeping *E.* × *reflexa*. This last makes a contrasting shape to the vase-like growth of the dogwoods. A vigorous shrub rose such as *R.* 'Highdownensis' or *R.* 'Cerise Bouquet' can be planted at the back of a group of dogwoods and the pleasant foliage of the roses and their flowers add interest and contrast to the scheme.

Corokia These little New Zealand shrubs are worth planting for their dark twigs and grey leaves. The flowers are inconspicuous. They need to be placed in a group for emphasis and are attractive with groundcover such as *Alchemilla mollis*, or the less vigorous *A. conjuncta*. Until recently *C. cotoneaster*, the wire-netting bush, was the only variety I had tried, but I have now been given *C. macrocarpa*, which is more beautiful but also more tender; it is described in Chapter 10.

Corylopsis The *Corylopsis* genus is closely akin to the hazel – *Corylus* – but is not planted frequently. Various species, depending on their size, are suitable for the garden. *C. glabrescens* can grow to about 4.5m/15ft and there are good examples of it in the arboretum at Westonbirt. I had no idea when I first planted it that it grew so large, so unfortunately lost it by moving it in the spring. Now I have the smaller *C. spicata*, and *C. pauciflora* which grows to about 1.5m/5ft and as much across. These three are relatively late introductions from Asia and all have drooping yellow cup-shaped flowers

Above *In early spring* Corylopsis pauciflora *has delicious, cowslip-scented, pale yellow flowers. Since it seldom grows to more than 1.5m/5ft in height or across, this member of the witch hazel family is suitable for any size of garden. It flowers in sun or shade and I find that it grows well even in a limy soil.*

Right *Smoke bushes (the genus* Cotinus), *although slow-growing, eventually make rounded billowing shapes. The tiny flowers, massed in panicles, give a cloudy smoke-like effect. There are several good bronze or purple-leaved cultivars which are useful for specific border colour schemes.*

carried in the early spring just before the leaves. They are handsome shrubs for the woodland or for a shady mixed border where they can be left undisturbed.

Corylus The native hazel is a pleasant but not outstanding shrub which can be useful as a screen and is attractive in late winter when covered with yellow catkins. One of the most popular varieties is *C. avellana* 'Contorta' which grows in a strange twisted shape and is planted mainly for its oddity value rather than for its beauty. Here I grow only *C. maxima*

'Purpurea', which has large leaves of a dull purple colour. It is a useful foliage plant for putting in a group or as a contrast to fresh pale greens or red and pink flowers. Shrub roses with grey-green leaves or with fiery red flowers blend well with it and the tea-leaf willow, *Salix phylicifolia*, also makes an excellent foliage association, with its small shining green leaves with glaucous undersides and its dark stems.

Cotinus The rounded leaves of *Cotinus coggygria*, the European Venetian sumach or smoke tree, which comes in various forms, give good autumn colour and are bronze to green most of the season. There are two purple-leaved forms, but it is worth getting hold of the almost translucent 'Royal Purple' or 'Notcutt's Variety' in preference to the plain rather dull and heavy purple of the more ordinary 'Foliis Purpureis'. 'Royal Purple' is a plant which can be used over and over again for different foliage purposes and it gives one of the best and clearest reds in the autumn. I have grown it intertwined with *Clematis* 'Nelly Moser' and the tender rose *R.* 'Anemone' on a warm wall, not because the *Cotinus* needs the protection but because of its invaluable foliage colour.

Similarly, in another place I have allowed the orange-scarlet flowers of the tender *Eccremocarpus scaber* to straggle through the purple foliage, much to my delight and admiration but to shocked gasps from some visitors. Behind the *Cotinus* is a huge mass of the climbing rose 'Madame Grégoire Staechelin' with its abundant and breathtaking pink heads tumbling into the plant in front. In yet another more exposed area *Rosa* 'Paulii Rosea' creates a rather similar effect, and *Hemerocallis* 'Pink Damask' is in the foreground. It also associates well with *Alchemilla mollis*, and the little grey-leaved *Hebe* 'Pagei' makes another excellent contrast. The American *Cotinus*, *C. obovatus*, has the most vivid of the autumn colours, with shades varying from scarlet and orange to purple. What now belong to the *Rhus* genus will be touched on in Chapter 8.

Deutzia Members of this group, like the spiraeas, have slightly unpredictable flowering habits. They come into bloom in early summer and form their flower buds so early that they are sometimes caught by late spring frosts. Also, as with the late-flowering *Spiraea veitchii*, a very dry spell may deprive them of moisture necessary to make the buds swell. When originally introduced from the Far East the *Deutzia* was treated as a half-hardy cousin of the *Philadelphus*, and although it was in garden cultivation by 1822, Loudon still wrote in 1848 of *D. scabra* as a greenhouse shrub for forcing, like *D. gracilis*. Hybridizing has produced many compact arching bushes which are well worth having when they bear very slightly tinted purple leaves and rose-pink flowers. Although deciduous, they make a dense bush and a graceful shape and the flowers are valuable, particularly in a garden where few traditional midsummer herbaceous plants are grown. One of the best species is the summer-flowering *D. chunii*, which is an arching bush with long thin grey leaves, pink flowers with yellow anthers, and peeling pale brown bark. Completely opposite in habit is *D. setchuenensis* which has an upright form, pale green leaves and white flowers in corymbs in midsummer. It is reputedly tender but, except for having brittle wood, seems quite hardy here. In a cold garden deutzias should be given a place at the top of a slope.

Disanthus This is one of the medium-sized acid-loving shrubs which gardeners on lime much regret. It is a monotypic genus from Japan, *D. cercidifolius*, with leaves like a Judas tree but colouring a more vivid scarlet in autumn than almost any other shrub. I can visualize a group adding considerably to the autumn attraction of any garden with acid soil, but in England the shrub is rarely seen.

Elaeagnus The North American species known as the silver berry is one of the best grey-leaved deciduous shrubs for foliage combinations. It is a suckering shrub, *E. commutata* (syn. *E. argentea*), with narrow oval leaves of glistening silver. The young shoots are covered with brown scales. It flowers in spring but, although profuse, is not so fragrant as the deciduous Asian variety *E. umbellata*, which, with much less interesting leaves, scents the garden with delicious fragrance. *E. commutata* can be grown next to the red-orange flowers of *Euphorbia griffithii* in front of the apple-green leaves of *Griselinia littoralis*; or beside a planting of the more shrubby *Euphorbia mellifera*; or again, it may be allowed to sucker freely to form a contrast in texture with the equally grey but felted leaves of *Salix lanata*. It is such an exceptional plant that it will set off any foliage. *E. umbellata* has almost yellow young growth and is much taller and more straggly in shape. *E. angustifolia*, the Russian olive, has silver leaves and its form *E.a. caspina* has very fragrant yellow flowers.

The evergreen *Elaeagnus* most frequently seen is *E. pungens* and its vivid variegated form *E. p.* 'Maculata'. But I prefer the elegant grey-green leaves of *E. × ebbingei*, which is a hybrid of *E. pungens* and *E. macrophylla*. Actually the three are very similar with possibly an advantage in favour of the hybrid which has pale silver undersides to its leaves. Both the parent species are Asiatics. *E. glabra* is another evergreen very similar to *E. pungens* in leaf, but it will climb as much as 4.5m/15ft into a suitable tree. It is seldom grown but is effective against the dark foliage of an evergreen yew or ilex. *E. × reflexa* I have seen only at Trelissick in Cornwall where it makes a large wavy bush with a pendulous habit; it is a hybrid of *E. glabra* with *E. pungens*. The more rounded evergreens make excellent shapes and contrast well with horizontal plants such as *Viburnum plicatum* 'Lanarth' or 'Mariesii', or with upright trees of vase-like form. They are all wind resistant and suitable for exposure to sea gales, but can be severely damaged by frost.

Enkianthus These make beautiful and elegant branching shrubs for acid soil, and have the typical pendulous cup-shaped flower of the *Ericaceae* family. They all have vivid autumn colours and formal shapes.

Escallonia Escallonias are from South America and there are many good garden hybrids. Not all species are hardy inland but with their attractive shining green leaves and pink, white and red flowers, they are useful evergreens for hedges or specimen plants. I describe only those which I grow here.

One of the most tender, with long narrowly oval leaves of a translucent green with a pink vein, is *E. bifida* (syn. *E. montevidensis*). I was given this plant from the coastal garden at Abbotsbury and it flourishes here with protection from other shrubs. The white flowers are carried in panicles in later summer. I grow it with the blue-green foliage of *Euphorbia characias wulfenii* and with the suckering *Elaeagnus commutata*, which makes a good combination. On the other side is an *Olearia nummulariifolia*, which has thick small yellowy leaves making a strong contrast with the lax form of the soft leaves of the *Escallonia*.

E. rubramacrantha is a useful and tough shiny-leaved variety with rose-crimson flowers, which will thrive in sun or shade, and makes an excellent hedge, always looking healthy and glowing. It is a parent of many hybrids. *E.* 'Apple Blossom' is a small slow-growing shrub with pink and white flowers, very attractive to bees. *E.* 'Iveyi' is one of the best and larger varieties, with glittering smooth oval leaves and beautiful panicles of white flowers in midsummer. It is often used for hedges near the sea and is marked in Hillier's *Manual* as unreliably hardy, but seems to develop well in our rather sheltered inland garden. I have used it as a dark hedge to shelter grey-leaved plants but it is equally desirable as a single tall specimen, since the particularly glossy leaves make a perfect foil to almost all duller greens and often provide a focal point in a bed or border. The 'Donard' hybrids make more open cascading shrubs, with small leaves and flowers of different pinks and reds; *E.* 'Donard Seedling' has flesh-pink buds which open white. I have grown it as a hedge behind groups of *Hippophae rhamnoides* and the grey-leaved Gallica rose 'Complicata'. The shrubs are underplanted with *Geranium macrorrhizum* and this scheme has the merit of saving on both time and labour except for the occasional removal of rose suckers and cutting back the *Escallonia* every few years after the flowering season.

Euonymus Here we are concerned with the deciduous species, which are grown for their splendid autumn foliage and fruits, and with the Japanese evergreen, *E. japonicus*, which has many different leaf colours and is used primarily for hedges and seaside planting. The European spindle, *E. europaeus*, is a British native. It colours slightly and bears many red fruits. If it is already in your garden it is worth keeping, or some of its forms are, but it is far surpassed in value by the Asiatic *E. alatus*, which has distinctive corky wings on

Euonymus planipes, a spindle from north-east Asia, has a well-shaped regular habit, and its leaves turn brilliant red and yellow in autumn before falling. The fruits, typical of the genus, are scarlet and break open to reveal yellow seeds. Plant several specimens in order to be sure of cross-pollination and obtaining fruit. There are other spindles that also contribute glorious leaf and berry colours each season, particularly the easy-to-grow more compact European native, E.alatus, with broad corky wings on its branchlets.

the branchlets and turns a translucent scarlet in autumn, particularly if given an open exposure. It responds well to being trained into an espalier shape against a sunny wall. If you have the space, plant it in a group of at least three; it is the alkaline alternative to the acid-loving *Disanthus*.

E. planipes (syn. *E. sachalinensis*) is a taller bush with scarlet berries and good autumn colour, while the Japanese species, *E. yedoensis*, is a small tree which bears pale pink fruits with orange seed coats and has scarlet foliage in early autumn. The evergreen *E. japonicus* can grow also into a small tree, but is more generally used as a hedge which is kept closely clipped. It has many interesting variegated forms but the type itself has smooth shiny oval leaves of great charm. It looks magnificent planted in a group instead of as a screen, and is quite happy in shade.

Fatsia *F. japonica* (syn. *Aralia japonica*) is an excellent evergreen shrub with large shining palmate leaves. Its attractive variegated form has white rims to the lobes of the leaves, but is more tender than the green type. It gives a strong subtropical effect, but is quite hardy and at its best when grown in a dark corner. It looks perfect overhanging the pale green arching stems of Solomon's seal, and itself carries panicles of creamy-white flowers in the late summer. Although evergreen, it drops its leaves in rather an untidy way and they are so large that they need removing from the ground below before they can damage emerging plants. The Italian Arum, *Arum italicum pictum*, is similar to the British native lords and ladies but has white marbling on the green leaves and so contrasts well with the plain green of the *Fatsia*.

Griselinia *G. littoralis* is another of those New Zealand evergreens which are happiest away from inland frosts: choose a frost-free site at the top of a slope. Its leaves are one of the best colours of pale apple green and it makes a delightful wall shrub or group of shrubs as well as a seaside hedge. At Abbotsbury I have seen it as a 9m/30ft tree. There is a translucent quality about the green of the leaves which makes it excellent for blending with grey foliage; it is more distinguished than a shrub such as *Euonymus japonicus*. A species with a larger leaf, *G. lucida*, is smaller and more tender.

Hamamelis I do not want to spend too much time on the witch hazel since I do not much care for its shape or leaves, nor for the flowers themselves, which are rather spidery-looking with yellow petals and a red-brown calyx. Many winter flowers, although strongly scented, are not particularly attractive in appearance since soft petals would be damaged by frost. For the scent itself *H. mollis* is probably the best; a hybrid of it, *H.* 'Pallida', has paler prettier flowers.

It will tolerate considerable shade, so should be tucked away where it does not show too much but is sufficiently close to a doorway or path to enable the full delicious fragrance to be appreciated in winter.

Hippophae The sea buckthorn, *H. rhamnoides*, is a European native. There is no problem in growing it; once established it will send out suckering roots which will even penetrate tarmac. If you want a thicket on the windy side of the garden this is an ideal shrub, which although deciduous carries orange berries in winter – as long as there are male and female plants together – and has sharp spines on its young growth to discourage intruders. The silver willow-like leaves make it extremely desirable as a foliage plant, in spite of its invasive tendencies, and it is a useful alternative to the weeping pear, *Pyrus salicifolia* 'Pendula', when an upright habit is required rather than a drooping one. I find it makes an excellent plant to grow with arching shrub roses, and in particular 'Complicata' which sends out long branches carrying the large pale pink flowers to weave through the buckthorn. However, I have had to use weedkiller to control the wandering shoots which invade paths, and have planted it with a total groundcover as it is painful weeding near it.

Hydrangea This is clearly a group about which it is important to be extremely selective and I must say at once that no member of the Hortensia group of *H. macrophylla* will ever cross my doorstep, or garden boundary fence. For some reason, when the Continent of Europe decided to adopt the English style of landscape garden, and incidentally destroyed many beautiful French and Italian gardens, this vulgar, and showy plant – newly introduced from Japan in 1790 – was, and indeed still is, planted everywhere. Basically it is a woodland shrub revelling in shade and moisture so it seems an unfortunate choice.

The classification of the various species is confused, particularly in the *macrophylla* section: dividing them into lacecaps, which have flat corymbs of fertile flowers surrounded by a ring of sterile florets, and hortensias with mop heads of sterile florets, is the simplest way to draw a distinction. Dealing with this common hydrangea first, before going on to the more exciting species, there are many good forms which grow strongly and flower freely. Colours vary with the soil, the more acid soil producing intense blue, especially if aluminium sulphate is added, while limy soil produces pink flowers. If you want to play safe, choose the white varieties. *H. m.* 'Lanarth White' and *H. m.* 'White Wave' are both excellent and make thickets for the woodland garden. The *H. serrata* varieties are more suitable for a small garden and some of its forms have good bronze foliage colour in autumn. The rather tender *H. m.* 'Tricolor' has pretty variegated leaves marked in green, grey and pale yellow. This is tender when young but once established will survive late spring frosts. All the hydrangeas are susceptible in their early years and are best planted on slopes. I have put this variegated hydrangea next to a group of *Geranium psilostemon* and the magenta flowers go well with the foliage of the hydrangea.

Most of the species we grow here are Asians. An exception is the North American *H. quercifolia*, which makes one of the most ornamental medium-sized shrubs, but needs protection in a mixed bed or, in cold areas, the shelter of a wall. It has magnificent autumn-colouring leaves, shaped like those of an oak tree, and flowers freely with white panicles of mixed fertile and sterile flowers. I have grown it against a low wall near to plants with huge leaves like the rheums, but with its roots safely removed from too much winter moisture, and also in a group underplanted with a plain green hosta and contrasting with the fresh leaves of the Rugosa rose 'Roseraie de l'Haÿ'. It is a semi-evergreen here.

H. heteromalla bretschneideri makes a fine large spreading shrub which has white lace-cap flowers, beautiful peeling bark and attractive downy foliage. *H. robusta* is similar but has darker and more hairy bronze leaves; it is possible however that my plant is *H. aspera*. *H. sargentiana* has a strange gaunt habit of growth and is extremely slow; unusual rather than beautiful, it is the sort of exotic bush that one should happen on unexpectedly in a woodland glade. It has huge velvety leaves, not at all densely carried, and peeling bark, and should not be crowded by other shrubs.

H. petiolaris, a Japanese species, is a deciduous climber which will cover banks or flat surfaces and clamber over stumps and walls with self-clinging rootlets; it bears great greenish-white corymbs, with sterile white florets around the edge. Another interesting climbing variety is *H. integerrima* (now *H. serratifolia*) which is evergreen with entire leaves but less exciting flowers. It is rarely grown in Britain.

Finally, one of the best for flower and foliage is *H. aspera villosa* which, contrary to what is recommended for most hydrangeas, thrives in full sun as long as the roots are protected by a cool mulch or the leaves of low-growing plants. Its leaves, stems and flower stalks are covered with long soft hairs and the flowers are large and flat and pinky mauve. It is a valuable shrub for late summer colour and in the winter its peeling white bark is a distinctive asset.

Kolkwitzia This is a monotypic genus of which the only species, *K. amabilis*, was introduced by E. H. Wilson from western China in the form of seed, and first flowered in Veitch's nursery in 1910. It has a strange habit, densely twiggy with drooping branchlets. It is named after a German botanist; the epithet *amabilis* means lovable. The trumpet-shaped flowers are pale pink and the soft hairy leaves pale green with pink tinges. It flowers best the year after a really hot summer and, given heat to ripen the wood, can probably survive extreme cold in winter.

Lathyrus The everlasting pea, *L. latifolius*, is suitable for growing over banks and through dense cover; the only problem is that it needs cutting back in winter to remove untidy dead stems. As it twines itself vigorously around other plants care must be taken not to damage them when struggling with the pea. I have it growing over the edge of our big reservoir where, although it still needs tidying annually, it does no harm. The usual form is magenta but there are more attractive pink- and white-flowered varieties.

Ligustrum Hastily passing by the common privet, *L. vulgare*, I must emphasize the value of some of the Asiatic species in this genus. Here I have forms of the common evergreen *L. ovalifolium* which, in gold and silver variegation, are valuable and tough plants for dark corners in woodland and need little light or sunshine. The following species are listed alphabetically.

L. henryi is a compact pyramid-shaped evergreen with neat variable leaves, ovate lanceolate in some cases and the larger ones with a slightly retuse tip are dark green above but pale on the underside. In late summer it bears large panicles of white flowers. Not altogether dissimilar is *L. japonicum*, but this has more leathery leaves and makes a much wider and more spreading shrub or small tree. *L. lucidum* has an attractively fluted trunk and is worth growing as a tree; it is useful in the same sort of circumstances as *Phillyrea latifolia*. A Chinese semi-evergreen, this privet is more free-flowering than *L. japonicum*, but of less value as winter foliage. There is a good example of it in the Chelsea Physic Garden where it is probably sufficiently sheltered to keep its leaves.

Lonicera The tougher varieties of *Lonicera* or honeysuckle are perfectly suitable as deciduous shrubs or as twining climbers for growing in rough corners or groupings with other shrubs. The two evergreens *L. pileata* and *L. nitida* make useful thickets in woodland if grown in a mass and the latter is also well known as a popular, if unimaginative, hedge. The evergreen climber *L. japonica* 'Aureoreticulata' has strange mottled green and yellow leaves, not really very pretty, but its intricate way of growing makes it useful for foliage; it also suckers readily and will make a dense cover on a sunny bank. The winter-flowering honeysuckle makes an untidy bush in summer suitable only for the outer garden, but has very fragrant flowers, as its name *fragrantissima* tells you. I wish I also had the species *L. standishii*, named after the famous nurseryman John Standish and brought back from China by Robert Fortune in 1845.

The native deciduous *L. periclymenum* and its Dutch forms are all at their best trailing over stumps or fences in woodland, while the evergreen *L. japonica* 'Halliana' has scented white to yellow flowers all summer in shade or in the open. *L. tragophylla* prefers shade and has the purest yellow flowers but unfortunately no scent. *L. × tellmanniana*, a hybrid of this, with bronze-yellow flowers is a tender evergreen and perhaps not so suitable for the outer garden. Like the scarlet trumpet honeysuckle, *L. × brownii*, it deserves a warm wall to get the best flowering.

Olearia Skipping impatiently past the Ms and Ns, both of which crop up with magnolias and myrtles, *Nandina* and *Nothofagus* in their respective chapters on tender plants and ornamental trees, we reach the genus which, above all, contains many excellent and under-utilized evergreen shrubs, with varied foliage and charming trusses of daisy flowers.

Some olearias need protection and must be relegated to the wall border, for example *OO. chathamica*, × *mollis*, *moschata*, *semidentata* and *traversii*. Actually this splitting up applies only to some gardens, as of course *O. semidentata* (now *O.* 'Henry Travers') and *O. traversii* are hardy near the sea. The following I can grow in the open, but with some protection from other shrubs: *O. albida* (although it is happier against a wall) with its pale green, slightly undulating leaves, rather similar to those of *O. paniculata* (syn. *O. forsteri*) but with less sheen; the completely hardy *O. avicenniifolia*, which has dark green leaves, felted underneath, a long flowering period and makes a large shrub of up to 3.6m/12ft; *O. rani* (syn. *O. cunninghamii*), which flowers here all through May with large branched loose flat heads of white daisies, and has narrow dark green leaves with white beneath; and *O. paniculata*, one of the best for bright green undulating foliage, resembling *Pittosporum tenuifolium* but growing in a more sprawling fashion.

O. × haastii is the hardiest of all the genus and is much used for seaside and town planting. It is a little dull but flowers freely and has neat oval leathery leaves and a compact habit. *O. ilicifolia* is a slow spreading shrub with sharply toothed leathery leaves, white underneath. *O. insignis* (now *Pachystegia insignis*) is reputedly tender, with thick felted shoots and large entire leaves, green above and white and felted below. One of the hardiest is *O. macrodonta* which has attractive foliage, sharply toothed, very grey above and white below. It grows into a large shrub and is particularly good for massing in extensive groundcovering groups.

O. nummulariifolia has small thin closely packed leaves and is very hardy, but less exciting than the olearias which have the large leaves with felted undersides. *O. solanderi* is nearer to it than any other variety and looks remarkably like *Cassinia fulvida*. *O. × scilloniensis* is a very free-flowering hybrid, with grey leaves, and covered in trusses of white flowers in early summer; it is from the *stellulata* group, now called *phlogopappa*, all of which have great flower trusses. *O. capillaris* has interesting wiry stems, small narrow obovate leaves, and insignificant loosely carried white daisies.

Finally, the best of all is a hybrid named *O.* 'Zennorensis' after a garden in Cornwall. It has narrow pointed sharply toothed leaves and its young shoots are covered with brown felt, giving the bush and leaves an almost pink look. It makes a sturdy shrub and is protected here by the woody *Euphorbia characias wulfenii*. For safety's sake, I have put rooted cuttings in a sheltered wall site just in case we get a really hard winter. This and other tender olearias are included in Chapter 10.

I grow olearias for leaf interest and variation – the flowers are really a bonus – and I find they mix well with smooth green leaves and, being evergreen, are valuable for winter foliage effects.

Osmanthus This is another race of evergreen shrubs which have excellent foliage and extremely fragrant flowers. They are all from Asia except for one North American species which is too tender for outdoors in Britain. *O. fragrans*, which comes from China and Japan and was one of the first to be introduced to Europe, must have a sheltered wall preferably in a coastal garden. I have seen it only in Italy. It has typical large slightly toothed leaves and the most scented flowers of all the genus carried in a cluster on a stalk, whereas all the others carry their flowers in the axils of the leaves.

O. armatus, introduced by E. H. Wilson in 1902, is a large branching shrub up to 6m/20ft, with thick long leaves, armed with spiny hooks and teeth when young but later becoming entire. We have an old bush here, planted, I imagine, soon after its introduction to Britain, which now has an elegant fan-shape, slightly bare at the base. I have grown a *Rosa longicuspis* through it and it makes a focal point at the end of a flagged walk, covered in midsummer with a curtain of rose blossom and later in the autumn bearing its own small but fragrant flowers. (I am now convinced that one plant in this garden that has always been identified as *O. armatus* is in fact *O. yunnanensis*, which explains why I have found toothed as well as entire leaves on it. It also has beautiful pink-bronze young growth and certainly flowers later than September which is the time given for *O. armatus*. I am delighted to think that I in fact have both species.) Both

The golden-leaved form of Philadelphus coronarius contrasts well with the purplish-red young foliage of the evergreen Photinia × fraseri 'Red Robin'. Philadelphus, known in the past as syringa, or mock-orange for the scented flowers, have in general rather undistinguished foliage; those with variegated or golden leaves are the exception, although the latter should be grown in shade as the leaves are easily scorched in full sunlight. By the end of the summer the golden tints have turned to green.

the following year. I prune it as well by cutting branches of blossom for the house. *O. heterophyllus* is a holly-like bush with coarsely spined shiny leaves. Its insignificant flowers in late autumn are fragrant and welcome at that season.

I grow *O. h.* 'Purpureus', the young shoots of which are purple, and *O. h.* 'Variegatus', which has leaves bordered in cream. They are slow growing but excellent foliage plants.

Osmanthus × burkwoodii was formerly known as × *Osmarea burkwoodii* and is a hybrid deriving from an inter-generic cross between *Osmanthus delavayi* and *Phillyrea decora* (now *Osmanthus decorus*). It has leaves halfway in size between the two and flowers very similar to those of *O. delavayi*, although appearing a little later, on terminal stalks as well as in the leaf axils. It is better to grow both if you have plenty of space, but *delavayi* in my opinion is a better shrub even if less hardy.

Philadelphus The old common name of this plant is syringa. The original *P. coronarius* comes from the Caucasus and was introduced to western Europe at the same time as the true *Syringa* came from eastern Europe, and Gerard classified them together. This is the reason why the *Philadelphus* has for four hundred years been called 'Syringa', but the confusion still seems strange since we know that by 1623 Bauhin had sorted out this botanical mix-up and that his conclusions were confirmed by Linnaeus in 1735. If you want an English name call it 'Mock Orange'.

Two American species, *P. coulteri* and *P. microphyllus*, have become the parents of innumerable hybrids of varying degrees of beauty in fragrance and flower form. There are two varieties of *P. coronarius* itself which are valuable as foliage plants, but one of these, *P. c.* 'Variegatus', is extremely difficult to grow successfully. The other is one of the finest deciduous golden-leaved shrubs, besides having the typical creamy-white scented flowers of the species. *P. c.* 'Aureus' has very bright yellow leaves in early spring which gradually turn green through the summer. At its best grown in a shady corner, it is perfectly hardy, and suckers freely to make new plants. In full sun it is almost too startling a colour and by midsummer often has scorch marks. I have put it against a dark background next to the whitebeam, *Sorbus aria* 'Lutescens', and this makes an attractive picture in the spring with *Euphorbia amygdaloides robbiae* and *E. pilosa* in the foreground, with flower colour almost identical to the leaves of the *Philadelphus*. The fragrant *P. microphyllus* itself is suitable only for a border or rock-garden; it is small, with delicate leaves and twigs.

We found many of this genus in the garden and they all have good old-fashioned scent. Instead of regularly cutting out the older wood, every few years I do a total chop to the

O. yunnanensis and *O. armatus* need perpendicular trees planted nearby for contrast.

O. delavayi is perhaps the most popular *Osmanthus*, with dark glossy sharply toothed oval leaves and scented white flowers with a cylindrical tube, resembling those of a jasmine, which cover the bush in spring. This shrub is quite hardy when established but like many evergreens is best planted out in spring the first year. It can be used for a dark hedge if given an annual clipping after flowering, and thus keeping its compact shape as well as ensuring free flowering

ground. This means no flowers the following year but seems to refresh and enrich the bushes. Of course this drastic treatment is possible only in a large garden where you can always keep some varieties in perfect flowering condition and which ones you choose is really a question of personal preference. Many of the hybrids have inherited a purple blotch from *P. coulteri*, the leaf is not exciting and the winter appearance is excessively dreary. They seed abundantly all over the garden, so even if I had known which varieties we had to start with I would be confused by this time, but I prefer single flowers to double.

Phillyrea *P. angustifolia* and the tree *P. latifolia* are from southern Europe, North Africa and Asia Minor, but have been grown in Britain since the sixteenth century. *P. angustifolia* was a popular shrub during the seventeenth-century topiary craze and makes effective neat dome-shaped bushes. It has been used in this way around a pond at Iford Manor in Wiltshire. If grown as a dark evergreen hedge it needs plenty of cutting back, especially at the base, in order to make it

Above The arching stems of Rubus cockburnianus are purple but overlaid with a whitish bloom to give a grey effect during the winter months. The small pinnate fern-like leaves, with white under-surfaces, give a similar appearance throughout the summer, a foil to rosy-purple flowers and black fruits.

Right Pollarded willows provide glowing bark colours all through the duller winter months. The scarlet willow, Salix alba 'Britzensis' (syn. S.a. 'Chermesina'), should be pruned every two years to get the maximum colour effects of its young shoots.

really dense. If you want to edge a small formal area or create a gateway effect, this shrub always seems to me more attractive than one of the regular-shaped conifers, which are much more frequently used. Also, it has a sheen on its leaves that yew does not have, and it grows more quickly than box.

Polygonum *P. baldschuanicum* (syn. *Bilderdykia baldschuanica*, now correctly *Fallopia baldschuanica*) is known as the Russian vine. This rampant deciduous climber is a most useful plant for a bank, or for covering an ugly building. It really

is only for the larger garden but looks delightful in late summer with its froth of white flowers and is at its best when allowed to grow freely into a large tree.

Rosa The rampant species of roses which are suitable for growing up trees or over banks and in free-standing mounds are all of Asiatic origin and are described in Chapter 9 on shrub roses. Many of them are semi-evergreen as well as having strongly scented flowers and clustered fruits.

Rubus I grow only two of this genus of ornamental brambles. One is a species from central China called R. cockburnianus, which is useful for its extremely white bark and white bloom on the new shoots each year. The leaves are attractive, fresh green and pinnate, and it suckers very freely, quickly making a thicket. The old wood needs cutting down in the winter, which is a painful task but, if it is not done, the whole effect of the new grey shoots is spoilt. The other *Rubus* here is a thornless hybrid, R. Tridel 'Benenden', with arching branches and pure white single flowers 5cm/2in across, of great beauty for the spring garden. It does not grow densely

but makes a satisfactory clump under trees, with ground-cover of the smaller periwinkle.

Salix There are many excellent willows, including trees with attractive bark, small creeping mountain shrubs and medium-sized bushes which are not too fussy as to soil. The last group concerns us here. Although the white willow is a familiar native which grows into a small tree, it has one form which is outstanding in leaf and bark, S. alba 'Britzensis' (syn. S. a. 'Chermesina'). This is slow growing, prefers damp soil and has branches of scarlet colour; it needs pruning every few years to encourage this so is best grown in a group for a large garden, but it can be effective as a single specimen in a smaller one. S. magnifica has beautiful and unusual leaves, which so much resemble those of a magnolia that it is often mistaken for one. It looks well in a damp area with plants such as rodgersias. Originally from western China, it is another of Ernest Wilson's notable introductions. I lost it here after two years as I had chosen too dry and windy a site.

Another shrubby *Salix* is the native tea-leaf willow,

S. phylicifolia, which has very dark twigs and grey-green leaves, with a bluish bloom on the undersides. The catkins appear before the leaves in the spring. It is an underrated garden plant, but I find it makes a tidy compact shape and contrasts well with shrubs with dull purple leaves like *Corylus maxima* 'Purpurea'. *S. sachalinensis* 'Sekka' has polished brown stems and green leaves.

Sambucus There are several varieties of the common elder, *S. nigra*, which are worth planting in the outer garden for their foliage. All have the typical elder leaf smell. I am wary about their use as I find that elder seedlings are among my greatest weed problems in groundcover, however dense. The golden elder, *S. n.* 'Aurea', which grows in Scottish hedgerows, is attractive, but the two variegated forms, *S. n.* 'Marginata' and *S. n.* 'Aureo-marginata' are even nicer, particularly if cut back hard to the old wood fairly frequently.

The most vivid foliage belongs to *Sambucus racemosa* 'Plumosa Aurea', which has very elegant deeply fretted golden leaves and should be pruned annually. It is one of the best golden-leaved deciduous shrubs and is suitable for a bed or border in quite a small garden. *S. nigra* 'Guincho Purple', discovered as a seedling in a hedgerow in Scotland and introduced to Ireland by Vera Mackie, has bronze foliage.

Schisandra I first saw this interesting deciduous twining climber in autumn at Rowallane in Northern Ireland where it was covered with red berries carried in long clusters. I think it was *S. rubriflora* and must have been a female form as only this bears berries. My plant is a male, and although it has an attractive habit and is ideal for scrambling up trees I only get the red flowers in the spring and no berries. The flowers are carried on drooping stalks, and the leaves are long, toothed and pointed, and glabrous.

Schizophragma This genus, as represented by *S. hydrangeoides*, is superficially very much like the climbing hydrangea, *H. petiolaris*, and is a native of the same district of Japan. Its leaves are more coarsely toothed and the flower heads less flat and slightly larger. It is rather a difficult shrub to get going and is at its best in the rough or wild conditions most nearly approximating its native habitat; it seems reluctant to grow up a shady wall, preferring the branches of trees. However, after the first three or four years it makes rapid progress. I have not tried it on a bank in the open but I suspect this would be the ideal situation.

Sorbaria This a is rather underrated small tree or shrub with pinnate leaves and long feathery panicles of white flowers in late summer. The form I have has pale golden leaves, especially in early spring, and suckers very freely. The branches have a reddish tinge when young, so it may perhaps

be the variety *S. aitchisonii* rather than a form of *S. arborea*. It is a much better plant than the one normally seen which has dull coarse green leaves.

Spiraea This is a vast genus containing many valuable flowering shrubs for the wilder garden, most of which have an elegant arching habit. Those we grow here are at their best planted in great dense masses. There are spring, mid-summer and late-summer flowering forms, all of which need a slightly different pruning schedule; but on the whole they can be left untouched for many years. A valuable spring flowerer is the bridal wreath, *S.* 'Arguta', which carries clustered white flowers all along the stems. This is a popular hybrid. *S. veitchii* is a superb 3m/10ft shrub with long downy arching branches, covered in midsummer in dense flat corymbs of tiny white flowers. It is at its most magnificent grown in a mass, possibly with an arching shrub rose, and likes to have rich moist soil. If the early summer is dry and if the soil conditions are poor, it may fail to give a satisfactory display. I have planted it here in two different borders but now wish I had kept it for a group in the outer wilder area.

S. japonica 'Anthony Waterer' is of quite a different type and responds to hard pruning every spring as it flowers on the current year's growth. It has almost crimson flowers and there is a form with variegated foliage which makes more of a low thicket, and will flower freely even in shade.

Stachyurus I have seen only one species of this interesting spring-flowering genus, *S. praecox*, but immediately decided it was a 'must' for the garden. It is a perfectly hardy shrub from Japan, which carries drooping racemes of primrose-yellow cup-shaped flowers. The leaves are pointed and slightly spiny but the bare branches in winter are an attractive reddish brown.

Staphylea This is a small tree or shrub given extra interest in late summer by the strange bladder pods which contain the seeds. It has an upright branching habit and, in the species we have here, *S. holocarpa*, white drooping flowers opening in May from a pink bud. The variety *S. h. rosea*, which I have seen at Hidcote, is more attractive as its young growth has a bronze tint and soft pink flowers. Like innumerable other plants of great garden value this is one of Ernest Wilson's introductions in the early years of this century. We are fortunate here in that a great deal of interest was taken in the garden just at the time when so many exciting new species were being discovered in the Far East.

Stauntonia This is an evergreen twining genus from northeast Asia which needs a sheltered spot and could arguably be included with the wall plants in Chapter 10. As it much prefers to grow over and into other trees or shrubs it can be given

Schisandra grandiflora rubriflora *is a deciduous twining climber with pale pink flowers in early summer. In autumn the berries are scarlet but will only be borne on the female plant if a* male *is also grown nearby. Schisandras prefer to drape themselves over other strong host plants but will succeed on a fence or wall.*

a sunny site in the outer garden providing that it is sheltered by its host plant or plants. The species *S. hexaphylla* which I grow here has white flowers tinged with violet with an exotic fragrance. Unfortunately it does not produce them freely, and in our garden despite its luxuriant leafy growth it has not flowered and this may well be because the heat reflected from the wall is not sufficient.

Stephanandra This is an outstanding shrub for foliage and for its arching habit and dark almost red stems. I prefer *S. tanakae* to *S. incisa* since it has the right scale for this garden and makes splendid arching bushes with lobed leaves of a fresh green which shows up well in shade. The smaller *S. incisa* has more toothed leaves and grows densely but without the grace of *S. tanakae*. They both make an excellent con-trast with dark evergreens and I believe that if I grew them in the open I would also get autumn tints; but they are essen-tially woodland plants and best adapted to massed planting.

Symphoricarpos This is a genus of small thicket-forming North American shrubs which, except for the more delicate-leaved species *S. orbiculatus*, best in its variegated form, is suitable only for woodland. This is the coral berry from east-ern America; what is known in Britain as the snowberry was a later introduction from the western states and became a feature of Victorian shrubberies. However, it suckers and pushes itself forward too much, and although grown for its white or pale pink fruits is otherwise dull.

Syringa It is unnecessary to describe the common lilac, *S. vulgaris*, and the hybrids are too numerous to list. Notcutt's Nursery has a considerable number. Some of the species, such as the Himalayan lilac *S. emodi* and its variegated form, are worth growing for their larger leaves and later period of flowering. The Canadian hybrid *S.* × *josiflexa* 'Bellicent' has particularly delightful open panicles of rosy-pink. The small *S. microphylla* from China grows only to about 1.5m/5ft and has dark scented flowers, and the Persian species is a slender shrub with lilac and white flowering forms. Pages could be written about the improved hybrids, but although they are hardy shrubs for the wilder areas, they provide interest only in their flowering season, so should not compete with plants which also have exciting bark and/or foliage. The common lilac can be a suckering pest if planted too near the house, and is most effective where its lower branches are obscured from the immediate view by more important foliage plants but where its flowers and fragrance can be appreciated.

Viburnum This genus has almost everything: flower, foliage, fruit and form. Of course not all these qualities are combined in every species. Two comparatively small repre-sentatives, one of the species *V. davidii* and the other the hybrid *V.* × *juddii*, have already been described (page 55). In this chapter the best of the larger and hardier ones that I grow are included, keeping for Chapter 10 the most tender and sweet flowering which need a sheltered wall, and earn their place there by sheer merit, but cannot survive an open situation except in a warm garden.

Probably the most sensible way to tackle this large genus which contains so many excellent and important species and hybrids is to treat it in some some form of chronological order, related to the date of arrival in Britain.

The laurustinus, *V. tinus*, which everybody knows, is a native of the Mediterranean area, and has been used in English gardens at least since the sixteenth century. Originally it was thought to be a member of the sweet bay or

Viburnum plicatum 'Mariesii' has very strong architecture, with branches reaching out in horizontal tabulated layers. Given space, it makes an admirable corner plant or focal point. In early summer, bushes are wreathed in white, the florets gathered in globular heads all along the branches. Deciduous and completely hardy, with good form, leaves which colour in autumn and spectacular flowers, this shrub, or the smaller V.p. 'Nanum Semperflorens', has a place in every garden.

laurel family and many years elapsed before it was realized that it and the other European natives, *V. opulus* the guelder rose and *V. lantana* the wayfaring tree, were also part of the same genus. *V. tinus* is useful for hedges in mild areas, but its chief contribution is its winter flower, with flat corymbs opening from delicately pink buds, and excellent dark green glossy foliage. There are several forms but the most worthwhile is the variegated one, which has creamy-yellow leaves, vivid red stems and a pyramidal shape with drooping branches right to the ground. It is more tender than the type and makes the best shape if grown against a wall, but is perfectly hardy here in groups of shrubs; it was, of course, given some protection the first few years.

The maple-like leaves of the wild guelder rose turn a rich colour in autumn and it has red translucent fruits. It is very welcome in a large garden but if space is restricted there are many better plants. Its variety V. o. 'Roseum' (syn. V. o. 'Sterile'), which has creamy-white sterile 'Snowball' flowers, is far surpassed in merit by the more tender Chinese V. macrocephalum and the Japanese V. plicatum, especially its best form V. p. 'Grandiflorum' (incidentally, V. plicatum is the correct botanical name for V. tomentosum), which have huge globular heads. Both varieties were introduced by Robert Fortune in 1844. All forms of V. plicatum are deciduous; the beautiful V. p. 'Mariesii' introduced by Veitch's nursery in 1879 has long spreading almost horizontal branches with large flat inflorescences of fertile flowers, surrounded by sterile ones, all borne on erect stalks above the leaves and completely covering the branches. This is one of the most remarkable flowering shrubs and its unusual horizontal habit makes it a useful architectural plant. It also has good colouring in the early autumn. The variety V. p. 'Lanarth' flowers and comes into leaf later, so is less likely to be damaged by frosts coming after a mild early spring.

V. odoratissimum and V. japonicum are evergreens, of which the former and more tender was already in cultivation in 1818, the first of the truly fragrant ones to be grown, although originally only in hot-houses. Both these have outstandingly beautiful glossy green leaves and dense trusses of flowers. V. japonicum needs protection from other shrubs and we lost it here in its first season by giving it too windy and exposed a site; V. odoratissimum is in the sheltered corner of a wall and greenhouse and has not flowered yet. The next group to arrive were all evergreens of merit except for one deciduous species, V. betulifolium, which has distinctive berries. They were brought back from the Far East by Ernest Wilson in the first decade of the twentieth century.

V. cinnamomifolium will grow into a 5.5m/18ft shrub and has glossy leaves resembling V. davidii (see page 55) and similar fruits, but distinctive red-brown stems. V. harryanum is a smaller bushy shrub with neat almost round leaves and small white flowers in late spring. It is unusual rather than beautiful. V. henryi has an open form of growing, with glossy narrow leaves and very attractive panicles of white flowers in early summer followed by bright red fruits which eventually turn black. This is another splendid plant, and hardy.

V. rhytidophyllum is the toughest of the evergreens and has large corrugated leaves, very glossy on the upperside but hairy beneath. The flowers are cream and carried in wide flat corymbs in late spring; the fruits are best if you grow more than one plant and are very desirable, being a bright red at first, fading to black. It grows to 6-9m/20-30ft, so is only for the large garden, where however it is an effective addition either as a single plant or grown in a group. The small and graceful V. utile is chiefly known as the parent, with V. carlesii, of V. × burkwoodii which combines the evergreen leaves of one parent with the fragrance of the other. It also has charms of its own as the leaves have a sheen and delicacy unusual in the genus and it flowers freely in late spring.

The strongly scented V. carlesii is a shrub grown chiefly for its early flowers, and several improved forms have been developed, including 'Aurora' which is very free-flowering. V. farreri, or V. fragrans as it is generally called, in my opinion is overrated as a winter-flowering shrub as so often its fragrant pink to white flowers are damaged by frost or rain. However, it has an excellent upright shape and veined bronze-coloured leaves which redden in the autumn. The improved form of the hybrid V. × bodnantense called 'Dawn' is a much more desirable plant and has more frost-resistant pink flowers.

This has been a long list, but all those mentioned are good garden shrubs and in many cases, if space is limited, you can combine foliage and fruit, or flowers and foliage, in your choice. The horizontal branched varieties are among the most important of the deciduous form-giving plants for design purposes, besides having breathtakingly beautiful flowers. They all like rich soils but prefer lime to acid. The more erect ones are not weed suppressors but can be grown in large groups with a dense perennial groundcover.

Vitis The best and most rampant vine for growing through and over shrubs and trees is undoubtedly V. coignetiae. The wide heart-shaped leaves can be almost 30cm/12in across, smooth and veined on the surface but downy underneath. In the spring the young leaves are faintly bronze coloured and they turn crimson and scarlet in the autumn. It is at its most spectacular growing through the branches of a tree, but care must be taken not to allow it to overwhelm a weaker shrub. It needs full sunlight to get the best colouring, and is perfect growing in a tree which is dead or past its prime.

Weigela Frankly I do not understand the botanical differences which divide this group from Diervilla and to most of us the distinction does not much matter. The weigelas have interesting foliage and I grow them for their value as leaf contrast with plain green or grey-leaved plants. The pink or red flowers also make a pleasing picture, set as they are all along

the branches on short shoots. They are tubular or funnel-shaped and are borne profusely, especially if the flowering shoots are removed each year directly after the blossom is over. This gives an excellent excuse for picking hard and they make long-lasting flower sprays for the house.

We found various rather dull weigelas in the garden when we arrived and the only ones I have added have all been members of the *W. florida* group. *W.* 'Florida Variegata' is one of the prettiest and easiest to grow of all variegated shrubs; it seems to be as hardy and strong-growing as the green forms, but, if anything, makes a neater more compact bush. Its pale pink flowers, which nestle among the creamy-edged leaves, blend well with pink and red shrub roses, in particular with some of the Rugosas that have fresh green leaves. Equally delightful with it are grey-foliaged plants and although I do not normally like the mixture of pale pink and blue flowers, the *Weigela* blends with a grey-leaved plant with light blue flowers such as catmint. There is a colour scheme of red and pink tulips combined with forget-me-not which is very popular but crude. Another smaller *Weigela* is *W. f.* 'Foliis Purpureis' which has bronze rather than true purple foliage. It also has pink flowers and is perhaps best planted in a group of at least three and underplanted with something like the variegated *Astrantia* or variegated *Ajuga*. The golden-leaved hybrid, *W.* 'Looymansii Aurea', needs to be given a shady position and once it has established itself grows strongly but in a lax habit. Both it and the ordinary green forms with white, pink and dark red flowers are most suitable for planting in groups with other vigorous shrubs; *W.* 'Florida Variegata' on the other hand will look equally well in a mixed border or in a mass but needs full sun, while the bronze-leaved variety requires careful placing between other small shrubs or herbaceous plants.

Wisteria There seems to be no doubt that wisterias should have a hot sunny position if they are to flower well, so in a cool district it is best to give them the heat of a wall, or at least to grow them on some sort of support in an area where there is a relatively warm micro-climate. Nothing can be

more beautiful than the festoons of long pendulous racemes in lilac, pale mauve or white, whether on a balcony or railings, or over an old tree; but they will not succeed in a shady woodland area.

The two species usually in cultivation are, quite straightforwardly, the Chinese and the Japanese. *W. sinensis* is the stronger grower and will climb up to 30m/100ft into a tree. You can distinguish between the two species if you have old plants in the garden as the Japanese *W. floribunda* twines with its stems in a clockwise direction and the Chinese *W. sinensis* anti-clockwise. The form *W. floribunda* 'Multijuga', which has the longest racemes, as much as 90cm/36in, would be my choice for a new plant on a hot wall; but if choosing one for an old tree I would pick the more vigorous *W. sinensis*, probably its white form. If you are prepared to prune twice a year it is possible to grow *W. sinensis* as a standard; first do a hard pruning for shape in winter and then shorten the long leafy shoots in late summer. The flower buds begin to swell early in the season, before the leaves, so even on a hot wall it is advisable to plant any of these varieties with protection from the eastern sun.

Left In late summer two clematis mingle and intertwine with a bronze-leaved vine on a wall. The small-flowered, dark purple Clematis viticella *flowers profusely above the foliage of* Vitis vinifera *'Purpurea', the Teinturier grape, while pale blue* Clematis *'Perle d'Azur' climbs up through the vine's foliage.*

Above The white form of the Japanese wisteria, Wisteria floribunda *'Alba', has very long racemes and flowers which are faintly flushed with lilac. This Japanese wisteria is more spectacular than the Chinese species but is less vigorous and takes longer to get established.*

Chapter 7

TREES AND SHRUBS
FOR THE GARDEN FRAMEWORK

REES, WHETHER EVERGREEN or deciduous, have regular outlines which, depending on their size and general suitability for a garden, give permanent shape and body besides framing the distant skyline. They are part of the framework of the whole design. They can be columnar, pyramidal, weeping, mop- or broad-headed, spreading, fan-shaped or horizontal in growth. Many desirable trees, especially conifers, do not take their final shape until they are mature. Similarly, evergreen and deciduous shrubs can have regular outlines, but with more emphasis on solidity as they often branch from the base to form a vase- or fan-like shape.

There are a few firms who specialize in growing trees on beyond the size at which they are normally sent out from a nursery. Careful methods of annual 'wrenching', and trenching around the roots to assist the growth of small fibrous roots in the seasons before transplanting, help the tree to re-establish itself quickly after it is moved. These trees can be successfully moved when already large enough to give immediate form-giving value to a new garden. This means that other smaller plants start with the correct size relationship to them to give an immediate impact.

Depending on the scale of the garden all the trees and shrubs described in this chapter, besides being used to balance with buildings or to contrast with groups of differently shaped plants, can be used as important corner or gateway plants, either connecting two parts of a garden or, which is of increasing importance today even for a country garden, helping to screen something undesirable in the landscape beyond. The evergreens, of course, give all-the-year-round colour but deciduous trees and shrubs can form equally agreeable skeleton branch shapes, although they are not so effective as screens.

Specimen trees of regular shape can be effective as focal points at the end of a framed vista. They can be used as a pair to frame a distant vista in the landscape beyond the garden. Towards the end of the great wave of conifer importations of the nineteenth century, William Robinson condemned the prevailing fashion of using conifers as specimen trees with no relationship to other planting schemes inside a garden, and ridiculed 'the idea that every choice tree in our pleasure grounds should be set out by itself like an electric lamp-post'. It is the same with all specimen trees; the more regular the outline, the more important is the need for the tree to act as contrast or to harmonize with other plants or buildings. These symmetrical trees or shrubs are a definite architectural form and need to be used in an architectural manner.

Of the trees which contribute in this architectural way to a garden, those with foliage of gold, purple and glaucous blue should be avoided as they make too great a contrast with the natural colours of the normal countryside. Their vivid leaves should be used in special designs and foliage schemes, where they are deliberately contrasted, or are part of a hidden section inside the garden proper.

All the plants included in this chapter contribute a regular outline of shape to the garden, or have the massed effect of a broad-headed spreading tree, which is of equal importance for balancing with buildings. They are arranged in three sections: conifers; evergreen trees and shrubs; and deciduous trees and shrubs (including large broad-headed trees).

As many genera contain plants with more than one shape, each section is arranged alphabetically, with suggestions as to the best use to make of each individual species or variety.

Conifers

Most conifers will ultimately grow into large, often broad-headed, trees. Spreading cedars, pines and soaring Lawson cypress, for example, are invaluable in a mature garden

Above the lower pond at Hadspen, three trees demonstrate contrasting form, habit and foliage: the grey-leaved pear, Pyrus salicifolia 'Pendula'; Malus hupehensis, a crab with pink clustered buds opening to white flowers; and the architectural Asiatic dogwood, Cornus controversa 'Variegata', with cream-edged green foliage carried on horizontally-layered branches. Rosa filipes scrambles through the crab apple to make a glorious picture at the end of June.

where they can add romance – even mystery – and at their best look picturesque.

Although young conifers and 'dwarf' cultivars are effective when used in pairs or groups to frame other garden features or, occasionally, to provide a focal point, I am wary of their use in garden design. Often they seem to have little function except to give vertical emphasis and, personally, I dislike the fashionable labour-saving conifer and heather garden.

Calocedrus The incense cedar, *C. decurrens*, makes a dark narrow column which in our landscape looks best amid a group with trees or large shrubs of vase-like shape. It has soft green foliage which provides an attractive background to pale deciduous leaves and autumn colours.

The well-known and frequently photographed planting in the Westonbirt Arboretum in Gloucestershire gathers strength from the use of the branching *Parrotia persica* as a foil both in contrasting shape and form (see page 114).

Calocedrus comes from the south-western states of America, and needs plenty of moisture and rich deep soil.

Cedrus A fully developed cedar is one of the most magnificent of all trees, but like many of the giant conifers does not reach its true shape until almost mature. All except the Deodar, *Cedrus deodara*, make a pyramidal shape when young, that is for the first sixty years or so depending on the conditions given. This means that the lower branches grow out in an almost horizontal way and the branches shorten as they reach the top. Once they achieve their final characteristic spreading shape, cedars are vulnerable to strong gales and heavy falls of snow. They are most effective if grown as specimens in a lawn, but like true forest trees would much prefer to be grown in woodland with some protection from neighbours when young.

Cedrus atlantica and its form *C. a. glauca* come from the Atlas Mountains and finally have the most fastigiate shape of all the species. The needles of *C. a. glauca* are a clear grey-blue and the tree looks best against a dark background; it is too vivid and unnatural a colour for use as a specimen since it stands out too harshly against the muted colours of the English countryside.

C. deodara is a native of the Himalaya and is the most difficult to establish in Britain. It needs a sheltered spot and plenty of water for the first few years. If conditions are right it grows very gracefully with pendulous ends to the branches and is an attractive green, not too dark and gloomy. There are several forms but the plain green upright one is best.

C. libani, the cedar of Lebanon, is more spreading than *C. atlantica* when mature, and therefore more suited to a large garden. In Italy I have seen it draped with a white Banksian rose, whose roots were nourished on a higher terrace of a steeply descending garden.

Chamaecyparis This is the false cypress, which is distinguished from the true *Cupressus* by its flat rather than round branchlets. The most usually grown species is *C. lawsoniana*, which has innumerable foliage forms. It grows quickly into a tall columnar tree and can be very effective. First introduced from north-west America in 1854, it has since been used extensively for screens and hedges. However, when grown in a straight line it makes too rigid an outline. As it ages it grows shabby at the base and has a slightly more spreading shape. The average conditions in the British Isles do not suit it since it needs high rainfall, combined with good drainage and protection from wind in a natural forest.

C. lawsoniana and all its different foliage forms give very quick protection from unsightly buildings or from excessive noise, but they are not a long-term tree in a northern climate. They are best planted in a clump or group, as a contrast to shrubs or trees of spreading shape. There is an attractive form *C. l.* 'Triomf van Boskoop' which has glaucous blue foliage and looks excellent against a dark background of yew.

Cryptomeria *C. japonica* is a beautiful tree when mature. Its form *C. j.* 'Elegans', seldom growing higher than 6m/20ft, has feathery bronze foliage which makes it more suitable than some other conifers for contrast with foliage of deciduous shrubs or trees, and it blends easily into a background of rounded or branching shrubs in a mixed border. It prefers an acid to an alkaline soil, and is not reliably hardy.

Cupressus The true cypress is one of the best of all conifers but no variety is a hundred per cent hardy in Britain. The Italian cypress, *C. sempervirens*, is a well-established part of the Italian landscape, where it contrasts in shape and colour with the grey-leaved olive. It is a columnar tree with steeply ascending branches and, in its wild form, dark green foliage. Here it would not survive planted in straight avenues, exposed to wind, but if planted in a clump, with rounded evergreen shrubs such as *Elaeagnus macrophylla* or *E.* × *ebbingei* to give it protection, will thrive in most situations. It is one of the best evergreens for a vertical accent in contrast with broad masses on the horizontal plane, whether of buildings or in plant material. Vita Sackville-West suggested that the same effect could be obtained by using the Irish juniper, *J. communis* 'Hibernica', but I find this has a distinctive bluish tone which does not fit into every scheme. The more usual plant to use is the dark green Irish yew, *Taxus baccata* 'Fastigiata' (see page 106).

Cupressus macrocarpa, the Monterey cypress from south-

In evening light at Tintinhull, an old cedar of Lebanon, Cedrus libani, *is silhouetted against the sky. Of all the true cedars, the Lebanon species develops the most picturesque spreading habit to shape the skyline and provide shade in many mature English gardens. It grows more slowly than the Atlas or Himalayan cedars but is ultimately the most rewarding of lawn specimens.*

shaped and coloured leaves and an excellent habit of growth. Surprisingly it is seldom grown in Britain although it creates few shade problems so is suitable for a small garden, but it is used extensively as a street plant in America. Slow to get going, it also has a habit of losing its leader every spring if we have late frosts, or frost-laden winds. It is probably best in a climate with more extremes of heat and cold where it is not tempted into premature growth during a warm spell in the winter, and where it can be more certain of hot sun during the summer to harden or ripen the wood.

The fossilized remains of this plant have been discovered all over the world, including Great Britain. A living specimen was finally found growing in Asia, where it is considered a sacred tree, and introduced to Europe in the eighteenth century; it reached Britain in 1758 and was first grown in the nursery garden of James Gordon in the Mile End Road, London.

Its unique fan-shaped leaves turn a clear yellow in the autumn, and it is tolerant of industrial and urban pollution. The more common male form makes an excellent broadly fastigiate tree, of very neat and regular appearance, and there is a variety with an even more columnar shape. Female ginkgos are generally broader in outline.

Juniperus The junipers are distinguished from most other conifers by bearing fruit rather than cones and these can be used for culinary purposes or for flavouring gin. There are so many species and forms that the exact one to be used for architectural accent must depend on individual choice, as well as on the site.

The horizontal varieties such as *J. horizontalis*, the creeping juniper from America, *J. sabina*, the savin from Europe across to the Caucasus, and *J. × media* 'Pfitzeriana' from eastern Asia, are used extensively by the landscape gardener. These evergreens make good corner plants and useful contrasts to vertical growers or to bushes of rounded shape.

One of the most effective ways I have seen the Pfitzer juniper planted is in a group at Knightshayes, where it blends with the horizontal line of a steep bank. Its branches are held at an acute angle with pendulous tips and it makes a wide, totally weed-suppressing mass, eventually reaching a spread of about 4.5m/15ft.

J. horizontalis is really a flat creeping groundcover. It has many good foliage forms from glaucous blue to grey-green, varying greatly in intensity depending on the amount of sun or shade it receives. It prefers acid soil. *J. sabina* with its strong rather disagreeable aromatic leaves is another low grower, which branches to a spread of 3m/10ft or so. The blue-green form, *J. s.* 'Hicksii', makes a bush very similar in

ern California, has bright green foliage and grows extremely rapidly, and though conical when young will eventually form a broad-headed tree. It is one of the least satisfactory conifers in a northern climate as the foliage gets badly marked by cold winds. If you can put up with its rather motheaten appearance, it is hardy in coastal districts, and provides shelter for more attractive plants.

Ginkgo G. *biloba*, the Chinese maidenhair tree, is a monotypic genus of deciduous conifer. To the average gardener, it looks remarkably like a deciduous tree with attractively

habit to the Pfitzer juniper, but needs careful siting to absorb its rather glaring foliage colour.

The common English juniper, *J. communis*, usually makes an upright shrub and is a useful conifer for vertical accents, in particular the so-called Irish juniper, which is probably of Scandinavian origin (see page 102), but strikes a rather formal note. The prostrate form *J. c. montana* is hardy and thrives throughout the northern hemisphere in cold mountainous areas.

Metasequoia M. *glyptostroboides* is another deciduous conifer which is a monotypic genus, and like the ginkgo has been found in fossilized form by botanists for many years; it was thought to be extinct until discovered growing in central China in 1947. In its young state it is not unlike a larch tree. Its leaves are linear and carried on short branchlets so that they give the appearance of being pinnate and feathery. They emerge bright green in the spring and become pink and brown before falling in the autumn. It is extremely fast growing, hardy, and very easily propagated from cuttings. In my opinion, it is rather a poor relation of the splendid swamp cypress, *Taxodium distichum* (see page 106), which is much more distinguished in appearance but also much more difficult to grow successfully as it needs special conditions. The *Metasequoia* forms a regular pyramidal shape, casts little shade and makes an attractive specimen tree in a small garden, or a deciduous screen in place of poplars, where the invasive roots of this genus might do damage to the foundation of buildings.

Pinus While young, the trees in this genus are all conical in shape, with distinctive upright or hanging needles, but their true beauty and romantic outline do not become apparent for many years. They come from widely varying climates and each individual species needs a specially chosen site. On the whole they are happiest in full sun, and able to withstand strong winds. In Britain the more tender species can be grown only in coastal gardens.

P. armandii is an ornamental tree from the Far East; when mature it has a regular outline which is attractive as a formal shape. The leaves are drooping and slightly glaucous.

P. montezumae has long grey-green leaves and a domed crown, and makes an unusual mound when young, de-

Metasequoia glyptostroboides, the dawn redwood, is a deciduous conifer long known as a fossil relic. It was only discovered in the wild in 1941 and quickly introduced to gardens. Growing very fast and with a strong conical shape, it provides a welcome accent at the end of the lily pond at Hadspen.

veloping into a magnificent tree in its native Mexican mountains but unreliable in a variable climate. It is more of a plantsman's tree than one for the garden architect and is grown mainly on account of its distinctive appearance.

P. nigra, the tough Austrian pine, is often used for woodland shelter, but its variety, *P. n. maritima* (syn. *P. n. calabrica*), the Corsican pine, is more suitable for growing as a specimen or group in the ornamental garden. It was introduced by Philip Miller into the Chelsea Physic Garden in 1759, but although coming from southern Europe it has proved extremely hardy in Britain, and has an elegant and more delicate appearance than the type.

P. pinea is the umbrella-shaped stone pine from the Mediterranean which develops into a flat-topped wide tree – a useful and rare shape in many landscapes. It is not easy to establish here, and like many of the genus needs protection from frost when young.

Pinus radiata (syn. *P. insignis*), the Monterey pine, is too tender to survive hard frosts in inland areas, but is useful as a shelter belt in coastal areas and able to withstand strong sea gales. It was introduced by David Douglas in 1833. A quick grower, it has a fresh green appearance, making a dense head eventually, and a dark brown bark. Here, where we have such excellent frost drainage, it is doing well. I am not, however, recommending it for a normal inland garden, and the mild winters of the last years may be the only reason for it looking so comfortable and well-established.

P. sylvestris, the Scots pine, with its warm reddish bark makes one of the most beautiful and romantic outlines of all trees when mature. It is well worth waiting for but has a disappointing branching conical shape when young, and for many years contributes little.

Pinus wallichiana, the Bhutan pine, of which there is a splendid example at Anglesey Abbey, is a broad-headed tree with graceful drooping foliage.

Podocarpus This is a difficult genus and the only two species I know come from Chile. It resembles a yew more than other conifers but has paler softer leaves which clothe the tree right to the ground. Both *P. andinus*, with glaucous undersurfaces to its leaves, and *P. salignus*, which has a more drooping appearance, need the protection of other shrubs or small trees when young. There is a free-standing specimen in the Savill Gardens in Windsor Great Park, which is the best example I have seen. Both species grow at Abbotsbury on the Dorset coast.

Sequoia The Wellingtonia, *Sequoiadendron giganteum*, has feathery leaves which bear some resemblance to a *Cryptomeria*, and is remarkable chiefly for the girth it attains. As a form it is conical in its juvenile state, and not wide-spreading when mature. It has beautiful reddish-brown bark. Unfortunately, it was often planted as a specimen tree after its introduction to Britain in 1853, whereas it thrives best on a moist slope as part of a forest. In ideal conditions it can add 1.2m/4ft a year to its height, but when too exposed quickly begins to lose branches and look rather moth-eaten.

The smaller redwood, *Sequoia sempervirens*, although still preferring a woodland site, is a more graceful garden tree, and has drooping well-clothed branches of a delicate appearance. It is semi-evergreen, and often loses some of its leaves in winter.

Taxodium *T. distichum*, the American swamp cypress, is one of the most beautiful of all trees for a large garden. It is a deciduous conifer with young bright green foliage, which turns pink and then bronze in the autumn, and red bark. It needs plenty of moisture, and in its native swamps develops strange knee-like growths which stick up above the level of the soil or water. Here it can help to drain low-lying marshy ground by its absorption of water. It prefers acid soil, and makes a regular fastigiate shape which broadens as it ages.

Taxus The common English yew, *Taxus baccata*, needs no description. As a branching mature specimen tree it makes a splendid decorative dark green mass, well-clothed almost to the ground. Grown in a continuous line and clipped as a hedge, yew is one of the most distinctive and decorative ways of making a formal straight line in a garden. It is equally useful grown as a shelter belt, as we have it here, but the trees probably need two hundred years to reach full maturity. Its advantage for us is that, planted in a line across a slope, it provides perfect protection for the upper area, and still allows the frosts to slip away under the low branches. The north side of the slope is bounded by a high wall, and inside the enclosure so made is a warm micro-climate for growing tender plants.

A variety of *Taxus baccata* which makes a strong horizontal shape is *T. b.* 'Dovastoniana'; it holds its branches in long tiers with weeping branchlets at the tips. There is an excellent example of its golden form, 'Dovastonii Aurea', at Tintinhull, where it has been used as a corner plant with an architectural accent. This variety has golden tips to its leaves and gives an overall golden effect.

T. b. 'Fastigiata', the Irish yew, is a clone found accidentally in County Fermanagh in 1750. It has a similar habit to the Italian cypress, and has come to have rather funereal associations since it is so often used in graveyards.

Tsuga This is the hemlock spruce, (of which I know only the eastern hemlock, from the eastern states of North America),

T. canadensis, which grows happily on lime. It has the normal habits of a conifer except that it branches at the base, instead of developing a single trunk, which puts it into the class of narrow fan-shaped profiles and makes it a useful tree for contrast with rounded and cone shapes. Its variety *T. c.* 'Pendula' is a most attractive, very slow growing mounded plant which will in time reach 6m/20ft in width.

Evergreen trees and shrubs
Broadleaved evergreens with regular and architectural form provide permanent textures and colours. Besides having interesting leaves they may also contribute flowers in season.
Cotoneaster The large evergreen *Cotoneaster × watereri* 'Cornubia', a hybrid of *C. frigidus* (probably with the willow-leaved *C. salicifolius*), can grow up to 7.5m/25ft; the two cultivars raised at Exbury, *C. × w.* 'Exburiensis' and *C. × w.* 'Rothschildianus' are probably almost as big. The latter has beautiful yellow fruits which give it an added interest during the winter. All three have a spreading fan-like habit branching from the base and making a good structural contrast to dark green conical shapes or to trees with broad heads. They are useful at the edge of a garden where a more rigid and vertical line is not wanted, and they are very hardy and wind-resistant. *C. × watereri* 'Pendulus' is a relatively recent weeping hybrid which is not particularly distinguished in itself, but good as a wind-break to shelter more tender plants with different habits of growth.

It is easy to be enthusiastic about *C. horizontalis* and unquestionably it must be included in the list of plants which make a strong architectural contribution. It has a spreading 'herring-bone' shape and bears dark red berries. It is not evergreen in every situation but in our garden very seldom loses its leaves. The same is true of *C. conspicuus*, which is one of the prettiest of the arching mound-like cotoneasters (see page 38), and particularly attractive on a dry bank.
Drimys *D. winteri* is an outstandingly beautiful small tree or shrub, which grows with horizontal branches to make an almost perfect pyramidal shape if free standing. It has large leathery leaves, slightly glaucous beneath, and in early summer is covered with scented ivory flowers. Unfortunately it can be grown as a specimen only in warmer regions, and here

The austere, dark green, fastigiate Irish yew (Taxus baccata 'Fastigiata') with a flat top makes a strong outline in contrast to scrambling sweet peas and fuchsias at Garsington Manor near Oxford. Italian cypresses and junipers planted in formal rhythms can also be used to make a series of architectural statements.

it has to have the shelter of a high wall, where it still contributes its graceful shape and acts as a strong landmark in the planting scheme. I grow *D. lanceolata*, which has smaller leaves, intensely fragrant when bruised, red stems and less conspicuous white flowers. It stands in an open space and also makes a pyramid shape. *D. winteri* comes from South America and *D. lanceolata* from southern Australia. There is a variety of *D. winteri*, *D. w. andina*, which appears to be completely hardy and more floriferous than either of the other two, but although it makes a neat compact mound it is hardly architectural.

Embothrium The Chilean flame tree, *E. coccineum*, has long glossy bright green leaves and its form is just regular enough to qualify it for inclusion in this chapter. When young it does make a cone shape but the growth becomes untidier and more lax later on. Chiefly grown for its startling crimson-scarlet flowers, it is often planted in woodland glades with rhododendrons and azaleas which like the same conditions. Mrs Reed has one on the outskirts of her splendid plantsman's garden at Liskeard in Cornwall, and seeing it there made me realize how useful it can be as a small evergreen tree for a town garden.

Eucryphia The eucryphias are in the main acid lovers and have both evergreen and deciduous species. They grow as rather narrow cone shapes with leathery oblong to lanceolate leaves. The flowers are ivory-white and freely carried. *E. cordifolia* will grow to over 9m/30ft, and has heart-shaped leaves. Its hybrid *E. cordifolia* × *lucida* is very vigorous and has more lanceolate leaves, glaucous beneath with slightly wavy edges. Both these are lime tolerant. *E.* × *nymansensis* and its form 'Nymansay' have a particularly compact habit and are also lime tolerant. *E. moorei*, the only evergreen species with pinnate leaves, is a tender but very attractive small tree. There is an excellent example at Trewithen in Cornwall.

The deciduous species is discussed on page 113.

Griselinia The hardiest species of this attractive genus is G. *littoralis* which will grow into a 9m/30ft tree of great gracefulness and charm if in the right conditions near the sea, but it is more usually seen as a hedge. Its apple-green leaves are smooth and soft, and therefore very susceptible to frosts when young. As it gets bigger it may grow branching from the base, or a single dark trunk will make an attractive contrast with the shining pale leaves. It is grown in the garden at Zennor in Cornwall where the winds sweep off the Atlantic, and like most of the plants in that garden is from New Zealand. Although I have seen other superb examples, its dark buff bark and windswept shape are at their most effective at

Zennor. But the best tree I know is at Abbotsbury on the Dorset coast, where it is in dark woodland surrounded by tall trees, and the leaves appear at their palest in contrast.

G. *lucida* has larger leaves with a more varnished surface. There are two variegated varieties of G. *littoralis*, but neither has very attractive markings.

Ilex There are several good forms of holly which make excellent regular shapes, and among the best is I. × *altaclerensis* 'Camelliifolia', a cross between *Ilex aquifolium* and the more tender *I. perado* from the Azores. This is a beautiful shrub or small tree with a pyramidal outline and almost spineless leaves of a glowing dark green. It also fruits abundantly. Like many other of these similarly shaped plants, I. × *altaclerensis* 'Camelliifolia' is most effective if planted as a pair, framing a view or a gateway, depending on the scale of the garden. It needs to be planted at least 9m/30ft from its partner in order to keep clear the view or path between; its outline is spoilt if it has to be clipped.

There are many other hardy hollies which can make regular shapes, but on the whole I prefer those with entire rather than toothed leaves. The Hillier Arboretum has an excellent collection. Hollies come in almost every shape and size, including weeping forms which could be useful for landscaping.

Ligustrum There are two evergreen members of the privet family which grow either in a regular fan-shaped way or develop into a small tree with a trunk (but see also page 114).

L. *lucidum* is a native of China and does not often get much above 6m/20ft in Britain; it has large lustrous pointed leaves about 15cm/6in in length and half as broad. Once popular for planting in London squares, it is still often grown as a street tree – especially in southern Europe. It flowers in late summer, with great white plumes. If space is no problem these plants would be excellent for use as a gateway pair, especially when branching from the base. In fact, I have used the Japanese privet, L. *japonicum*, which is slightly less big in scale and will grow only to about 4.5m/15ft, in this way. The leaves are smaller and darker and sometimes likened to those of a camellia, but in my opinion they are much less smooth and glossy. L. *japonicum* also has large panicles of white flowers, followed by black fruits. The trunk is attractively fluted.

For the deciduous L. *sinense* see page 114.

Magnolia Only one evergreen magnolia, M. *grandiflora* and its various forms, is included here. The deciduous varieties which come in Chapter 8 are woodland plants, at their best grown with some shade between other plants, rather than used for shapes in the garden. The evergreen M. *delavayi* is

The creamy-white flowers of the evergreen Magnolia grandiflora, *from the south-eastern states of North America, are produced all through the summer in warm climates.*

It is less free of flower in the average English garden and benefits from being trained back to get extra heat and protection from a high wall.

also discussed in Chapter 8 with the ornamental trees.

M. grandiflora is from North America. It has handsome green leaves, glossy green above, and in some of its finest forms, such as *M. g.* 'Ferruginea' and *M. g.* 'Goliath', hairy and buff-coloured beneath. It is usually grown as a wall shrub in Britain but, in warmer regions and in southern Europe, it looks splendid when grown as a specimen. It makes a formal regular pyramidal tree and bears large cream flowers intermittently through the summer.

Osmanthus There are two members of this family which by their regular vase-like shape and large size merit inclusion here as architectural plants. *O. armatus* has long thick, rather rigid leaves, with toothed edges, and bears fragrant almost hidden flowers in autumn. It grows more compactly than the larger *O. yunnanensis* which has softer entire leaves and a laxer form of growth. It flowers in midwinter, and is very fragrant. Both have translucent pale young growth with a pink-red tinge, reminiscent of a *Photinia*.

Phillyrea This is probably my favourite tree, and we are lucky to have found a healthy specimen in the garden here. The most superficial way to describe it is as a small version of *Quercus ilex*, the evergreen oak; it can be used for smaller gardens where the oak would create too much shade.

The species which becomes a tree is *P. latifolia*. The leaves resemble those of an olive, but are a darker green and more shiny, shimmering and fluttering in the wind. Here it has grown to about 7.5m/25ft, and others I have seen are about the same size, including a magnificent clump at The Vyne in Hampshire where the group is planted as a mass at one end of the house and is, I think, the plain variety, *P. latifolia*. The original one in my garden may well be *P. l.* 'Spinosa' as it has very narrow serrated leaves, definitely slightly different from *P. latifolia* of which I now have a few more small examples. Known as the 'farmyard tree', it was introduced to the British Isles before Gerard (i.e. before 1597), from the Black Sea area, and is frequently mentioned in early catalogues throughout the seventeenth century (see John Harvey, *Early Gardening Catalogues*) but for some reason has been much neglected in recent years. It is quite easy to propagate from cuttings so may return to popularity.

The smaller *P. angustifolia*, from the Mediterranean region, was also known in Tudor times and featured in the topiary craze at the end of the seventeenth century, as it could be cut into elegant compact cones. You can see it so cut at Iford Manor, near Bradford-on-Avon in Wiltshire, where it is used around a pond; it is much more interesting in texture than the more frequently used dumpy conifers.

Photinia The Chinese hawthorn, *P. serrulata*, when well grown is one of the best evergreen large shrubs, with excellent foliage and very attractive white flowers, carried in corymbs like a *Viburnum*. It can reach 9m/30ft, and the best examples I have seen are in the warm western counties of England and in Italy. The leaves are at least 15-20cm/6-8in long and 5-7cm/2-3in wide, very shallowly toothed. The young shoots, which are produced from early spring throughout the growing season, are a bright coppery-red, which gradually fades to green. They are not affected by frost. The only other shrub which has remotely the same quality is the *Pieris*, which produces its fiery red young leaves at the same time as its dangling lily-of-the-valley flowers. The *Photinia* does not flower until quite old, but the flowers are then followed by red fruits. From its earliest age it makes a bushy lax shape, but with a basically conical habit. There are some good forms of it at Knightshayes, mostly of the Japanese species *P. glabra*, which was introduced to the West in 1903, a hundred years after the Chinese variety. A hybrid of the two has produced *P. × fraseri* which is more tender, like its *glabra* parent, and has coppery rather than red growth.

Pieris The varieties of *P. formosa*, from the Far East, have the best coloured young foliage. These are all acid-loving shrubs which grow to about 2.4m/8ft, with a delightful spreading habit which introduces a firm line into the rounded shapes of a rhododendron glade. The branches are held in horizontal layers. It is essentially a woodland plant which, although able to withstand extremes of temperature, is susceptible to changes in a variable winter climate. Unlike the *Photinia*, the new growths, if encouraged to shoot early, may well be affected by renewed cold spells. For this reason it needs to be planted on a frost-draining slope, and hidden from the early morning sun which damages the young leaves by thawing them out unnaturally early in the mornings. *Pieris formosa*, and another Asian shrub, the deciduous *Enkianthus*, are both good foils to more bushy shapes, and very much more delicate in appearance than some of the horizontal viburnums or dogwoods.

Pittosporum These are New Zealand shrubs which tend to be treated as being suitable only for very favoured sites in coastal districts, but which could in fact be grown much more frequently. Some of the most tender varieties are described in the chapter on wall shrubs.

The hardiest that we grow here is one with perhaps the least firm architectural outline. A pleasant spreading shrub at first, it later becomes a small round-headed tree. *P. dallii*, which I first saw on a wall at Hidcote, can be grown as a free-standing specimen, and has dark elliptic leaves, the leaf stalks a distinct maroon colour, and the young shoots glabrous and pale. The white flowers are fragrant and packed into a terminal cluster, which makes them more conspicuous than the flowers of most of this genus. It was introduced from New Zealand in 1913.

P. tenuifolium, with its many forms, grows as a hedge here, but with the protection of a background of yews, and, in another part of the garden, in a sheltered and favoured spot. It grows very quickly, and each plant makes a splendid conical or pyramidal shape with attractive undulating foliage. Even if used as a hedge it is most effective if not planted too close together, in order to maintain its distinctive and symmetrical outline. The leaves of the type are pale, shining green, intensely undulate, and set on black twigs. The flowers carried freely in late spring are a strange chocolate-purple colour and very fragrant, but clustered in the leaf axils and not, therefore, very noticeable. The form 'Silver Queen' has extremely pretty foliage of silver-grey but, although not so far damaged here by hard weather, it literally grows at half the pace of the type. It is not therefore suitable for mixing to make a hedge, and as it has a slightly more rounded and mound-like shape is best grown in a group, preferably against a dark background.

P. 'Garnettii' has variegated silver-white leaves, spotted with pink, and makes a compact rounded cone. It seems to be a robust plant.

P. tenuifolium 'Purpureum' has purple foliage, and I have given it a wall position, but have seen it free-standing at Knightshayes. It has a rather bizarre appearance in the spring as the young shoots are bright pale green, carried at the end of the stiff purple branches. The curled edges help to protect the leaves from fierce sun. The only other plants which have wavy and curled edges to the leaves similar to *Pittosporum tenuifolium* are some of the *Olearia* species, which also come from New Zealand.

Prunus There are two forms of the common laurel, *P. laurocerasus*, which, although not large, do give a definite shape for certain planting effects. *P. l.* 'Zabeliana' has a horizontal growth somewhat reminiscent of the Pfitzer juniper, but less dense. For woodland planting, where the formality introduced by all conifers is less satisfactory, this shrub is a useful and ornamental alternative. It has dark green narrow leaves and flowers freely, even in the shade of yews. Another form, 'Otto Luyken', has paler and brighter green leaves and is more compact.

Quercus The evergreen oak, *Quercus ilex*, is one of the few evergreen varieties of this genus which can withstand a northern climate. It is desirable in every way, although it does create dense shade and therefore would not be suitable for a small garden. Furthermore, it does change its leaves, even though it maintains its foliage all through the seasons, and in a large tree this creates a lot of work, especially if the tree is grown as a specimen in a lawn. It will grow into a beautifully shaped tree, and the young pale growth makes a delightful and lightening contrast with the darker older leaves. A Mediterranean tree, it has been grown in Britain since the sixteenth century. In warm climates it makes a very pleasant hedge, and is used for arbours and shady walks. In Britain it is more difficult to grow it as a hedge as pruning encourages young growth to such an extent that the summer is neither hot enough nor long enough to ripen and harden the

The Japanese maple, Acer palmatum, *grows to become a large shrub or broad-headed small tree, suitable for the framework of small gardens. These maples are useful in borders and as lawn specimens in larger gardens, the leaves turning vivid shades of red and orange in the autumn. They prefer a well-drained acid loam and do not thrive on chalk.*

young green shoots, so they suffer damage in winter.

Grown as a specimen tree it is perfectly hardy once established, and in coastal gardens is often planted in beautiful groves for shelter. The whole landscape of the valley near the sea at Abbotsbury is dominated by these beautiful trees, which only occasionally get scorched by the salt-laden winds. The underneath of the leaves is heavily felted and the leaves are carried sufficiently loosely to flutter in the wind, showing the contrast in surfaces.

Deciduous trees and shrubs

I include here only trees and shrubs which have a definable architectural shape. At Hadspen I grow many other woody plants which are used in border associations and as specimen trees.

Acer It is difficult to know exactly in which category to put the whole maple family, as some make spreading or mound-like shrubs and some make medium-sized trees which are ideal for small gardens and may give the form and balance there which is equivalent to that of broad-headed trees in a larger garden. Those like the Norway maple and the sycamore make excellent wind-resistant trees for the outer gar-

den. Nearly every species has forms with interesting colour and bark. These are described in Chapter 8; in this section shape and habit are the main criteria of choice.

The Japanese maple, *Acer palmatum dissectum*, is a very slow-growing shrub, and combines weeping branches with a rounded rather artificial appearance. Its final combination of delicate dissected foliage with a skeleton winter structure of twisted but compact form, is most unusual, and takes many years to develop. It is probably at its best as a corner plant in a mixed bed or border, where it contrasts strongly with shrubs or herbaceous perennials, which make a carpet near it. A moist woodland soil is the most suitable and it thrives if given protection by other trees. The leaves are divided, and can be purple, bronze or pale green. The pale fresh green forms give vivid autumn colours.

The Norway maple, *Acer platanoides*, makes a handsome large tree, which grows quickly and is therefore useful on a new bare site where some mass is needed immediately. There are quite a number of forms, varying from broad-headed to more fastigiate, and from those with lobed leaves to those with more dissected. The green foliage varieties usually turn a clear yellow in the autumn. Personally, I prefer to have

interesting foliage colours as focal points in a mixed planting, or against a dark background, rather than as one of the main form-giving features of the garden.

The sycamore, *Acer pseudoplatanus*, needs plenty of space but is tough and provides shelter in cold uplands. Its worst feature is its tendency to seed prolifically but, except in woodland, this is not a great problem in the garden. Most of the varieties with attractive coloured leaves are rather less vigorous and suitable for the smaller garden, or as part of a planting scheme of trees and shrubs in the larger area (see page 79). The American box-elder, *A. negundo*, has pinnate leaves and is the fastest grower of the genus. It makes an attractive more pyramidal shape than the others, and so is useful in most gardens whatever their size; like the sycamore, the forms with variegated foliage are much slower growing (see page 120).

Aesculus Everyone knows the ordinary horse chestnut, *A. hippocastanum*, which in its common form has white flowers, carried in erect candles in late spring. The pink form, *A. × carnea*, is a cross with the American buckeye, *A. pavia*, and makes a pretty pyramid for a large garden. *A. pavia* itself is a smaller tree with more delicate foliage, which casts much less shade: it has been rather neglected by gardeners in general.

A. indica, the Indian horse chestnut, has panicles of upright pink flowers in early summer and in general a more erect fastigiate habit of growing. A particularly good late-flowering form of it was raised at Kew in 1928, and named 'Sydney Pearce' after the Assistant Curator. It can be seen just inside the main gates. The leaves of *A. indica* are larger and smoother than in the ordinary European variety and the panicles of the flowers are longer.

Betula Although most of the birches are included in the chapter on trees of interest for their bark, they are among the small trees most used for growing in town gardens, blending well with every sort of architectural style. The only one for this section is the weeping birch, *B. pendula. B.p.* 'Youngii' ultimately makes a beautiful dome-shaped tree, but it is a slow grower, and always looks slightly ridiculous when very small. The variety *B. p.* 'Tristis' is more erect.

Cercidiphyllum The Japanese variety of this graceful and

The katsura, Cercidiphyllum japonicum, *has a regular pyramidal outline even when mature. The attractive foliage emerges pink-tinged in spring before becoming a clear summer green. In autumn the leaves assume yellow and scarlet tints and, as the sugar rises, smell of crushed strawberries. Forms which develop multiple stems are invaluable for certain landscaping situations.*

shapely small tree is the one usually grown but it differs little from the Chinese variety brought back by Ernest Wilson twenty years later, in 1907, for the Arnold Arboretum and eventually arriving in Britain. Its leaves, as you may guess, are very much like those of the Judas tree, *Cercis siliquastrum*, but are opposite rather than alternate; they emerge earlier in the season, turning a delightful yellow or pinky-yellow in the autumn. Until of considerable age, it makes an excellent pyramidal shape and is ideal as a single specimen in a small garden, or effective if planted in large groups to contrast with trees with spreading heads or rounded bushes. It needs plenty of moisture in the growing season, but is otherwise a very thrifty and easily grown tree.

Cornus Most of the dogwoods are shrubs or small trees with a shrubby branching shape, of great importance in the garden for their beautiful and varied foliage and pale flowers. Two species are important especially for their architectural habit, developing as trees or shrubs with their branches in almost horizontal layers. Both green and variegated forms of *Cornus controversa* and *C. alternifolia* are garden-worthy. They are superlative trees, attractive when clothed in fresh green or silver and green foliage, and still effective in their winter skeleton form. They have flat corymbs of small flowers in late spring, and black fruits in the autumn. The best example of the green *C. controversa* that I know is at Trewithen in Cornwall, and there is a well-grown variegated one in the Botanic Gardens at Bath. My own variegated form is one of the delights of the garden here; although only eight years old it is already 3.6m/12ft high and the lower branches have a spread of about the same. It is one of the most outstanding trees for architectural purposes, but is difficult to obtain, and difficult to propagate which makes it expensive.

Enkianthus This is another member of the *Andromeda* or *Ericaceae* family, and requires conditions very similar to those needed by the *Pieris* of the same group, or by rhododendrons and azaleas. As they are best in some form of woodland planting they are not useful as specimens for definite shapes in a formal garden, but their layered branches make an excellent contrast and foil to the usually rounded and evergreen rhododendrons. They grow to about 3m/10ft, and have some of the most exquisite colouring of all autumn leaves. They need acid soil, rich, moist and well drained.

Eucryphia There is only one deciduous variety of this excellent Chilean genus worth growing, namely *E. glutinosa*, which has pinnate leaves, paler than those of *E. moorei* but rather similar. It has a regular shape like the evergreen forms (see page 108), and equally beautiful creamy flowers and autumn tints.

Fagus If you stand back and look at a specimen of the European native beech, it makes an almost perfect, very broadly based pyramid shape. To achieve this regularity of outline it is worth taking some trouble with original staking and general care. It does create dense shade under its canopy, but evergreen ground cover, such as *Epimedium, Vinca* and *Ruscus*, is perfectly at home around the base of the trunk.

F. sylvatica is the European common beech and this has variegated leaf forms as well as purple and cut-leaf. If I was starting from scratch in a garden, I think I would establish, as speedily as possible, a *Fagus sylvatica heterophylla*, of which there are several more or less cut or lobed varieties. The coloured leaf beeches have to be carefully placed, and although the purple beech is glowing and bronze in the spring, later in the summer it gets very dull and heavy.

The fastigiate variety, the Dawyck beech, is symmetrical and erect, and useful for a small garden, or for growing in a group among trees with broader heads. The weeping beech, *Fagus sylvatica* 'Pendula', is one of the best weeping trees, but it is slow to grow and develop. The purple weeping variety makes a small tree with a mushroom head. There are good examples of both at the Westonbirt Arboretum.

Ligustrum The evergreen varieties of privet, which grow in a vase-like form, or with a single trunk, were mentioned on page 108. The Chinese species, *L. sinense*, is similar to *L. japonicum*, except for being deciduous and more free flowering. There is a fine bush of it in the Chelsea Physic Garden and another at Kew.

Liquidambar The American sweet gum *L. styraciflua* makes a slender pyramidal tree, with deeply lobed leaves very much like those of a maple. The leaves have a shining green colour, and, if you are fortunate and have a good form, turn scarlet in the autumn. It colours best if fully exposed to sunlight. In winter it is easily recognized by its distinctive corky bark, most evident on the twigs of the branches. It likes a moist soil, and can be grown in quite swampy ground as long as it is not in a frost pocket.

Liriodendron *L. tulipifera* is a well-known and very handsome tree from North America which has been grown in Britain since the seventeenth century. No garden of more than half an acre should be without one. Its fine straight trunk branches into a spreading head and balances suitably with any groupings of buildings or with other trees. It makes very little shade and has distinctive leaves and flowers. The leaves have flattened ends like broad fish-tails, and the flowers are tulip-shaped and greenish-yellow. The foliage becomes quite pale after the first frosts. There are many good examples of this tree, notably at Stourhead in Wiltshire.

There is also an attractive variegated form.

Liriodendron chinense was introduced from China by Ernest Wilson in 1901; I have never seen it but am greatly tempted to try one as the Asian varieties of so many genera are superior to the North American ones, and many of my favourite plants seem to have been introduced to the West by 'Chinese Wilson' as he was called – hence the 'sinowilsonii' found in plant epithets.

Parrotia There is only one member of this family in general garden use, *P. persica*, which makes an attractive vase-like shrub or small tree, contrasting well with vertical columnar evergreens. It is a striking bush at all times, with leaves resembling those of the hazel but turning to shades of crimson and orange in the early autumn. The bare branches in the winter show patchy bark, reminiscent of a London plane tree, *P. × acerifolia*. In early spring it bears frost-resistant dark red flowers, consisting of clusters of stamens. They are like those of the evergreen shrub *Sycopsis sinensis*, which flowers at the same time here, and is also a member of the *Hamamelis* family, but keeps its dull puckered leaves all winter. I like to think we have the biggest and best *Parrotia* in the country; unfortunately we do not know when it was planted but it was probably before the 1914-18 war.

Platanus The London plane, *P. × acerifolia* (syn. *P. × hispanica*), is a well-known feature of town planning, with its attractive mottled bark and maple-like leaves. *P. orientalis* has been cultivated in Britain since the sixteenth century, and may well be a parent of the former. It makes a very large stately tree with a broad head and marbled trunk and is excellent for a large garden. The leaves are more deeply lobed than those of the ordinary London plane. It is very long lived, and provides a suitable mass to balance with a large building or group of buildings.

Populus Some of the poplars are grown purely for their decorative or aromatic leaves and these are described in Chapter 8. For a small garden it may be best to avoid the genus altogether because of the destructive nature of their invasive roots. If, however, you have plenty of space, these trees planted in groups or in lines have a valuable architectural quality and a speed of growth hardly matched by any other. As shelter or for screens, especially to hide a straight and ugly line such as a tennis court, poplars are invaluable, quickly breaking high and disfiguring horizontal lines. (If you do use

Tall poplars, Populus nigra, line the drive at Royaumont in northern France. Outlined against a grey sky, their staccato shape and regular spacing give formal definition to relaxed woodland-type planting which needs a strong background frame.

them for hiding a tennis court remember to make sure the roots are on a lower level.)

All poplars have a pyramidal shape, which in most varieties spreads out to a broader head as the tree ages. The two best 'screeners' are *P.* × *candicans*, a hybrid of the American balsam poplar and retaining some of the leaf aroma, and the Lombardy poplar, *P. nigra* 'Italica'. The latter makes the most fastigiate shape of all trees. *P. trichocarpa* is the fastest grower, has peeling bark, and turns a pale yellow in the autumn. All these are well clothed throughout the year with branching foliage down to the base of the tree.

Pterocarya This is a tree for a relatively large garden, and one which thrives provided it has rich moist soil. All the species have pinnate leaves, rather similar to those of a walnut, but a more attractive fresh green colour. The one I grow, *P. fraxinifolia*, was taken as a cutting from the great tree at Abbotsbury. The tree is frost-tender for the first few springs if tempted into early growth, but seems to add about 6ocm/24in to its height each year. It has attractive long green catkins and winged fruits. Although apt to throw up suckers at a considerable distance from the main trunk, it is generally very little trouble once established. There are some splendid specimens along the water at Syon Park.

Pyrus I include here only the grey weeping pear, *Pyrus salicifolia* 'Pendula', one of the most beautiful of all small weeping trees. It can be grown as an effective contrast to horizontal lines, such as grass or still water, and is equally satisfactory in a cascade effect with a waterfall or steps to continue the same line. Its silver-white willow-like leaves make it an admirable foil to dark foliage. One of the most successful plantings is at Knightshayes, where it stands almost alone on flat mown grass inside an enclosure formed by a dark green yew hedge, with a pond and nothing else to distract the eye. Contrast of foliage colour and texture is given by the three different plants – yew, grass and pear. Contrast of architectural form is provided by the horizontal and vertical lines of the hedges, clipped to make a battlemented top, water and grass and the cascading tree. The effect is an example of restrained and planned design. Alas, too often the pear is used without adequate thought for contrasting or blending shapes; but it is one of the most popular trees of the landscape artist, and there have been some excellent group plantings in public parks.

Salix Many of the willows are described in other chapters but the weeping form *S. babylonica* is another useful tree for architectural form. It was traditionally supposed to be the tree beside which the Israelites wept in exile, hence the name, but now that is believed to have been some form of poplar. Napoleon was buried under a willow and it is therefore sometimes called Napoleon's willow. It is often planted in association with water, but makes an equally effective contrast with a horizontal lawn or any smooth surface. Very few weeping trees are at their best in a mixed planting, crowded by other bushes.

Tilia The pendent lime, *T.* 'Petiolaris', is one of the best weeping larger trees, growing much faster than the weeping beech. It will flourish in any soil and any conditions. It has the regular shape of a broad pyramid, with branches slightly up-curving at the extremities, but strongly pendulous. The leaves with long stalks flutter in the breeze and display the paler undersides. It has two disadvantages: first, it sheds its leaves and sticky flowers all through the summer, and second, the flowers are narcotic to bees, so if the tree is near water the bees in their drugged state fall in.

Viburnum The horizontal branched viburnums are among the most useful shrubs for emphasis. They make perfect corner plants, or frames for gateways, and also can be used to clothe banks, continuing the line of the slope.

The wild form of *V. plicatum* (syn. *V. tomentosum*) from which all these horizontal spreaders derive was not introduced until 1865, while *V. plicatum*, although only arriving in the West in 1843, immediately after the end of the Opium War opened China to botanists, was already then a hybrid and cultivated in many Chinese and Japanese gardens. The branches are held in tiers, and suppress all weeds with their heavy foliage and dense flower heads. The white sterile florets are clustered along the boughs in late spring, and the leaves colour bronze and pink in the autumn. There are several good forms, some with more tabulated branches than others. In my cottage garden I planted *V. plicatum* 'Lanarth' without realizing that its spread would increase to as much as 3.6m/12ft. Even here, when I knew this, I have used a pair for framing a pathway and have put them too close to the edge. There are several other good forms, and I once ordered the pink form 'Pink Beauty', but was sent the white form in error and never followed it up. These shrubs look equally effective as a contrast to rounded, vertical or weeping shapes, and are invaluable in the garden and for introducing a measure of formality into woodland planting.

At Knightshayes Court in Devon, a solitary weeping pear (Pyrus salicifolia 'Pendula') makes a focal point above a circular reflecting pool in a small green-hedged garden room. Its silvery-grey leaves and flowing lines contrast with the dark formality of the surrounding yew topiary, the top surface of which is clipped to resemble castle fortifications. Such restrained planting is inspirational.

Chapter 8

ORNAMENTAL TREES AND SHRUBS

SOME TREES AND shrubs may not have a distinctive shape or habit but deserve to be grown as specimens for their decorative foliage or bark. Few of us have sufficient space in our gardens to plant all the ornamental trees we would like to. If we have the scale, we may well lack the means to undertake extensive plantings and the expense of maintenance. Furthermore, we may have doubts about the future of our individual gardens; not only is it likely that trees for which we now find a place will not be enjoyed by our own successors, but only too possible that the garden itself may be swept away to furnish a site for industrial or urban development. We all live in a state of such insecurity about the future that even looking twenty or thirty years ahead seems too unrealistic to allow of the idea of planning large-scale ornamental planting, especially of trees which are slow to mature. Here in the heart of the Somerset countryside, the hazard of urban or industrial encroachment is not a real one, at any rate in the foreseeable future. The greatest deterrent to planting is rather the risk of failure through future lack of maintenance.

Up to a point this is a situation with which I have had to deal already, as we took over a garden which had been planted with skill and vision but which, after approximately thirty years of excellent upkeep, had suffered nearly as long a period of comparative neglect, due to wartime difficulties and shortage of knowledgeable labour. Many small and interesting trees were, of course, lost, but the larger trees survived and flourished, and would now delight the heart of the Edwardian grandmother who chose and placed them with such care. She thus created the bones and structure of the garden, and to such good effect that we were encouraged to reclothe this skeleton with many of the smaller and rarer trees and shrubs which had vanished in the intervening years, besides using new varieties and improved forms.

The Chinese form of the Asiatic dogwood, Cornus kousa chinensis, *is more lime-tolerant than the species and will grow to make an elegant spreading shrub in most soil conditions. In early summer the white bracts, pink-tinted at first, are held on erect stalks completely clothing the branches which grow in elegant drooping layers. The leaves turn bronze and crimson in autumn.*

Even in a small garden, apart from trees of architectural value, discussed in the previous chapter, there is often room for one or more trees with interesting flowers, foliage and bark which can make important focal points, or give height in a mixed border of shrubs and herbaceous perennials. If you choose the groundcover material wisely – it can be either builders' stone, gravel, grass or other flat horizontal plants – it would be perfectly possible to make a simple and beautiful garden of this ground surface with a few trees as the only extra ornament. The tree or trees should blend or contrast with the architectural mass of the house, as already said, but can have the additional advantages of leaf colour and texture, peeling or striped bark, and possibly flowers and fruit in season.

Here, where we have plenty of space, partly in reclaimed beds and borders now planted with a mixture of heights, depths and foliage contrasts, and partly in a sloping area below the walled vegetable garden which had been used in the past for orchard and extra cabbages, we have planted small trees to complement the mature large ones. In the old orchard we have sown grass, and planted specimen trees, leaving some areas rough to simulate beds about 20cm/8in high and level, but mowing tightly to make sweeping paths which curve through the whole section and have gentle corners to make mowing simple. Every bend has a suitable corner tree to accent it and give it purpose, with another tree ahead acting as a focal point to lead one on before again changing direction. At present, for ease of upkeep, there are no bulbs in the grass to regulate the times and the evenness of the mowing, and their absence in fact leads to a simplicity of design which gives the eye an opportunity to concentrate on the trees themselves. Each area of rough grass contrasts with the smooth paths in exactly the same way as would more detailed flower beds, or flat beds of any other growing material. The rough grass is mown at intervals of three or four weeks. Elsewhere in the garden we have sections of grass for naturalized bulbs, including summer-flowering native field orchids, and these areas cannot be cut until the end of August, after the orchids have seeded.

While a tree is young, it is essential to keep clean a circle or square at least 1m/3ft across around its stem, as it will not be able to compete with coarse grasses for food and moisture. Here we surround a circle cut in the turf with rabbit netting, as we frequently have trouble from roe-deer, squirrels, hares and now and again rabbits. The netting also serves as a cage to hold mulch, which saves the young exposed trees from drying out in the summer and protects them from cold in the winter; the cage itself also gives some screen against cold winds. Trees with long tap roots are in less need of this extra help as the roots will not be affected by any grass or weed competition. It is important to keep the edges of the cut turf tidily trimmed as the whole effect can be ruined by unkempt borders, in just the same way as edges of grass next to beds or paths can make or mar the whole appearance of the garden. The area surrounding the young trees, besides being mulched, can be kept clean by spot spraying of paraquat. I am told that it is safe to use the systemic aminotriazole, which works by translocation and penetrates to the roots, although I am so wary of possible contamination of the soil that I do not use it myself. Once the young tree is well established it is possible to use a solution of simazine, which will sterilize the top few inches of the soil and prevent germination of annual weed seedlings.

When planting the young tree, be sure to make a hole sufficiently wide and deep in which to spread out the roots. Add some organic manure or other humus-forming matter, and make certain that the subsoil is loose enough to ensure good drainage. If necessary make a mixture of good friable topsoil, particularly if your own is very clayey or liable to compact. Perhaps most important of all is to remember to stake the trees with stakes at least 1.2m/4ft high, even if the plant is much smaller, and tie it carefully with some soft and expanding material. I find that even the black rubber ties if overlooked for too long can seriously damage the stem of soft wood. Sensible and thorough staking is all the more important if there are wind-funnels or if the whole area is exposed.

Before deciding on which tree to plant you will need to know the degree of acidity or alkalinity in the soil as measured by the pH index (see Chapter 2). For permanent plants such as trees with deep roots, this cannot be substantially altered to suit the individual plant or tree. Hardiness too must be considered, and this is especially important when planting specimen trees in the open where they cannot benefit from the protection of their neighbours. Trees from countries with extremes of temperature and high altitudes find it difficult to adapt to warmer winters, when they are tempted into early growth, and when they are very young they have few reserves to draw on if their spring shoots are cut back. Trees from warmer countries are unlikely to make premature growth but obviously can withstand only a certain amount of frost.

Let us now look at a few trees which are of particular value and interest for foliage and bark, leaving flowers and fruits to be considered as of more or less secondary importance. This is not because I do not appreciate both, but simply because I have to be selective, and foliage (including autumn colour), bark and the skeleton structure of trees extend the theme of this book. This means omitting altogether the genus *Malus* and passing rapidly over *Prunus*, while trees such as *Davidia* have crept in since their 'flowers' are to be counted as bracts, not petals. This applies also to some of the best dogwoods.

Acer The maple family covers such a range that one can almost certainly find a species inside the genus to suit any site or garden, whatever its size. See also pages 79 and 111.

A. cappadocicum, from the Caucasus and the Himalaya, will grow to at least 15m/50ft, has excellent glossy lobed foliage which turns yellow in autumn, and in some forms has attractive young red growth. *A. davidii*, *A. griseum*, *A. grosseri* and *A. g. hersii* are primarily grown for their handsome bark, but all have pleasant summer foliage and striking colours in autumn. The odd man out of this group is the paper-bark maple, *A. griseum*, which has flaking and peeling cinnamon-coloured bark, and looks marvellous against the sun. It is a small tree with a neat and regular shape, and trifoliate leaves which colour in autumn if given a position in full sun. The other three mentioned have handsome striated bark of green and white, and elegant leaves held on pink or red stalks and turning red in autumn. The leaves of *A. davidii* are veined and toothed but ovate in shape and not lobed.

The palmatum maples are probably the most frequently grown in smaller gardens, but actually are happiest in woodland conditions. They are very slow growers but compensate for this with the most fiery colours of all in autumn. *A. p. coreanum* has an attractive shape after a few years and is a relatively quick grower; its leaves turn dark crimson in autumn. Of the *heptalobum*, or seven-lobed group of the palmatums, I have only *A. p. h.* 'Osakazuki' which has brilliant scarlet leaves at the end of the season. The coral-bark

In Princess Sturdza's garden in northern France, maples with green, bronze-purple and golden foliage demonstrate the subtleties of leaf colour and texture which make more fleeting seasonal flower effects seem relatively unimportant. Maples need a moist well-drained soil and do best in acid rather than alkaline conditions, often producing spectacular fiery autumn tints. The Japanese maples benefit from some protection from cold winds.

Maple, A. *palmatum* 'Senkaki' (now correctly A. *p.* 'Sango-kaku'), is beautiful at every time of the year. The coral-coloured young stems glow through the winter. In summer it is clothed with pale fresh green leaves, which turn pale canary-yellow in the autumn. There are some particularly fine examples of it at Knightshayes.

The sycamore has many excellent foliage forms, all of which grow less vigorously than the type. The young leaves of A. *pseudoplatanus* 'Brilliantissimum' are an exciting pink when they unfold in the spring. The tree needs careful siting, either as a focal point or, better still, against a dark background in a mixed planting. The leaves really look like flowers from a distance. Unfortunately they fade by the end of the summer to an ordinary green. 'Prinz Handjery' is almost as vivid but the underside of the leaves is purplish. One of the most attractive in habit and leaf is A. *p.* 'Leopoldii', which has been rather alarmingly described as having 'leaves yellowish-pink at first, later green, speckled and splashed yellow and pink'. I dare say this is an exact description, but if I had not seen it elsewhere growing with quite subdued colours, I would certainly never have acquired it. It makes a good sober-looking tree here and appears to have green with white to cream markings on the leaves. Another sycamore with good leaves is the golden A. *p.* 'Worleei', which is one of the best golden foliage forms, very bright in the early spring, fading to green through the summer. Eventually it makes a big tree and is more upright.

Ailanthus The tree of heaven, A. *altissima*, is so often grown in suburban gardens as a foliage plant that one tends to forget that if allowed to develop it makes a handsome tree of up to 24m/8oft. The trunk of a mature *Ailanthus* has an attractive grey bark. The leaves are very large and ash-like and on the juvenile plant, or on one that is pruned heavily each season, will be about 90cm/3ft in length. Like the *Paulownia* it can either be encouraged to behave as an exotic and tropical-looking bush, or in a suitable climate it can be allowed to develop its true habit, with smaller leaves but a graceful shape. It is unfortunately very brittle and needs some spring shelter to do really well, but is an excellent town tree. There is a variety A. *a.* 'Pendulifolia' which has drooping leaves and makes an elegant lawn specimen.

Albizia A. *julibrissin* is the only species of these deciduous trees with mimosa-like foliage that will thrive in temperate climates and even this does much better when we have hot summers. The doubly pinnate leaf is bright green with a bronze tinge. Found from Persia eastward to China, the species has been grown in Europe since 1745. It is a beautiful tree for a sheltered corner, but needs some protection during the first years. The pale pink flowers, carried in fluffy heads, are also very attractive.

Alnus There are few members of the deciduous alders which have distinguished foliage. We grow only one here, A. *cordata*, from Corsica and southern Italy, which has glossy shimmering leaves and a regular conical shape. When grown as a group they can be used for screens, and are an excellent alternative to Lombardy poplars; also, being more conical and less columnar, they are very useful for outlines. The *Alnus* has been grown in Britain since 1820 and could be more often planted. It will grow in heavy moist soils.

Aralia The devil's walking stick, A. *spinosa*, is deciduous and makes an unbranched trunk, which in winter is armed with stout spiny stems. It suckers very freely, so you can either allow a thicket to develop or cut these shoots off as they appear and encourage the tree itself to grow to about 3.6m/12ft. The Japanese species A. *elata* has forms with variegated foliage; the leaves are doubly pinnate, up to 1.2m/4ft in length, and marked with silver or gold splashes of colour. They are usually grafted bushes, and for the best results the tendency to sucker must be strongly restrained.

I have grown the slow and difficult golden variegated form A. *elata* 'Aureovariegata' in a bed of *Acanthus mollis*, where it thrives and produces white panicles of fluffy flowers in late summer. There is a beautiful example of the even better silver variegated form, A. *elata* 'Variegata', at Knightshayes.

Arbutus The strawberry trees, including A. *andrachne* and A. *menziesii*, are difficult to establish as they are very tender when young. They are grown usually for their fruit, but I find the cinnamon-coloured bark one of their greatest attractions. The hardier shrubby species, A. *unedo*, is described on page 80. The hybrid between it and the Greek A. *andrachne*, A. × *andrachnoides*, is the best for a temperate climate and also the most lime-tolerant, inheriting this characteristic from A. *unedo*, which is the only member of the *Andromeda* or *Ericaceae* family to thrive on our soil. The hybrid has unusually attractive branching stems of a red-cinnamon colour.

Berberis I include only one species of *Berberis* here for its beauty. B. *temolaica* has dark shoots, beautiful glaucous blue-grey leaves, and an erect habit; it should eventually make an upright shrub of about 3m/10ft, but is slow. The fruit is red and egg-shaped and said to be very ornamental. My plant has yet to bear any.

Betula Without exception these deciduous trees have outstandingly beautiful stems, ranging from the white of the native European B. *pendula* (syn. B. *verrucosa*, meaning 'warty') to the exciting pinks and orange of the American

The weeping form of the ordinary silver birch, Betula pendula 'Youngii', is mushroom-domed and provides a contrast to more broad-headed or upright shapes. It is most effective when paired to frame a path or gateway or a single

specimen can create a focal point. Trees with a pendulous habit are often grown beside water where they droop over the horizontal surface to provide contrast and reflection.

example of the latter in the Edinburgh Botanic Garden. *B. albo-sinensis septentrionalis* has shining orange-brown bark with a distinctive pink sheen. I have planted all these in groups of three to get the maximum effect, but it takes four or five years of patience before the bark begins to peel and reveal its true quality. An annual scrub with soap and water will apparently improve the glowing colours, but I cannot quite see myself doing this.

The ordinary native European birch has an excellent purple-leaved variety which is not often grown; it is worth having where such foliage colour is acceptable since the tree has an airy open effect quite unlike the heavy foliage of so many trees with leaves of this colour. The weeping varieties are mentioned on page 113.

Carpinus I grow only one of the hornbeams, although if I were considering a new hedge I might well choose the normal variety of *C. betulus*. *C. betulus* 'Fastigiata' is well worth growing however for its regular form, which quickly becomes pyramidal rather than upright, and for its grey fluted trunk

and Asian species. The small fluttering leaves also colour to a pale yellow in autumn. The best American species, *B. papyrifera*, the canoe or paper birch, has white peeling bark, possibly the whitest of all. Of the Asians, perhaps the most remarkable bark belongs to *B. ermanii*, pink on the trunk, orange-brown on the branches; and the leaves are glossier too than those of the native species.

Two splendid Himalayan birches, *B. utilis* with a creamy peeling trunk and *B. u. jacquemontii* with white stems and peeling bark are also worth mentioning; there is an excellent and attractive serrated leaves of a fresher green than in the type. There is a good example at Forde Abbey in Dorset.

Castanea The deciduous sweet chestnut, *C. sativa*, is only just lime-tolerant, but will survive periods of drought, as must be obvious from the way it thrives in southern Europe. It is a native of the Mediterranean region and was introduced to Britain by the Romans. Unfortunately, the summers are seldom hot enough to produce good-quality nuts. I have planted a decorative variegated form, *C. sativa* 'Albomarginata', with a strong white margin to the leaf, which I saw at Kew, and I think this may make a more interesting foliage tree than the variegated elm, *Ulmus procera* 'Argenteovariegata', which has a more mottled and splashed marking and is also subject to Dutch elm disease.

Catalpa This genus contains small shapely trees of Asiatic or North American origin; the Asiatics were not introduced to Britain until the first years of this century and are rarely grown. The American bean tree is commonly used for street planting in the eastern states of America, and the group in Westminster Palace Yard in London proves their reliable tolerance of urban pollution. The golden variety of *C. bignonioides* has larger leaves than the type and is very decorative, but I find it grows very slowly and that the tips of the branches are often affected by late frosts. It comes into leaf rather late in the spring but is excellent as a focal point for emphasis. The ordinary green *C. bignonioides* has attractive white flowers with yellow and pink markings, but seldom bears them freely and never when young.

Cercidiphyllum see page 113.

Cercis The Judas tree, *C. siliquastrum*, must not be dismissed just because it is to be found in so many old gardens. The leaves are distinctive and the axillary flowers crowd the branches in late spring, usually just as the leaves are emerging. Coming from the eastern Mediterranean it loves sun, and the branches get brittle as the tree ages. There is a white-flowered form which is even more attractive than the slightly muddy rose-pink of the type.

Cornus The horizontal trees in this genus were mentioned in Chapter 6 and the shrubs are included in Chapter 4. The small trees described below are either American or Asiatic, and for once I think that one of the species from the New World, *C. nuttallii*, is better than those from Asia. It is a woodland tree from the western states of North America and has attractive dogwood foliage which colours well in autumn. The flowers appear in late spring and are themselves inconspicuous, but are surrounded by large white bracts which take on a slight pinkness when the tree is in full sun. They are not borne for at least six years and the plant takes

many more years to mature. There is a splendid specimen at Abbotsbury in Dorset.

C. capitata from the Himalaya is an evergreen branching and shrub-like tree, which is reputedly tender but seems to take quite happily to conditions in our garden. It is a much faster grower; mine, grown from cuttings about six years ago, are already 3m/10ft high. It flowers in early summer and the rather similar bracts, but slightly smaller and pale yellow, are followed by strawberry-shaped fruits in early autumn. The leaves are a pleasant green with a grey tinge and the tree will reach 12m/40ft in ideal situations.

C. kousa from Japan and Korea, and the Chinese variety *C. kousa chinensis*, are also very slow growers, and the latter is thought to be more lime-tolerant. They carry their flowers with showy white bracts more freely than the others; a good example will be completely covered with white decorations in early summer and since the branches are long and spreading will look very effective. I have seen an excellent example of the Chinese variety standing in a woodland glade at Westonbirt, and it looks charming too at Abbotsbury in a mixed planting with other trees and shrubs.

Davidia *D. involucrata*, the pocket-handkerchief tree, has its own rather strange charm with its very odd white bracts draped on it in late spring. Ernest Wilson was sent to China by Veitch's Nursery on his first botanical expedition to bring back this tree, which had already been seen by the French missionary David in 1869. This was the beginning of Wilson's infinitely rewarding and adventurous career just after the Boxer rebellion, during which he introduced many excellent new plants. The *Davidia* itself makes an attractive small tree, though its grey ribbed leaves with their silky undersides tend to hide the effect of the unequal-sized bracts, which are always carried in pairs. The form *D. i. vilmoriniana* has leaves which are hairless beneath. There is a wonderful example of it just inside the main garden at Hidcote.

Decaisnea *D. fargesii* is a rather unusual small tree or large shrub from China. It has distinctive large pinnate leaves and carries pale green flowers in racemes almost 45cm/18in long, followed by equally interesting long metallic blue pods.

Drimys See page 106.

Embothrium See page 108.

Eucalyptus If you are prepared to take a little trouble, it is well worth planting some of this extremely decorative genus. They have very handsome and aromatic foliage, and if you choose those grown from seed from high altitudes, they can be quite hardy in many situations. It is now generally considered a mistake to stake these fast-growing trees. Plant them as small seedlings to make sure they are wind-firm. If

A multiple-stemmed eucalypt, Eucalyptus niphophila, *displays the attractive mottled grey and cream patchwork bark pattern. The leaves are grey-green and* leathery. Known as the snow gum, this tree (hardy in most British gardens) grows less quickly than many of the genus.

plants obtained from a nursery are lanky, cut them to the ground in spring and allow to regrow. If staked, they seldom make a supportive root system. Many trees grow into an ugly shape through failure to give meticulous care to these requirements; even in this garden we have more than one example of what the lack of sufficient vigilance can produce in the shape of tall trees bent and moulded by the prevailing south-west wind. The bark as well as the foliage is of immense decorative interest. The leaves vary from a glaucous blue to pale green and silver-grey, and from small rounded to long sickle shapes. They also differ in colour and shape in juvenile and in adult plants. They all come from Australia and Tasmania and will not withstand many degrees of frost.

We grow what are probably the most hardy varieties, and as there are so many species I will mention only those that have proved a success here. They should never be given any form of feeding, as this leads to their pushing out too many new shoots which are frost-vulnerable. Pinching out leaders when the plants are small will help sturdy growth.

E. *coccifera* grows with a neat rounded head and is much less vigorous and speedy than most. The juvenile foliage is almost round, about 2.5cm/1in in diameter, and very glaucous, but later becomes a dark grey-green. E. *dalrympleana*, which I grew in our earlier garden, has most attractive patchwork bark. The leaves are bronze when young but get rather large and untidy. It grows very quickly and is difficult to keep in a good shape.

E. *gunnii* is reputedly the hardiest of all and makes a tall tree very quickly, but it can be kept as a bush with juvenile foliage by frequent cutting back. This young foliage is rounded and silver-blue, while the adult tree has sage-green sickle-shaped leaves. On two separate occasions I have obtained under the name *gunnii* plants of quite a different character, which are more compact growers and keep an intensely blue colour and small rounded leaves. Obviously a great deal of hybridizing takes place in natural conditions, and as all plants are grown from seed the results are often a surprise. In my case, as I have also a good tree of the true E. *gunnii*, I am delighted.

E. *johnstonii* is a favourite as it has glossy apple-green leaves, with grey undersides, and red bark. Unfortunately it is in a wind-funnel here and has a markedly wind-swept appearance. E. *mitchelliana* is a weeping variety known in Australia as weeping Sally with narrow grey-green leaves. Although it has not succumbed to hard conditions, it just does not thrive here, and has taken three years to reach 60cm/24in, which is very unusual in this fast-growing genus.

E. *niphophila* has white branches and very elegant grey-cream bark as the tree matures, but it too seems slow. Its leaves, which have pink stalks, are eventually long and green, but the juvenile foliage is oval and grey-green. It seems completely hardy against frost. E. *parvifolia* is also very hardy and has narrow blue-green leaves, which replace the small rounder ones very early in the plant's life. E. *pauciflora* has sickle-shaped leaves, and although hardy does not grow very fast. After six years it is still only 1.8m/6ft tall here. E. *perriniana* has intensely blue-grey young foliage, turning in time from round to oblanceolate but remaining glaucous.

E. *viminalis* quickly makes a heavy head and is susceptible to gales; one of my trees, 3m/10ft in height, has twice been found lying horizontal. It is an attractive species, with pale unstalked leaves which even when young are long and thin and become 10cm/4in in length and 1.2cm/½in wide when older. In Australia it is known as the ribbon gum.

If well grown, all these *Eucalyptus* make effective contributions of leaf and bark and are seen at their best against a dark background. This is no problem at first but many of the faster growers overtop surrounding trees in a few years, and then also become more vulnerable to fierce winds.

Eucryphia See page 108.

Fraxinus The manna ash, F. *ornus*, is well worth growing, not only for its panicles of creamy-white flowers, carried prolifically in early summer, but also for its attractive pale green pinnate leaves. The species F. *mariesii*, from China, is more interesting than the European native, having larger flower panicles and more delicate-looking leaves. *F. griffithii* has dark green leathery leaves and distinct four-winged shoots resembling those of the American species, *F. quadrangulata*, but comes from southeast Asia. I first saw it at Westonbirt and, although it is supposed to be tender, I have had it here for two years now.

Ginkgo See page 103.

Gleditsia The golden-leaved form of the honey locust, *G. triacanthos*, from the eastern states of America, is by far the most valuable of the genus for foliage effect. The type itself is frequently grown for street planting since it is indifferent to air pollution. It has many small frond-like leaflets which, particularly in its golden form *G. t.* 'Sunburst', give an airy and graceful appearance. The branches are armed with rather formidable spines; it grows very slowly, and the leaves come late in the spring. It is at its best in shade with plantings of other pale-leaved plants and with dark shiny leaves like those of *Acanthus mollis*. If you have a dark woodland glade, a collection of evergreen and deciduous golden foliage and textures is surprisingly satisfactory and not at all garish. Miss Jekyll made an excellent grove of this kind at Pyrford Court in Surrey.

Griselinia See pages 88 and 108.

Gymnocladus The hardy species, *G. dioica*, is a beautiful and graceful tree but for some reason rarely planted. It is a slow developer but very desirable with enormous bi-pinnate leaves of a delightful shade of pink, turning to fresh green and then yellow before falling. In winter, however, it has an untidy skeletal appearance as the leaflets fall off the main leaf-stalk. I am indebted to Richard Gorer whose description of this tree in *Hardy Foliage Plants* led me to plant it.

Idesia This is a monotypic genus of great beauty. *I. polycarpa* has leaves on long stalks, very large and regularly ovate with red veins, glaucous undersides and glaucous new growth. I first saw this tree, both male and female, at Abbotsbury from where I obtained cuttings and now have a tree about 4.5m/15ft high. I have the *Idesia* very near to a *Populus lasiocarpa* and the leaves are almost identical. The trees, however, have quite a different habit of growth. The *Idesia* has tabulated branches while the poplar is typically fastigiate to pyramidal, although rather less feathered and well covered than other poplars since the leaves of this species are carried much less freely. The female *Idesia* has large bunches of red berries, but my specimen has yet to flower.

Ilex See page 108.

Koelreuteria *K. paniculata* is the only species of the koelreuterias which is in common garden use, although several good forms of it have been introduced or have arisen in culti-

vation. It is a deciduous tree from China, already known in Europe in the eighteenth century but never very widely grown. The leaves are very delicate in appearance, pinnate, up to 45cm/18in long, and remarkable for their pink colour and ranging according to the pH of the soil from pale yellow and coral to scarlet. The young tree does not flower, but later, when about 3m/10ft high, will produce crowded yellow flowers in terminal panicles. It can eventually reach 12m/40ft but it is much more usual to see specimens of about 6m/20ft. A good form of *Cercidiphyllum japonicum* will have the same pinkish leaf colour in the spring and yellow in the autumn but, of course, quite a different shaped leaf and a much more compact and regular habit.

Ligustrum See pages 108 and 114.

Liquidambar See page 114.

Liriodendron See page 114.

Lomatia The only species of the evergreen *Lomatia* I know is the tender *L. ferruginea*, which has interesting dark green fern-like leaves with leaf stalk and branchlets covered with red down. The undersurface of the leaf is rust coloured. Originally from Chile and Patagonia it is quite often grown in Cornwall and on the west coast of Scotland. It is an acid-loving small tree and likes to grow among other small shrubs for protection.

Magnolia Whole books are written about this magnificent genus, and deservedly so since no other has so much to offer in the way of flower, foliage and shape. The exotic flower, in particular, is of great beauty. Magnolias are, however, slow to flower and relatively difficult to grow well, aspects which endear them to the serious gardener. All enthusiasts have a strong competitive streak, and if you have reared your own plant from cutting or seed, you have so much the more right to prize it highly and even perhaps to boast a little. The method of propagation using mist has made it possible to strike cuttings from magnolias whereas previously seed and layering were the only means of increase. There are two evergreen species in common garden use. *Magnolia grandiflora* has been described in the previous chapter for its structural use in gardens. Already documented as flowering in

Fallen petals from Magnolia × soulangeana strew the grass at Furzey in Hampshire. This large shrub with branches spreading from the base, bears the tulip-shaped flowers in spring before the leaves emerge. There are named clones to choose from; all have white, pink or rose-purple petals, each stamen a deeper purple at the base. M. × soulangeana is the most popular of all magnolias and can be grown as a lawn specimen or against a high wall. In alkaline districts it should be heavily mulched with a low pH compost.

Britain by 1735 it was one of the first three of this genus to be introduced into Europe from the south-east United States. For fifty years M. *grandiflora*, M. *virginiana* and M. *acuminata* were the only ones known in European gardens; indeed M. *delavayi* from China arrived only in 1899.

The leaves of M. *delavayi* differ considerably from those of M. *grandiflora*, being translucent matt sea-green or glaucous, and larger than those of any other evergreen tree which can grow in a temperate climate. It also has attractive white bark which mottles with age, but is seldom seen as it should be, being more often than not grown in bush form against a wall. In fact, it can grow into a tree of 12-15m/40-50ft, but perhaps only in its native Yunnan. The flowers are parchment-coloured and open towards the end of the summer. Undoubtedly more tender than the American species, it nevertheless flowers when still only small; I have a huge bud now on a bush barely 90cm/36in high, and only in its third season. Although it needs shelter, especially when young, it is essentially a woodland plant, and accustomed to partial shade from adjacent trees and shrubs. If grown in full sun against a warm wall, it will benefit from some protection against leaf scorch during its formative years. This is basically true of every magnolia, except perhaps M. *grandiflora*, which has much glossier leaves.

Of the American species M. *macrophylla* has the largest leaves of any deciduous tree or shrub that we can grow. The thin leaves, glaucous beneath, can be almost 60cm/24in long and 30cm/12in wide, and the flowers are the colour of parchment with purple markings at the base. M. *ashei* is very similar but flowers early after the leaves have appeared.

M. *fraseri*, which has leaves nearly as large as those of M. *macrophylla*, was introduced in 1786. It thus almost co-incided with the Yulan, M. *denudata* (now M. *heptapeta*), the first Asiatic species. This last arrived from China in about 1790, but on account of its early flowering habit was kept for greenhouse use until the 1820s or 1830s.

M. *acuminata*, the cucumber tree, arrived in Europe a year before the evergreen species, and was preceded only by M. *virginiana* (syn. M. *glauca*), which had been cultivated in England since 1688, and was flowering in Mr Collinson's garden at Peckham before the cucumber tree arrived. The leaves, long, green and pointed, are carried on branches which are at first erect but later become spreading; the greenish flowers are produced in early summer with the leaves. Its name refers to the shape and colour of its fruit.

M. *virginiana* is not the first recorded magnolia, but the first to be cultivated in Europe. The Mexican M. *dealbata* was certainly known in the sixteenth century because by then it

The Japanese shrubby magnolia, M.stellata, with star-shaped many-petalled white flowers borne on bare branches in early spring, is very slow-growing and takes many years even to reach a 2m/6ft height and spread. It is a perfect shrub for the smaller garden.

was already grown in the great Aztec Botanical Gardens in Mexico. Indeed, fossilized remains have been found which establish the existence of the genus for over five million years, and moreover, like the similarly ancient *Ginkgo*, it was spread over a wide geographical area, not confined as it is today to the north-east of America, and eastern Asia. But to return to the sweet bay, as M. *virginiana* is called, it will grow to 6-9m/20-30ft, its leaves are long and glossy and it carries its fragrant flowers intermittently from mid- to late summer.

Some of the most interesting magnolias are the deciduous Asian species. They are numerous and have been hybridized freely for garden use. M. *campbellii* is generally considered the emperor of all magnolias. The flowers are carried in winter, before the leaves, and have tulip-shaped petals unfolding into goblets of white or pink. It takes twenty years to flower from seed and since it is extremely susceptible to frost it can never be relied upon to give an annual display. A woodland position is essential and it needs a warm site sheltered from the eastern sun. It was first found in Sikkim in 1868, and prefers a rich moist acid soil.

The only comparable magnolia, which flowers a few weeks later and a few years earlier, is M. *campbellii mollicomata* which Forrest found in 1920. It is a form of M. *campbellii*, with hairier leaves and a pink flower. M. *heptapeta*, mentioned above as the first Asiatic magnolia to arrive, was closely followed by M. *liliiflora* (now M. *quinquepeta*), with which its name was confused. Drawings were made of the flowers by Kaempfer, and the plates published by Sir Joseph Banks were transposed, so that M. *quinquepeta*, which flowers later with its leaves, we classified as the lily tree, and M. *heptapeta* was thought to have purple flowers, coming into bloom before the leaves. From this species numerous excellent hybrids have been bred and there are many forms and seedlings. The most frequently grown M. × *soulangeana* is itself a hybrid between these two species. It has many useful and vigorous garden varieties including 'Lennei' and 'Brozzonii', which combine white and purple to produce various markings and colours.

M. *kobus* is a hardy small Japanese tree with a regular leafy habit of growth, which does not flower for about six or seven years (many authorities say it may take up to twelve). M. *kobus*, and what is thought to be only a variety of it M. *stellata*, are the best for soil containing lime. The former flowered here at six years, when it had already made a cone-shaped bush of nearly 3.6m/12ft, which is why I presume to contradict the authorities. Together with M. *stellata* it came from Japan in the 1860s. The flowers are white and many petalled. M. 'Kewensis' is a very desirable recently raised cross between M. *kobus* and M. *salicifolia*, the latter an acid-loving variety also from Japan, with narrow leaves and long thin petals which are produced before the foliage in spring. I have seen an excellent tree of M. 'Kewensis' in Mr Lionel Fortescue's garden in Devon.

M. *hypoleuca* (syn. M. *obovata*) is a Japanese species introduced at the same time as M. *kobus* and M. *stellata*, but it is calcifuge and harder to cultivate successfully. Like most difficult members of the genus it is very rewarding if you do succeed with it as it has slightly bronze young growth and a handsome regular shape. The flowers are cup-shaped and fragrant, with crimson stamens.

M. *quinquepeta* makes a medium-sized tree or large shrub. The flowers are held erect and continue to appear intermittently all summer, but most freely in late spring. The variety we have here, M. *q. nigra*, has very dark purple flowers with paler centres.

M. *sargentiana* and its variety M. *s. robusta*, are perhaps the most beautiful of all magnolias. Like the gigantic *campbellii* types, M. *sargentiana* needs to be grown so that its pink water-lily flowers can be seen against the sky, as it flowers before the leaves in spring. It was first introduced by Ernest Wilson to the Arnold Arboretum in 1908, from west China. The *robusta* form is reputedly easier to grow and has longer leaves and darker flowers.

M. *sieboldii* (syn. M. *parviflora*) has hanging egg-shaped buds which open widely and produce crimson fruit later. The leaves are very attractive, being glaucous and hairy beneath.

M. *sinensis* very much resembles M. *wilsonii* and although I grow both I think the latter is the better. It flowers sooner and although very similar with hanging cups and crimson stamens, is just that little bit more attractive. The leaves make it easy to distinguish between them as those of M. *sinensis* have a broad end and are crinkly green, while those of M. *wilsonii* are pointed and more glaucous. However M. *sinensis* is happiest in full sun while M. *wilsonii* prefers some shade, so you may find them both useful. They should be grown on a slope or above a bank, so that the beautiful inverted cup-shaped flowers can be appreciated from below. Both come from western China and were introduced to Britain through Ernest Wilson and the Arnold Arboretum.

M. × *soulangeana* is a very popular, quick growing, early flowering hybrid. It makes a wide spreading shrub-like tree and bears tulip-shaped flowers very freely before the leaves in spring. M. *stellata* is slow growing and suitable for the smaller garden. It is seen frequently, a compact bushy shrub rather than a tree, with white many-petalled flowers, borne profusely in spring just before the leaves. There are two varieties with pink and dark flowers respectively. M. × *watsonii* (now M. × *wieseneri*) is an excellent but difficult hybrid of M. *hypoleuca* and M. *sieboldii*. Its flowers more closely resemble the former, and it is the most fragrant of the whole genus.

Nothofagus This is a rather neglected genus which contains small evergreen and deciduous trees of great distinction and charm. Known as the southern beech, it comes from the Southern Hemisphere and the leaves, although smaller, much resemble those of the ordinary *Fagus sylvatica*. It is difficult to propagate and therefore expensive to buy, but its neat appearance and habit make it suitable for much wider use, particularly in small gardens as none of the varieties makes dense shade. The evergreen species are naturally the most tender and dislike a windy position. Most of them grow slowly, while the deciduous ones are very fast-growing, as well as less exacting as to climate, and make an excellent elegant shape with a head which branches freely from a single trunk. Most of the evergreen species will suffer in a hard winter.

N. *betuloides* and N. *cliffortioides* are both evergreen and the former is one of the hardiest. It will make quite a large tree, with dense dark green leaves, shiny above and pale beneath, about 2.5cm/1in long. The leaves of N. *betuloides* are also finely toothed, which distinguishes it from the smaller and tenderer N. *cliffortioides*, in which they are half the size and entire. This latter species is doing well here.

N. dombeyi can be semi-evergreen and grows quickly, more like the deciduous varieties. *N. antarctica* and *N. obliqua* are the two best of these, and grow as much as 90cm/36in a year, with glossy attractive leaves which turn yellow in the autumn. I have found them easy to grow; they rapidly assume a regular shape to make a notable contribution to the general appearance of a garden. Where there is more space they can be grown in groups.

Nyssa The only species I know is the deciduous *N. sylvatica*. When young it makes a columnar tree but becomes more broad-headed as it grows older. Its chief beauty lies in its glossy green leaves which turn a brilliant scarlet in autumn. It likes rich deep soil of an acid type and needs full sun to get the best colouring. From the eastern states of America, it is quite hardy in Britain if given the right conditions.

Osmanthus See page 109.

Paulownia There are two Chinese species of this genus which are generally grown, *P. tomentosa* and *P. fargesii*. They can be cut back regularly and so used just for foliage effects, particularly when it seems likely that, if allowed to grow towards their natural tree shape, they will fail to flower. They can produce striking erect terminal foxglove-like panicles of pale purple or lilac. Unfortunately the buds, formed the previous autumn, may be damaged by frosts during winter or early spring. This means that two years out of three there will be no blossom. However, even if not cut back, the leaves are very large and attractive, up to 23cm/9in long on an adult tree of 10-12m/30-40ft and perhaps twice that size on a tree grown purely for foliage effect. The shoots are very downy and the leaves of *P. tomentosa* soft and lobed, those of *P. fargesii* heart-shaped and pointed. The latter, a more recent introduction, flowers earlier and seems to be more adapted to a temperate climate.

Both species need a site that is sheltered, particularly from the east, and preferably on a slope as the flowers are borne at the top of the tree. To get the maximum benefit from the rarely emerging blooms try to plant the tree so that you can look down on it. Personally I am very happy to grow them as foliage trees, as they make an excellent bushy shape and the leaves are velvety and decorative; however, I do not really care for the artificiality of the plants which are cut back to stimulate the leaf size.

Photinia See page 109.

Platanus See page 114.

Populus The architectural merits of poplars are mentioned in Chapter 7. Here the emphasis is on their decorative qualities and the fragrance they contribute through their aromatic leaves.

The true balsam poplar, *P. balsamifera* (syn. *P. tacamahaca*), was introduced from America before 1689 and is more scented than any of its hybrids.

P. × candicans 'Aurora' has attractive variegated leaves with glaucous pink growth, but needs cutting back if the leaves are to remain big and well-marked. If you have plenty of space, you can of course allow the tree to sucker and thus keep tall, less well-coloured trees growing next to new young plants. Personally I much dislike rather haphazard cutting back – something quite different from the true art of topiary, which was essentially for very formal gardening – because trees cut back just shoot again and spoil the natural line.

P. lasiocarpa, from central China (see page 126), has beautiful veined leaves, bright green and downy, and is one of the most interesting Asian poplars. I do not know the supposedly very similar *P. wilsonii* which comes from the same district.

P. trichocarpa, an American species, is one of the quickest growers of the balsam type, with attractive peeling bark and yellow leaves in autumn. I have used a group here to screen the ugly lines of a tennis court, planting the invasive roots on a lower level.

Prunus This is a difficult genus to ignore altogether and equally difficult to describe adequately in a few words. The garish pink colours of many of the Japanese cherries do not appeal to me; I prefer the white or white and yellow flowers which are found among the species. I am therefore omitting the Japanese and more recent hybrids, even when they have excellent habits, while admitting that they do provide colour and form for many gardens. The only two I grow are the pale yellow 'Ukon' and the large single white 'Tai-haku'.

The cherry plum, *Prunus cerasifera*, has a purple-leaved form 'Pissardii', with dark red young foliage which becomes heavier and more purple through the summer. The flowers are white, opening from a pink bud. Not a particularly distinguished plant perhaps but one of the lightest and prettiest of small purple trees or shrubs to use as a foil with grey, green or gold. It can also be effective if draped with a pink or blue clematis.

P. conradinae flowers at the end of winter and has an elegant shape, two characteristics which make it a valuable species for every garden. *Prunus lusitanica*, the evergreen Portugal laurel, is often used as a large shrub for the outer garden but also makes a beautiful specimen tree. The variety *P. l.* 'Variegata' is most attractive, with cream-edged leaves.

P. maackii should be planted in a group and grown for its outstanding golden-brown bark, which flakes as it gets older. This tree needs a solid background and I have placed it in

Prunus 'Tai-haku', the great white cherry from Japan, frames the view of a country garden in spring. Its flowers are very large and open while the young foliage growth has coppery tints. Later in the autumn the leaves turn yellow and orange and the bark is decorative all through the winter. It will reach a height of 6-8m/20-25ft in as many years.

front of a bank of pale green bamboo, against which the glowing bark will show up. *Prunus padus*, the European bird cherry, has graceful racemes of white blossom and makes a regular and neat shape. *P. serrula* (syn. *P. s. tibetica*) has shiny mahogany bark and narrow leaves like a willow; it rivals *Acer griseum* in decorative value. *Prunus subhirtella*, the spring cherry, includes not only winter- and spring-flowering varieties but also three or four weeping forms which give good architectural structure when their long pendulous branches are bare.

Quercus On the whole oaks grow extremely slowly, so that although they may eventually make a large and stately tree, they can be included here for new plantings. *Quercus* is a huge genus, like *Prunus*, so it is best to be selective and mention only a few species which are valuable as foliage trees.

Q. canariensis (syn. *Q. mirbeckii*) is one of the fastest growing oaks, and is happy on any soil. The only really good example I have seen is at Anglesey Abbey, where it is magnificent on the heavy Cambridge loam. It has grey bark and shining green leaves, pale beneath, which hang on during the winter. Although known as the Algerian oak, it is also found in Spain and Portugal.

Q. coccinea, the scarlet oak, is very slow growing, demands acid conditions and in fact has turned up its toes with me. However, it is a most attractive tree from North America, introduced to Britain as long ago as 1691, and turns the most vivid colour in autumn. *Q. ellipsoidalis* has fresh pale young growth which also turns scarlet in autumn, while its trunk is barer than that of *Q. coccinea*. *Q. ilex*, the evergreen oak, was described in Chapter 7. *Q. robur*, the English

oak, has many different forms, among the best of which is Q. r. 'Concordia' which has golden leaves all through the summer but is so slow that it should perhaps be classed as a shrub rather than a small tree.

Rhus The *Rhus* genus contains many very variable types of plants, from the American creeping poison ivy, *R. radicans*, and the poison oak, *R. toxicodendron*, to the more welcome *Rhus typhina*, which is best if allowed to grow as suckering undergrowth.

R. potaninii is a small tree from central and western China, introduced in 1902 by Ernest Wilson. Its pinnate leaves will turn a rich red in autumn. Having a spreading head, it will make an attractive tree of up to 7.5m/25ft, which is just about the height of one I know in a garden in Gloucestershire. There is a splendid specimen at Knightshayes. New trees are easily obtained from the suckers.

Robinia The robinia, or *false acacia*, has become thoroughly naturalized in Europe since its introduction from North America in 1601. It was originally brought to France and named in memory of the French king's gardener Jean Robin, who first cultivated it. At that time it was classed as an

Above The attractive leaves of Sorbus 'Joseph Rock' become richly tinted with a mixture of 'hot' orange and red in autumn, making a 'setting' for spectacular clusters of creamy-yellow fruits which turn amber as they mature.

Right The wide spreading fan-like branches of Styrax japonica are clothed with fresh green foliage and bear bell-shaped white flowers in early summer. It requires a lime-free soil. Plant on a slope so that the branch pattern and flowers can be admired from below.

Acacia, hence its common name. The most well-known variety is *R. pseudoacacia*, which has delightful fresh green pinnate leaves and a white flower carried in long racemes. Although not a very long-lived tree it will grow in any soil and withstand any sort of industrial or urban pollution; in the United States where it is known as the black locust tree it is extensively used for street planting. The clone called *R. p.* 'Frisia' has startling golden leaves, but is particularly vulnerable to wind, being even more brittle than the type. And there is also an attractive hybrid of *R. pseudoacacia*, *R.* × *ambigua* 'Decaisneana', which is smaller and has pale pink flowers.

R. hispida, the rose acacia, is normally a large suckering shrub, but can be grafted on to a stem of the false acacia and then makes an attractive small tree. The leaves are darker green and it has pink trusses of the largest flowers in the genus.

Sorbus This is another huge genus from which I will pick a few of my personal favourites. They are easy to grow and happy in any soil; only the whitebeams, varieties or close relations of the native *Sorbus aria,* grow into large trees. *Sorbus aria* itself could have been included in Chapter 7, as it has a regular conical shape when young, spreading when older. Its simple almost entire leaves vary in colour from grey to pale green, with tomentose undersides which are spectacularly white in the spring. One of the best is *S. a.* 'Lutescens', which is also hairy on the upper surface of the leaf, while some of the other closely related species have remarkably lobed or toothed leaves.

In the *Aucuparia* section the leaves are pinnate and the fruit is generally much prized, as well as the excellent autumn foliage. The native *Sorbus aucuparia,* the mountain ash or rowan, is happiest on an acid soil, but many of the species from Asia are able to tolerate some lime, perhaps not much more than that found in a neutral soil.

S. cashmiriana has pinnate leaves composed of numerous small leaflets and bears clusters of white berries in winter.

S. insignis (syn. *S. harrowiana*) is a small tree from the Yunnan, introduced by Forrest as recently as 1912. It has pinnate leaves, with two to four pairs of leaflets of a much harder and glossier dark green and with paler undersides than most of the *Aucuparia* section. It is a quite outstanding species which I have seen only at Knightshayes, where its unusual and distinguished appearance drew my attention. Reputedly more tender than some of the ordinary ones, it has however survived here for two winters.

S. hupehensis has bronze-coloured branches and leaves, the latter turning red in autumn, and white berries slightly tinged with pink. *S.* 'Joseph Rock' has stunning yellow berries. *S. vilmorinii* has fern-like leaves which turn scarlet in autumn and pink berries which turn white. It is said that birds are more inclined to leave untouched those berries which are white or yellow.

These few are the ones that I have grown here, or in my previous garden, but there are many others which are probably equally satisfactory.

Stewartia Both *Stewartia* and *Styrax* are small trees with fastidious tastes that thrive only in conditions similar to those appreciated by rhododendrons. In an open woodland, with acid soil and adequate moisture through the summer, they

are most rewarding. *Stewartia,* though deciduous, is allied to the camellias, and the flowers are similar except that they are all creamy-white. If there is enough sun, they will flower freely; the leaves turn scarlet in winter.

Styrax The *Styrax* resembles an *Halesia* with pure white pendulous flowers. It prefers shade and moisture to full sun and dislikes severe frost. Ideally the soil should be neutral or acid. I know only two varieties, *S. hemsleyana* and *S. japonica,* of which the former is the larger and more vigorous.

Zelkova The *Zelkova* is closely allied to the elm and is a useful alternative. Considering that it has been grown in Britain since 1760, when it was introduced from the Caucasus, it is surprisingly little known. The species in question is *Z. carpinifolia,* which was in fact the only one known until *Z. serrata* was found in eastern Asia in 1861. There are good examples of *Z. serrata* in the Chelsea Physic Garden and at Anglesey Abbey. It makes a medium to large tree with a spreading habit, grey bark, and attractive acuminate leaves which are coarsely toothed. A species from central China called *Z. sinica* has pink-tinted leaves when young. All these three are slow growing.

Chapter 9

ROSES AS SHRUBS

IT WOULD BE quite impossible to write any sort of gardening book without including the rose. Equally, it would be far beyond the range of this particular book on country gardening to write about all the different types, species and hybrids of the rose. To keep to my main theme I describe only those roses which can be termed all-the-year-round plants, and are of value for their habit, shape, foliage, flowers and fruit. These can be used in mixed borders with other shrubs and herbaceous perennials, or as hedges, or in beds with strong low-growing perennial plants.

Not only has Graham Stuart Thomas been responsible for saving and preserving many of the old roses which are the ancestors of the modern Hybrid Teas and Floribundas, but he has also written extensively about them. In this section I mention briefly only those roses which I find most attractive and useful, but even in their choice and disposition I have been greatly influenced by his books. I have made no attempt to give the reader extra information here, I can do no better than to direct him to Thomas's books and will only give some suggestions for their association with other plants. I have described those roses which can be used as shrubs, and I have left out all the climbing roses of the Hybrid Tea type. The vigorous Ramblers are included if they are suitable for mounding up as huge sprawling shrubs, or for growing into trees and for groundcover in wilder parts of the garden.

There is no reason to decry the beauty of the vivid colours and perfection of flower shape of the modern bedding rose, but it does need special conditions for its culture if it is to be seen at its best. In the right setting bedding roses are magnificent, but they should be grown in formal beds, within a definite area of the garden, and preferably in an enclosure. They

Unlike highly bred bush roses which look their best in a formal setting, shrub roses can be grown in the wilder areas of the garden. They come into flower in early summer and give a wonderful display for a few weeks. Although few of the actual species have a repeat flowering period, there are many modern shrub roses which have been bred for a second flowering. Mainly with pink and mauve flowers which blend in the eye, they associate well with low-growing plants with similarly gentle colours and pale foliage.

must be in perfect condition, neatly and competently pruned, fed, and sprayed against disease and pests. It should also be understood that the rose garden will not be attractive between the autumn of one year and the spring of the next, as during that time there will be nothing to admire except dying foliage, followed by tightly pruned bare woody twigs. Unfortunately, except in public parks, or in the rare private garden, roses are seldom well-grown. Too often the roses are unhealthy, unskilfully pruned and unsuited to the site chosen. Of course, there are many ways of growing them which are an acceptable compromise between perfection and disaster. It is worth emphasizing that to grow roses well does entail a considerable amount of trouble and skill. However, there are many types of rose which can give beauty of a rather different visual form to a garden, and which do not need special care or sites, but still can contribute the essential characteristics of flower and fragrance.

Another interesting side to growing roses is their historical development, and their significance in an old garden as well as in the literature of every European country. Perfection of shape in bud and bloom, and perpetual flowering qualities were sought throughout many centuries. Even Gertrude Jekyll, when she wrote her book on the rose garden in 1902, would have been using mainly Hybrid Perpetuals, Bourbons and old roses. Much effort and skill was expended on the breeding of these roses in the nineteenth century but not much attention was paid to the most beautiful way of growing and arranging them. Although first raised as early as 1867, it was not until after the turn of the century that the new Hybrid Teas became readily available.

What we tend to think of as a traditional feature of the garden, the rose bed, border, or complete inner garden, is a comparatively recent innovation of the Victorian era, and was a result of the development of new skills and knowledge of rose-breeding, and the availability of more rose types.

In some ways one might be tempted to think of shrub roses and Hybrid Teas as belonging to entirely different genera. This is nonsense, of course, since just as the bedding rose has been bred and developed from species and old groups of hybrids, so also has the use of cross-breeding between species and Hybrid Teas produced particularly fine roses which we call modern shrub roses. These can often be used in place of old roses which seem prone to disease. So much skill has gone into the formation of the flower alone of the bedding rose that it bears little resemblance to the single delicate bloom of the original species, or to the fragrant massed and globular petals of many of the old hybrids. The colours, too, of the older roses are generally yellow, white, soft pink and mauve, occasionally dark purple, and some even striped. With artificial pollination it became possible, at the beginning of this century, to use the hitherto sterile Persian yellow rose to introduce new strains into the more muted colours of mauves and pinks; this has led to the often vivid flame colours so much prized today.

Shrub roses make graceful bushes and after the flowering season often carry attractive heps. They can be almost any height from sprawling 60cm/24in mounds to 3.6m/12ft branching specimens, which are ideal for standing alone on a lawn, or for the back of a planting scheme in a mixed border. The rampant species roses can be encouraged to scramble through old trees or to cover banks and fill rough corners. The leaves have enormous variation; some roses, like the sweet brier, *R. eglanteria* (syn. *R. rubiginosa*), have strongly scented foliage, others are coloured grey, or mauve tinted like *R. glauca* (syn. *R. rubrifolia*), or fresh green and wrinkled like the Rugosas, which also turn pale yellow in the autumn. The leaves are normally pinnate but can be fern-like with many small leaflets. The fruits too are very variable, some solitary, large and flagon- or apple-shaped, others carried in drooping clusters of red or orange.

Many shrub roses can be pruned to play their part in quite formal planting schemes; prune them as you would shrubs by cutting out the old or dead wood from the base, but not too often. The great arching bushes should not be pruned back, as one would cut Hybrid Teas, to an eye, as new growth from that point will spoil the symmetry of the curving branches. This might seem so obvious that it is hardly worth saying, yet it is often done in order to shape back roses which have been put in too restricted a site for their scale. On the other hand, although there is less regular work in care and culture, thinning out can be a painful and arduous task, and care must be taken not to damage adjacent plants when extracting rose branches which have become entangled in them.

Historical development

Before describing how these shrub roses can be grown it may be helpful to give a brief picture of their historical development and to show the influence each separate group or species has had upon another. From the gardener's point of

No garden should be without Rosa glauca (syn. R. rubrifolia); with a graceful arching habit and glaucous leaves it is the perfect rose for every situation. In early summer it bears sprays of pink white-centred flowers followed by decorative orange fruits. It usually seeds freely in the garden and will thrive in any odd corner.

view, it is important to establish the characteristics of the various groups, even if breeding, in the wild or artificially, has radically altered the basic habit of growth or flower of the individual rose. For each accepted historical group there are certain general characteristics which give the group an approximate cohesion. However, this is clearly from the amateur's point of view and not an involvement in botanical niceties. Actually Mr Thomas has done the work for us; thanks to him we can grow these roses with more than just a hazy idea of their parentage, and, but for Mr Thomas, many of them might have been lost for ever.

Most of our garden roses are descended from the Gallica rose which has been known and cultivated in Asia since the beginning of history. It is not a true species and may have been hybridized itself in the wild. Its basic characteristic is to be fairly compact in habit, making a bush about 90cm/3ft in height which flowers in midsummer. The flowers are held on stiff stalks, have upright heads and are very fragrant. In a mixed border it makes a neat small hedge or a good clump.

Quite early on, this Gallica became crossed, we think, with the species *R. moschata*, the true Musk rose from western Asia, and the resultant hybrid, the Damask rose, became the source of the fragrant Attar of Roses which is still produced today. The Damask characteristics are greyish-green foliage, strong hooked thorns and weak flower stalks, carrying heavy nodding double intensely scented flowers, often in clusters. The Damasks flower only in the summer, like the Gallica, except for one variety, the autumn damask, which later played a considerable part in the breeding of repeat and perpetual flowering roses. This group of roses came to Europe with the Crusaders, if not earlier. It was crossed with the native *R. canina* or dog rose (so called because a distillation of its roots was thought to cure rabies) to produce the Alba group and later the Centifolias.

The Alba rose flowers in early summer and has soft grey leaves which would make it desirable even if it did not have its attractive shape and pretty pale pink or white double or semi-double flowers. It has none of the strong and deeper colours of the Centifolias but makes a better shaped and healthier bush. The Centifolias are grown mainly for the marvel of their intricate double flowers, as the bushes are ungainly and often weighed down by the heavy flower heads. These are the rose flowers so often used for flower paintings and in portraits in the eighteenth century. The moss rose is a sport of these Centifolias, which are also known as Provence or cabbage roses. It has interesting green or red growth on the buds and stems, and appeared first sometime in the eighteenth century.

At this time other European species were known and in cultivation. Among these *R. glauca*, *R. pulverulenta* (syn. *R. glutinosa*), *R. eglanteria* and *R. villosa* (syn. *R. pomifera*) are all still grown in our gardens as true species or in improved forms. Both *R. pulverulenta*, which is seldom seen, and *R. eglanteria*, the famous sweet brier or eglantine, are grown mainly for their strongly aromatic foliage. *R. pimpinellifolia* (syn. *R. spinosissima*), the Scotch or burnet rose from which many new forms and hybrids were developed, makes a suckering thicket. The Austrian brier, *R. foetida* and the sulphur rose, *R. hemisphaerica*, from western Asia, were the only known yellow roses.

The Rugosa rose was not introduced from Japan until 1796, nearly a hundred years after the China rose, which was the first truly perpetual flowerer to come to Europe. The China rose has become the ancestor of most of our repeat-flowering roses, but, in some ways, adds to the botanical confusion, as it was not itself a true species. Its wild form was only discovered in central China in 1900. The Rugosa has strong characteristics, which in the main persist in its hybrids. It is a very hardy and thrifty plant, with apple-green, deeply veined leaves and very thorny pale wood. The flowers are deliciously scented and freely borne all through the summer, and usually followed by excellent coloured heps, tomato-shaped and rich in vitamin C. One of the most trouble-free roses, the Rugosa is also one of the most rewarding. In its wild forms it is totally disease-resistant, and suitable for planting as a hedge, and will survive seaside winds and salt spray. The flowers vary from white to pink and deep wine colours.

The China rose which, like the Rugosa, comes from all over north-east Asia, makes a small sturdy shrub with glossy green leaves; the form first imported, which had an important influence on rose breeding, was almost certainly already crossed with the Tea roses, which did not themselves arrive in Europe until the mid-nineteenth century.

Fortunately for posterity the Empress Josephine made a collection of every available rose at La Malmaison, and Redouté's paintings have enabled experts to identify many of these roses with mixed and confused parentage. Many were given French names and French nurserymen have since played a prominent part in rose breeding.

In 1823 the China rose made an accidental alliance with the autumn damask, in Reunion Island (then called Ile de Bourbon) in the Indian Ocean. This produced the Bourbon rose, and a further cross with another offspring of the same parents called the Portland rose led to the new and important race, the Hybrid Perpetuals. These roses became very popular and, like the Bourbons, vary considerably in habit characteristics; but all have some form of recurrent flowering. On the whole they make upright bushes, which need some support as the flower heads are double and heavy. Some pruning helps to encourage new young shoots, but the blooms are disappointingly easily damaged by wet weather, or may fail to open if there is a drought. I have found that, particularly in the pure air of the west country, they are subject to black spot, and I have replaced many old and attractive varieties with modern shrub roses which seem to be more disease-resistant. Strangely, there was very little incidence of this disease until after the introduction of the Austrian brier, itself seldom a sufferer, into later breeding.

The delicate Tea rose came from China in 1867 and led to

an orgy of crossing and re-crossing. This culminated in horticultural skills which made it possible to use the yellow rose for further hybridization and so develop the modern Hybrid Teas and later the Floribundas, which together became the most popular roses of the twentieth century.

Towards the end of the nineteenth and at the beginning of the twentieth centuries, many new species were introduced from the Far East; these are often extremely desirable in their own right. They have also been used to produce modern shrub roses by being crossed with Hybrid Teas. Similarly the latter bedding roses have been interbred again with individuals in the old groups, producing superb plants with the best characteristics of flower and shrub habit. The flowers are carried all season and have a resemblance to the highly developed and shapely Hybrid Teas, but the bush itself has the elegant habit and thriftiness of the species or group, and is disease-resistant.

Choosing and growing roses

When choosing roses for our own garden it is helpful to ask ourselves which particular qualities we are looking for. As with all flowering shrubs, beauty of flower, leaf, fruit and fragrance, as well as general shape and habit, are the main criteria. For roses, we must also consider the question of repeat or perpetual flowering and the problems of health. If you have plenty of space, it is worth remembering that the species roses, which flower only once, are in general free from disease, seldom even get greenfly, and look after themselves except for needing the occasional cutting back from the base. You can cover most of the flowering season by choosing species roses which have their peak at different times. In a smaller garden, where there is presumably more time for spraying to combat disease and pests, it may be best to grow shrub roses which are perpetual flowering but need more constant care. A compromise might be to get the best of both worlds and grow species mixed with climbing and trailing plants which flower at earlier or later moments in the season than the rose, and thus you will have a continual period of blossom. Clematis would be an obvious choice for this purpose as they cover almost every colour and some flower in almost every month.

On the north side of Tintinhull House, the double yellow pimpinellifolia hybrid rose, R. × harisonii (known as the Scotch burnet rose), flowers vigorously in spite of the deep shade. These early roses sucker and spread in rough corners and make low impenetrable hedges. The scarlet nasturtium (Tropaeolum speciosum) clambers through the rose stems to give a display in late summer.

Today, when we have to do most of the jobs in the garden ourselves, all plants must stand on their own feet with a minimum of propping up. Many roses are sent out by nurseries on an understock of *R. canina* or Rugosa 'Hollandica', which helps to give vigour to weak plants and to encourage uniformity of growth. This tough understock also withstands transplanting and damage in a journey. Unfortunately, it later sometimes sends up suckers from the roots, which in the end seriously weaken the health and vigour of the rose. If this occurs, they need to be cut out carefully, and this means not just cutting off at ground-level, but scraping back the soil to tear the unwanted sucker off the root. It is possible to use a contact weedkiller on these shoots if you can get them just as they emerge and this may well be effective. Of course some species roses, such as *R. pimpinellifolia*, are such colonizers that they can be grown on an understock to prevent spreading. Others, like the Gallicas, which are generally grown on a Brier rose to give them extra strength, if planted below the graft will sucker themselves and help to thicken the bushes. Once you have acquired a good stock of roses in the garden, or have access to those of a friend, it may well be best gradually to replace your old plants with those grown from cuttings, either from hard wood in the open in the autumn, or from soft wood in a mist propagator. In the end you will eliminate one more troublesome job.

If the ground is properly prepared to begin with, which includes being adequately dug and fertilized before the roses arrive, they will need just the same sort of care as the other shrubs. They like a protective mulch of organic manure, old leaves, or a covering of growing plants. In time, a mixed border containing rose shrubs, or a bed entirely devoted to them, can be completely carpeted with low-growing foliage plants, but you must remember not to plant the most invasive and vigorous herbaceous perennials with the weaker shrub roses. Some of the mints, the larger periwinkle, or *Lamiastrum galeobdolon* are too invasive. Hard pruning is seldom necessary but when you do have to cut back, remember to compensate the plant by extra feeding, as you are asking it to work hard to replace the growth removed. This you can do with handfuls of bonemeal or a balanced fertilizer, or, if the ground is totally carpeted, by the use of foliage feeds.

Plants should be encouraged to play the role for which they are naturally suited. When a rose is chosen, its site and its association with other plants in a border will partly determine how much or how little pruning is necessary. To make a mass of bloom and healthy foliage it may be advisable to leave the back members of a group almost untouched, while strictly cutting and shaping the foreground planting to create a cascade effect. This is particularly easy to achieve with roses such as the Hybrid Musks, which have a fan-like method of growing from the roots, and respond to cutting by sending up new shoots from the base. All these roses tend to get bare and woody, and the older the wood the more difficult it is to persuade a plant to make new growth.

Leggy bushes can have long shoots pegged down, covering the ground with leaves and flowers, creating an effect similar to that obtained with pruning, that is, a cascade of flower. Many of the untidy rather sprawling bushes, such as the Centifolias, the Bourbons and the Hybrid Perpetuals, respond to this sort of treatment. The pegging or tying down also encourages new shoots to be pushed up. Bushes can be trained to use fences, or other shrubs or trees, to give them support, just as the rose bushes themselves become hosts to smaller climbing and twining plants. The heavy flower heads will rest on the leaves of suitable foliage groundcover such as the herbaceous geraniums, *Alchemilla mollis*, hostas and astrantias. Later flowerers, such as Japanese anemones, will push their flowering heads through the lower foliage of the rose. Foliage associations and contrast are as important as flower combinations. Roses with beautiful leaves such as *R. glauca* or *R. villosa* look well with pink or mauve flowering plants such as *Cistus, Thalictrum, Dictamnus albus* and purple-leaved evergreens such as *Salvia officinalis* 'Purpurascens'.

Fragrance is not something that is tangible and can be measured; its characteristics and its intensity can be compared only with the scents of other well-known plants or plant foods. A great deal has been written about the subject, and we all know that, generally speaking, the most scent is given off by leaves and flowers in moist warm weather rather than in cold and dry. In all roses, except in the Sweet Briers, the scent is stored in the petals and not in the leaves. Aromatic leaves belong to plants which have to bear extremes of hot and dry weather, as the scent is in the protective oils which are contained in each leaf. For the scent to be released the leaf must be crushed or bruised, or at least, as in the case of the balsam poplar, rustled by the wind.

Roses release their fragrance as the petals unfurl, and the most heady and strong scents come from double roses such as the Gallicas, Centifolias, Damasks, and their Bourbon and Hybrid Perpetual descendants. On the other hand, you need to bury your face in these roses to get the full aroma. The delicious fresh scent of apples or pear-drops which comes from the Rugosas and the Musk type of species (including all the Asians) which flower late with clustered heads, is quite different. It is wafted through the garden in a way equalled only by *Philadelphus* or *Clerodendrum trichotomum*. Alba roses

have a delicate scent which floats around the bushes but does not travel far. The little Scotch rose, *R. pimpinellifolia*, has itself a delicious gentle scent, but its forms and hybrids seem to be almost completely without fragrance. Not before time, fragrance has crept back into catalogue descriptions and is now a quality taken into account in giving awards.

For comprehensive advice and lists it is best to consult the catalogue of a nurseryman who specializes in these shrub roses, or go to the books of Mr Stuart Thomas. The roses I describe here, and I have had to be very selective, I have grown either in my previous cottage garden, which had terraces admirably suited for tumbling bushes, or in this larger garden, where I am always anxious to save labour by dispensing with any unnecessary spraying or pruning tasks, and I have therefore concentrated more on large species or disease-free hybrids. Others are mentioned when it seems appropriate but many excellent ones have had to be omitted. As far as possible they are in their chronological order of flowering.

Early-flowering roses
One of the earliest to flower is the great species rose *R. banksiae* which, although widely grown, especially in warmer regions and in southern Europe, was introduced to the West from Canton only in 1807. It was named after Lady Banks, the wife of the famous Director of Kew, Sir Joseph Banks. In Mediterranean countries it is often seen draped over trees, banks and walls, but in cooler climates it will flourish only if given a warm sunny corner, with plenty of reflected heat from stone or glass, to ripen the wood. The first and true species was the double white variety, but the one most commonly seen today is *R. banksiae* 'Lutea', the double yellow form, which tends to be hardier. The single yellow came to England via Florence and the Riviera garden at Ventimiglia, La Mortola. This rose is at its best when allowed to tumble unpruned against a wall and mixed with other plants. It flowers at the same time as *Clematis chrysocoma sericea* in late spring; *C. alpina* and *C. macropetala* make good but less vigorous neighbours. The yellow-flowered varieties of the rose are, unfortunately, less fragrant than the white. It is virtually an evergreen so is useful on a sunny bank as dense cover. The foliage is fresh green and the shoots are thornless. All grey-leaved plants contrast well with the smooth leaves

Paul's Himalayan Musk, a seedling of Rosa brunonii, *is a rampant climber, growing to 10m/33ft or more. The pink flower sprays are very fragrant.*

Here, growing over a tree, it gives a fine display in midsummer behind a clear pink Gallica rose, R. 'Complicata'.

and thrive in the same conditions of heat and sun.

R. *laevigata* and what is probably its hybrid, R. 'Anemone', are also tender semi-evergreens suitable only for a warm wall. The leaves are larger, darker green and glossy, and the flowers of 'Anemone' are a vivid silver-pink, 10cm/4in across and single. I would like to grow the species itself twining among cordon apples, where its white flowers would look similar to those of a *Clematis montana*. The pink form, which is of garden origin and dates from about 1895, I grow here behind a large *Abutilon vitifolium* and next to a purple-leaved smoke bush, *Cotinus coggygria* 'Foliis Purpureis', and *Clematis* 'Nelly Moser' which flowers at the same moment.

There is a hybrid of R. *laevigata*, R. 'Ramona', which is less vigorous than R. 'Anemone' and flowers a few weeks later with petals of a deeper crimson.

Another group of early flowerers includes three species, R. *hugonis*, R. *ecae* and R. *xanthina*, which all have dainty fern-like leaves and brown arching stems. R. *hugonis* has branches wreathed in single pale yellow flowers and these are followed by small dark red almost black fruits. R. 'Headleyensis' is a seedling from this species with more creamy flowers and grows up to 2.7m/9ft high as opposed to the average of 1.8m/6ft for the type. R. *ecae* is a species from Afghanistan and has chestnut-coloured branches and buttercup-yellow flowers. R. *xanthina* has semi-double flowers but a very similar habit. Perhaps the best of all, with the freshest leaves and the most arching habit, is the selection from the single-flowered form R. × *spontanea*, 'Canary Bird'. This makes a splendid small weeping shrub and blends well with ground-cover plants such as *Brunnera macrophylla*, and provides an excellent contrast to bushy evergreen shrubs such as *Senecio* and *Elaeagnus*. All or any of these roses will make a pretty and thorny hedge, and the hybrid of R. *hugonis*, raised in the Botanical Gardens in Cambridge, R. 'Cantabrigiensis', is often used for this purpose. It is similar but with more of a cream than buttercup shade to its flower and very prickly stems. R. *omeiensis pteracantha* (correctly R. *sericea pteracantha*) is a slightly coarser shrub with white four-petalled flowers and pear-shaped fruits. It is grown chiefly for its translucent red thorns which are a winter feature of the young growth.

The third group of early-flowering roses is native to Britain, the Scotch or burnet rose, which Gerard called the Pimpinell rose and which is now listed under either R. *pimpinellifolia* or R. *spinosissima*. These roses flourish in the poorest soil and spread by underground stolons or suckers. They are very thorny, extremely thrifty, and make dense impenetrable hedges or thickets about 90cm/36in high. In wild

Above '*Frühlingsgold*', with pimpinellifolia *breeding, has rich golden-yellow flowers which pale to primrose after the buds open. Flowering before the real 'flush' of June roses, 'Frühlingsgold' coincides with blue ceanothus and tall mauve-flowered abutilons.*

Right *The brilliant crimson flowers of the species* Rosa moyesii *are followed by flagon-shaped orange-red hips. This tall vigorous shrub rose with ferny leaves and sharp thorns is suitable for growing next to shrubs (here with variegated dogwood) in mixed borders.*

conditions they have relatively small double white or pink flowers, while the fruits are reddish-black and not distinctive. But it is a tough little plant which needs to be grown either in a wilderness area of the garden or in a position where the roots can be contained by deep stones or a gravel path. In any normal planting scheme, mixed with herbaceous perennials or woody shrubs, it can become a pest or even a menace. It is very pretty when in flower but the leaves are an uninteresting deep green, not as ferny and delicate as those of the *hugonis* type. A form of it, R. *p. altaica* which comes from the Altai Mountains in Siberia, has much larger cream flowers, about 5cm/2in across, and grows to as much as 1.8m/6ft. I have planted it under old apple trees, through the branches of which the rampant species roses, RR. *filipes*, *mulliganii* and *rubus* scramble and cascade. The *pimpinellifolia* ramps underneath and solves any painful weeding problem as well as extending the period of flowering. It flowers first, followed by a short gap before *rubus* gets into its stride; R. *filipes* begins to flower in midsummer and R. *mulliganii* starts a couple of weeks later and continues into high summer.

In the same group as these roses are the splendid Frühlings hybrids which have been bred in Germany by Kordes crossing the Hybrid Tea 'Joanna Hill' with, in two cases, *R. pimpinellifolia altaica*, to produce 'Frühlingsanfang' and 'Frühlingsduft', and in the third with *R. p.* 'Hispida' to produce the best of all these early roses, 'Frühlingsgold'. There are many other Frühlings crosses but none so worthwhile as these three. 'Frühlingsgold' was first grown in 1937 and has grace of habit, fragrance, and freedom of flowering. The yellow nearly single flowers have coloured stamens and gradually fade to white. 'Frühlingsduft' has much more double flowers, slightly tinged with pink, and deep apricot in the centre when they first open. It grows in a less arching and graceful way than the 'Frühlingsgold' but it adds an extra colour tone to the pure yellow. 'Frühlingsanfang' has darker green leaves and single flat pure cream flowers. I have found it a slow starter, unlike the other two, but this spring, after five years, it is covered with blossom. It also carries maroon-red heps in the autumn. (Incidentally, nearly all single roses make better and more numerous fruits than double varieties, and it is even sometimes said that double roses do not fruit at all. This however is just a myth that has grown up over the years.)

All the Frühlings hybrids are particularly suitable for growing in half shade or almost woodland conditions. Their pale colours blend with greens and greys, while the mauve and pink shades of rose invariably look better in full sun. These roses are shrubs in the real sense of having value as arching-shaped bushes with attractive foliage and are not grown for their flower alone. They do all flower again at the end of the season but with much less profusion.

R. 'Maigold' is another modern *pimpinellifolia* hybrid. It is a rather lax but strong-growing shrub with large semi-double and bronze-yellow flowers, with a pink tinge at the edges. The leaves are glossy and it is at its best grown in a clump, perhaps three bushes together, in a wild area of the garden. Although not an easy rose to tie in and control, it is worth the effort for its early flowering period and for the vividness of its colouring.

A species rose which flowers early in a sheltered site is the delicate fern-leaved *R. webbiana* from central Asia. The small grey-green leaves and practically thornless stems are only rivalled for colour and decorativeness by those of the European species *R. glauca*. The flowers of both species are pink and single and the fruits are bottle-shaped. *R. glauca* does not flower until early summer but its leaves turn an almost glaucous purple in full sun and make an admirable blend of colour with pink-flowering shrubs and perennials (described on page 140). It grows tall rather than wide, and makes a good foil in shape and foliage colour to the weeping pear, *Pyrus salicifolia* 'Pendula', or a large bushy semi-evergreen such as the red-flowering *Buddleja colvilei*, which has blue-grey leaves. All of the small grey-leaved shrubs associate well with this rose. Those with yellow flowers can have the flower-buds removed.

An excellent European species which flowers before the main groups of roses is the apple rose, *R. villosa* (syn. *R. pomifera*). Whether the one we have here is *R.* 'Wolley-Dod' (syn. *R.* 'Duplex'), or the species, I am not certain. It makes a bush about 2-2.4m/7-8ft high and wide and has bluishgreen downy leaves which are very elegant and useful in a shrub border. The flowers are 5cm/2in across, clear pink from dark carmine-coloured buds. The fruits are appleshaped and crimson. I am thinking of using it instead of the Gallica hybrid, 'Complicata', as although this latter cannot be matched for beauty of flower, the foliage each season becomes disfigured by black spot.

R. moyesii is from western China and was only introduced to Europe at the beginning of this century. It is a very fine rose but needs plenty of space, sending out 3.6m/12ft or more long branches from the base, in a sort of fan shape. This stiff habit makes it difficult to place but its attractive leaves, divided into numerous leaflets, and its crimson flowers which later turn into flagon-shaped fruits, all combine in sheer quality to make it a desirable and striking shrub. It seldom flowers before June here, nor do its hybrids and seedlings. The one exception is *R.* 'Nevada' which by that time is already covered with its huge saucers of semi-double cream flowers, tinged with pink. This is a *moyesii* hybrid with a Hybrid Tea rose and makes a 2.4m/8ft bush, with arching brown stems and pale green foliage. It is one of the best and most floriferous of all modern shrub roses but is not entirely free from black spot in susceptible areas. In midsummer it has a second flowering and continues to produce some isolated blooms right through the autumn. It should be grown freestanding as a specimen in grass to get the full value of its arched branches, literally loaded to the ground with flowers; in a large area it can be most effective planted in groups. *R. moyesii* and its seedling *R.* 'Highdownensis' actually flower a little later but have been included here because of the earlier flowering of this hybrid. *R.* 'Highdownensis' has similar leaves to the parent plant but with a greyer tinge and an almost glaucous underside. The flowers are a paler and softer pink but it has the same bright flagon-shaped heps.

Another species rose which should come in with the summer-flowering roses, but creeps in here with the aid of its offspring, is *R. helenae*. The seedling is *R.* 'Lykkefund'. The parent is a vigorous rambling rose with trusses of creamy-white very fragrant flowers which are followed by drooping bunches of small orange fruits. The leaves are grey-green, unlike those of the seedling which are small and glossy. *R. helenae* has a determined and rather stiff habit, easiest to control if given an old tree into which to climb. *R.* 'Lykkefund' is much more ready to make a wide rambling mound, which is how I grow it here. The small, almost single flowers, held in clusters, are cream with a salmon-pink shade and with yellow stamens, followed by small orange heps held in upright bunches. Although suitable for a rough corner, it has more open growth than some of the later-flowering species, which will suppress all weeds.

Summer-flowering roses

There is no doubt that if you want totally trouble-free roses, grown as well-shaped bushes, the Rugosas can offer a great many advantages. Its general habit in its wild forms has already been mentioned (page 137) but it has also many useful and decorative hybrids. It was largely ignored during the first hundred years after its arrival from Japan, partly because in the age of Victorian lavishness its more thrifty qualities were not thought an advantage, but also because all attention was focused on the advances being made in rose-breeding during the nineteenth century. Some hybridizing was done in France and in America and in particular Rugosa 'Hollandica', a cross with *R.* 'Manettii', was used as an understock for other roses. In an old garden this may well be

the only Rugosa present; we found it here and it is not unattractive, with prickly pale green leaves somewhat resembling its species parents, bearing single dark pink flowers continuously through the summer, and making an upright rather leggy bush about 2.4m/8ft high. It was so often referred to as the Rugosa rose that the real thing tended to be overlooked. Now, with the increasing difficulties of maintaining large gardens, this splendid race has come into its own because it is easy to look after on a grand scale but is also useful in the smaller garden. Among the species there are bushes for every size of garden; among the hybrids this range has extended to types of roses which bear little resemblance to the parent Rugosa, but which have inherited many of its desirable and hardy properties.

For reasons of space I can give here only a list of the few I find most beautiful and useful for various purposes. The most frequently grown is Rugosa 'Blanche Double de Coubert', which has snow-white semi-double flowers and makes a splendid specimen, group or hedge. Its sport 'Souvenir de Philémon Cochet', which is now hard to find, is in some ways superior, as its flowers are more double and densely packed, with a very faint flush of pink in the bud, but difficult, I find, to propagate from either hard or soft wood cuttings. 'Roseraie de l'Hay' makes a 1.8m/6ft bush, with long well-shaped buds and rich wine-crimson flowers, most fragrant of all. 'Belle Poitevine' makes a more leggy and upright bush, has large semi-double flat flowers of very bright purplish-pink with cream stamens and is very similar to 'Souvenir de Christophe Cochet'. Rugosa 'Parfum de l'Haÿ', which has a more untidy habit and dark purple flowers, looks best in thickets in the wild rather than in a flower bed.

The pure white single flowers of *R. rugosa alba* are borne all summer and overlap with the large orange-red heps, and the pale pink single flowers of 'Fru Dagmar Hastrup' are followed by freely borne crimson heps. This latter bush is smaller than the rest and makes a neat well-covered shrub, suitable for growing in a mixed border with other shrubs and herbaceous perennials or for a hedge.

All these Rugosa roses have excessively prickly stems and make screens which are too painful for children or even dogs to penetrate. They are all hybrid forms of the rather variable *R. rugosa* itself and inherit the main characteristics of wrinkled foliage, scented and perpetual flowers, and excellent showy fruits. There are innumerable and very variable hybrids which do not immediately convey the Rugosa look, but which have useful qualities for specific purposes. *R.* 'Max Graf', for instance, is a hybrid with the trailing semi-evergreen *R. wichuraiana*, and makes dense growth for weed-

The climbing rose 'Leverkusen', a Kordes hybrid raised in 1954, is trained over a brick archway which frames a garden view.

This pale yellow rose, which has a second period of flowering each season, can also be planted as a free-standing shrub.

smothering in a small area, whereas *R. wichuraiana* itself would grow too large. It has glossy leaves and single bright pink flowers with white centres and yellow stamens. Although it flowers only once, it is so satisfactory for growing under the other shrub roses or shrubs and has such an attractive almost prostrate habit, that it earns its place in a garden

of every size. It looks very graceful arching out over stone and can be used in a planting scheme for a flat bed with grey-leaved plants or others with pink flowers.

R. 'Paulii' and its pink form R. 'Paulii Rosea', is a Rugosa cross with the native European *R. arvensis*, and has inherited the trailing habit of the latter with the thorniness and flower of the Rugosa. Unfortunately, it also only flowers once and bears no fruit, but the single white clove-scented flowers with yellow stamens completely cover the bush. It is one of the densest growers, impenetrable to weeds or pests and very useful groundcover for banks. It actually prefers to trail downwards and is ideal for a terraced garden or for growing over the edge of a pond, with its long 3.6m/12ft branches hanging down to the water. *R.* 'Paulii Rosea' is a less vigorous pink variety with silky petals and yellow stamens. More suitable for the smaller garden, it also likes to trail downwards. Here it has been grown so that it can tumble through the leaves of the purple-leaved smoke bush. The white form would be too strong a grower for mixing in this way, but it can be planted under other high shrubs as long as it has somewhere to send its trailing shoots. I first grew it hanging over a terrace in our cottage garden intertwined with *Clematis chrysocoma sericea*, which has an almost similar four-petalled flower. In fact, one of the later small-flowering species *Clematis*, such as the Viticella types, could be planted to grow through it.

R. 'Sarah van Fleet' is a Rugosa and Hybrid Tea hybrid and has upright thorny stems and clustered large pink double flowers. The hybrid 'Conrad F. Meyer' is similar but with more fragrant and more silvery-pink flowers. Both these shrubs are best at the back of a border, and are not as disease-resistant as the Rugosa parent.

R. 'Lady Curzon' is another Rugosa hybrid (with *R. macrantha*) which makes a tangled mound of branches about 2.4m/8ft high and wide. *R. macrantha* itself, although not a species but of uncertain parentage, is one of the most useful spreading shrubs for wild areas. It has pale pink rather flat scented flowers, while those of *R.* 'Lady Curzon' are smaller and darker pink and the stems and leaves have a distinct Rugosa look.

R. 'Raubritter' is another *macrantha* hybrid which should make a sprawling shrub, with strange small pink semi-double flowers which are folded in the same way as the flowers of the Bourbon rose, 'Madame Pierre Oger', but are about one-third the size. For some reason this plant, which grows in such a useful mound-like fashion, does not thrive here and I can hardly recognize the miserable specimens I have.

No garden can be without a member of the Sweet Brier family. The aromatic foliage gives delicious fragrance when touched or ruffled in the wind. *R. rubiginosa* is a European native and has been cultivated for many centuries. Under the name of eglantine, or *R. eglanteria*, it and its scent were constantly alluded to in poetry. It had a more practical use for perfuming the air to hide unpleasant odours.

The most popular of this group today are those known as the Penzance Hybrids, which were the result of breeding the sweet brier in the 1890s with some of the Bourbons and the Hybrid Perpetuals. Much of the natural fragrance of the leaf has been lost in the process. One of the smallest and most

Above *A prostrate growing rose with very prickly arching stems and single flowers of clear pink, Rosa 'Paulii Rosea' will trail downwards over a wall. On a bank, it can be used as a weed-suppressing ground-cover. The white form, R. 'Paulii', is more vigorous and will send out branches 6m/20ft long.*

Right *The popular Hybrid Musk 'Penelope' makes a vigorous fan-shaped bush up to 1.8m/6ft high, bearing coppery-pink buds and scented semi-double flowers of creamy apricot that fade before they wilt. It will flower again if carefully dead-headed, its later summer flowering coming when pale colours are scarce in the garden.*

useful of the original forms which is still obtainable is 'Manning's Blush', which does not grow beyond 1.5-1.8m/5-6ft, and has small double white flowers opening from a pink bud. Of the hybrids I grow only 'Amy Robsart', which has clear glossy foliage and deep pink flowers, followed by scarlet heps. It will grow to 3m/10ft. If planning a new garden I would seriously consider making a mixed hedge of these hybrids.

The modern 'Fritz Nobis' is of *eglanteria* descent, crossed with the excellent Hybrid Tea, 'Joanna Hill', and has huge double flowers of pale pink, scented like cloves, and attractive dark leaves. In the Ravens' garden it makes an elegant avenue, 2.7-3m/9-10ft high; it combines graceful habits with desirable flowers, but flowers later than the eglantines.

Another species, *R. forrestiana*, has arching stems and rose-crimson scented flowers, and small green leaves. It is a medium-sized shrub and looks its best with contrasting foliage of grey or dull purple. The new growth is a translucent red and its flowers are surrounded by strange leafy bracts

'Penelope' has copper-pink buds, glossy bronze young leaves and a vigorous habit and is deservedly one of the most popular. Rather similar, and a suitable companion in a bed, is 'Cornelia', with clearer pink flowers. 'Moonlight' has buds tinted slightly yellow, but opens to clear white; it is a more straggling bush, but suitable for tying into fences or allowing to grow through other shrubs. The flowers are smaller, but held in huge trusses, and the stems are dark red. 'Pax' is an even larger version, with semi-double scented flowers. 'Prosperity' and 'Pink Prosperity' are white and pink respectively and more like 'Penelope' in habit. 'Buff Beauty' is the most beautiful of all and the most free flowering; its cream-bronze flower heads and bronze young foliage growth provide a contrast to green- or grey-leaved neighbouring plants. All these Hybrid Musks carry small fruits in trusses, similar to those of the rampant species roses which flower a little later.

A modern rose with climbing and shrub-like forms is R. 'Aloha'. It starts flowering early and continues to produce its heavy heads of richly scented warm pink double flowers until late autumn. The flowers endure wet weather quite happily and are useful for picking. It will make a 2m/7ft bush and readily sends up strong new shoots from the base.

Although, as mentioned earlier, the Gallica rose is one of the ancestors of all our garden hybrids, the descendants often bear little resemblance to the original form. Those earliest cultivated are typified by old favourites such as *Rosa gallica officinalis*, *R. g.* 'Versicolor' (Rosa Mundi, the striped sport of *R. g. officinalis*) and 'Tuscany', which have all been grown for centuries. In spite of the tendency to disease, both black spot and mildew, I continued to grow the fragrant Rosa Mundi, which was first recorded in 1581. *R. g. officinalis* is the Apothecary's Rose, so called from its medicinal properties. It was cultivated at Provins near Paris, hence the common name Rose of Provins. The dried petals are used for conserves. The purple-crimson flowers are semi-double, while the sport has deep pink petals splashed and striped with white. It makes a delightful small hedge about 1.2m/4ft high, but because of its susceptibility to disease, might be better in a mixed border where its ugly appearance in late summer would be less noticeable.

'Charles de Mills', with flat cupped double flowers of dark maroon, and 'Tuscany Superb' both contribute a rare colour in roses. They were bred in France in the nineteenth century.

R. 'Complicata' is of Gallica descent and can grow up to 3m/10ft into a neighbouring tree or shrub. It makes beautiful arching sprays of clear pink flowers with a white centre and yellow stamens. It looks effective among grey leaves and

which also hold the bright red fruits that it carries well into the autumn. This is a most desirable shrub, recently imported (1918) from China, and is excellent next to an old European species such as *R. villosa* with its soft grey foliage. Both are appropriate for the mixed border, giving light shade and having a compact regular form.

Longer-flowering roses

The Hybrid Musk roses are of doubtful Musk rose descent, but they are extremely valuable garden shrubs for their branching fan-like habit and huge trusses of flowers which are carried in mid-June in England, and, if carefully dead-headed, again in two months' time. If you, like the majority of rose-growers, enjoy pruning and shaping your bushes, this group can give you as much satisfaction as the bedding rose, besides being much thriftier and healthier. Hard pruning does encourage new shoots right from the base, and these young growths generally have beautiful colouring. They have an excellent shape for combining with lower-growing herbaceous perennials. *Paeonia officinalis* and some of the species peonies look attractive with them. Herbaceous geraniums can be grown in massed groups under these roses to make a trouble-free weedless bed. Spring bulbs also have a chance to thrive, as the base of the roses remains open to the air and light. Hybrid Musks mix and tie in well between cordon apples, and can also be grown as a hedge. The flowers vary in colour from pure white, as in 'Pax', to some bright pinks and to the cream-bronze colour of 'Buff Beauty', but in many cases they fade to white before they wilt.

against a bush of contrasting shape such as the sea buck-thorn, *Hippophae rhamnoides*, which has very upright growth. The leaves of the rose are pretty, very light green and smooth, but unfortunately tend to get severely marked with black spot blemishes. *R.* 'Dupontii' also has Gallica ancestry but seems entirely healthy. It makes a large rather lax shrub, more compact than 'Complicata' and has 7.5cm/3in wide single flowers, which open pale pink around golden stamens but fade to white. It is a useful and ornamental bush for a wide border.

R. 'Constance Spry' is a modern shrub rose with Gallica blood, this time with a Floribunda as the second parent. It makes a wide bush with large heavy very double pink fragrant flowers. The young shoots have a coppery tinge. Support of some kind is necessary as the flower heads are so heavy that they can even break the stems, and the best method is to encourage the long sprays to twine among other plants. By growing it between the old cordoned apples I have – by chance more than by intention – given it the ideal support. It can be grown as a pillar rose, or with a framework to hold up the heads, but the untidy woody base needs to be concealed with vigorous perennials or low-growing shrubs.

The last and rather improbable descendant of the Gallicas which is grown at Hadspen is 'Scarlet Fire', a huge arching shrub profusely covered in June with scarlet saucer-like flowers 7.5cm/3in across. They are velvet in texture and lightened by yellow stamens. This is a spectacular plant for growing into a large shrub such as the purple-leaved hazel, as it needs the support of tall plants. It also looks attractive with grey leaves and a foreground planting of rounded evergreen bushes. The grey-leaved *Senecio* 'Sunshine' or *S. monroi* make an excellent contrast and hide the untidy leggy base of the rose. The colouring of the flower is so vivid that it needs a concealed corner as it should be met with unexpectedly, and not be part of the immediately visible garden scene.

The Alba roses start to flower early. The white double form *R.* 'Alba Maxima', sometimes known as the Jacobite rose, has beautiful grey-green leaves and a drooping regular habit. It needs to be blended into a white or grey border and not mixed with strident colours. *R.* 'Céleste' has larger leaves and delicate pale pink flowers, and is perhaps the most ex-quisite of all shrub roses. It can be underplanted with the fresh green leaves of *Geranium endressii* or the velvety ones of *G. renardii*. Recently I have used the feathery *Dicentra* 'Bountiful' around its base. 'Great Maiden's Blush' has pink flushed petals which gradually fade to white. The white 'Alba Semi-plena', the Rose of York, has always been the symbol of secrecy, although this may apply to any white rose. Alice Coats also points out that, dried white rose means 'Death preferable to loss of innocence'. All the Albas are worth growing and have an old-fashioned fragrance which clings around the bushes.

By early summer practically all the old shrub roses are in full flower. The Damask rose, *R.* 'Ispahan', makes an upright bush of no particular merit in shape but with the freely borne warm pink, almost lilac, flowers growing in great clusters along the stems. Grown for their flowers rather than for their shape as a specimen plant, Damask roses are best planted as an avenue or in a mass to give flower and scent. They would be ideal intermingled with rounded shapes of grey or green leaves and firmly underplanted with plain green hostas.

For beauty of flower and excitement of petal shape and formation, the Centifolias, the Bourbons and the Hybrid Perpetuals are hard to beat. When these qualities were combined, for the last two groups at least, with some measure of recurrent flowering, it is easy to see why other and simpler roses were pushed into obscurity. Very few of the most popular roses of the nineteenth century are grown today. 'Frau Karl Druschki' was not produced until 1901 and clearly has some Tea rose ancestry. It is still popular but unfortunately scentless. 'Reine des Violettes' is another Hybrid Perpetual with arching grey-green leaves and flowers more like the Gallicas. I am astonished to find how many of the old favourites from these groups I have banished in the last few years, and replaced with modern shrub roses which also have some of the characteristic muddled and complicated petals but are not so prone to disease. If you have the time to spray, however, roses such as 'Madame Pierre Oger', 'Louise Odier', 'Madame Isaac Pereire' and 'Madame Ernst Calvat' are all beautiful shrubs, with rich colours and scents.

There are two species which I always think of together but which really have nothing in common, except that, one being *R. macrophylla* and the other *R. roxburghii* (syn. *microphylla*) they have an obvious name association. *R. macrophylla* is a shrub characterized by large leaves composed of many leaflets and capable of growing to a height of 4.5m/15ft and nearly as much across. It is practically thornless and has large pink single flowers and pear-shaped fruits. The variety 'Doncasteri', with darker pink flowers, grows less vigorously

An old variety, the rose 'Rambling Rector', with fragrant white semi-double clustered flowers, and Rosa *'Complicata' line the bridge at Lower Brook House. Another 'Rambling Rector' grows over the little summerhouse to close in the view. This vigorous rose can be used to grow through trees or to cover unsightly buildings.*

and is more suitable for the small garden. *R. microphylla* or *roxburghii* on the other hand has flaking bark of cinnamon colour, with tomato-shaped orange fruits covered with spines. This rose is attractive in every season – the flowers are a pretty shell-pink – and grows to about 1.2m/4ft so is a useful shrub for the border.

The modern shrub rose *R.* 'Cerise Bouquet' is a *multibracteata* hybrid with 'Crimson Glory'. The species *R. multibracteata* is a wide arching bush with very prickly stems and fern-like foliage. *R.* 'Cerise Bouquet' has greyer leaves with grey-green bracts and larger fragrant flowers of intense vivid crimson with yellow stamens. It sends up long arching shoots with erect pinky-red flower-stalks. Like its two parents it flowers almost all summer. It needs space but if you have room for only one shrub rose this might be the best choice; it is also completely disease-free. Prune it from the base to avoid spoiling the arching shape. Plant it at the back of a border so that its branches rise above massed foreground planting, or use it in a group. It is less suitable for planting as a single specimen as it needs the support of other shrubs.

The Himalayan musk rose, *R. brunonii*, is a rampant rather tender climber, preferring to scramble through trees than climb against a sheltered wall. Its variety 'La Mortola', raised in the Hanbury gardens near Ventimiglia, is hardier, with pale grey leaves and richly fragrant clusters of white flowers. It can be encouraged to grow like a Banksian rose against a warm wall or into a light-foliaged tree.

The hardier *R. soulieana* is a Chinese species with a rather similar stiff habit. It has attractive small grey leaves and clusters of white flowers opening from creamy buds and followed by small orange fruits. It will grow to 4.5m/15ft but its stiff branches with sharp and painful prickles need to be kept away from paths and gateways.

Vigorous large-scale roses

The last group covers some of the larger species from Asia which bear their flowers in clusters and are suitable only if given space to develop naturally. Most of them flower in midsummer just after bush roses. Even in a small garden it may be possible to find room for at least one in an old fruit tree, or in an old conifer which has passed its prime. Many of them twist and turn on themselves and will completely cover an old tree trunk or a bank, or just make a huge humped mound. They are all very fragrant and bear clusters of small fruits through the winter. Space allowing, it is possible to have a long period of flowering each summer by using these roses. I will briefly describe my favourites among them.

R. rubus flowers towards the end of June in Britain, with clusters of white single flowers with orange anthers, followed by dark red fruits. 'Bobbie James' is similar but more tender and less rampant, and perhaps more useful where space is limited. I lost it after five years and have since discovered that this was due to honey fungus and not to lack of hardiness. It has a creamy shade to its flowers.

The famous *R. filipes* comes next, with pale green leaves and apple-scented flowers falling in curtains of blossom out of a tree. Its 'Kiftsgate' form has larger leaves and grows more strongly, and the young leaves are slightly coloured. It covers more space than the type but is a coarser plant, although magnificent when in flower and, later, in fruit. A variety with pink flowers but in other respects exactly similar to *filipes* is probably its seedling. Mine was grown from cuttings from the Margery Fish garden, just before Mrs Fish died, and I am not sure what it should be called, but it might be *R. f.* 'Gardener's Pink'. It has very healthy foliage and a more compact habit, better for the smaller garden. It flowers for many weeks. No underplanting is needed if these roses are planted over old stumps or banks, or just allowed to make a large sprawling bush, as they are semi-evergreen and will not permit invasive weeds to germinate.

R. 'Rambling Rector' has masses of small semi-double fragrant flowers in midsummer, coinciding with the 'Kiftsgate' form of *R. filipes*. *R.* 'Wedding Day' is one I have never grown, but from chance not prejudice. It will climb into a large tree and has good glossy green foliage and small white flowers, opening from creamy buds and hanging in clusters. *R. mulliganii* has dark shoots, long leaves, banana-scented trusses of flowers, which open here in mid-July, and scarlet fruits. It is a better and hardier plant than *R. sinowilsonii*, which was brought back by Ernest Wilson from western China a few years earlier, in 1904. (The great discoverer was known as 'Chinese Wilson', hence this plant's name.) *R. wichuraiana*, which is the parent of so many rambling roses, has almost evergreen shiny leaves and enjoys being used to carpet the ground; it will do an equally good job covering tree stumps or broken walls. Its stems will root as it travels along the ground. It is the latest flowerer and has 5cm/2in wide white flowers which are very fragrant, followed by small red fruits.

Roses grow in profusion at Lower Brook House, framing the doors and windows. Seen through foreground planting of the rambling rose 'Albertine' with glossy leaves and blush pink flower petals, Rose 'Tuscany Superb' has dark velvety flowers, climbing 'New Dawn' is shell-pink, and 'Alchymist' above the door has yellowy gold scented flowers.

Chapter 10

TENDER WALL SHRUBS
AND PLANTS

Y CONCENTRATING ON my ideal method of gardening – minimum work for maximum ground coverage and effect – I have taken it for granted that simplification and rationalization are the primary aims. The emphasis has been on plants that are grown more for their contribution to the whole scheme and plan of the garden, for their relationship to each other and for the simplicity of their upkeep, than for individual merit and excitement.

In this chapter, however, I describe the more tender plants, those which are risky to grow and need a little more care, especially when they are young, but are so rewarding that the element of doubt about failure or success is amply repaid by the extra pleasure and beauty if all goes well. When we choose tender plants for use in sheltered situations, it is wise to mix them with those other plants which, although they will survive without protection and without reflected heat from a wall, will do much better if given this extra help. This means that even if we have an unexpectedly hard winter, the borders will not be entirely bare.

Our garden, even though quite high up (135m/440ft), is extremely sheltered, with good frost-drainage, and contains inner areas with micro-climates ideal for attempting plants which are mainly recommended for seaside or Cornish gardens. The soil varies between about 6 and 7 pH, which makes it possible to grow almost anything except those plants which demand very acid conditions. At the same time, these inner rooms of the garden have inherent dangers for plants accustomed to climatic extremes. Any warm spell can tempt a dormant plant into starting growth, but when the weather changes again these young shoots will be cut

back, and if the plant is young it may lack the reserves necessary to make another attempt. A plant such as *Lobelia cardinalis*, for instance, which is normally frozen into the moist ground in its natural habitat in North America, there emerges unscathed in the spring, but here a false start, followed by a cold spell, may well be fatal for it. Similarly a long mild autumn in Britain will lead to much fresh sappy growth in the wood of shrubs and trees, without the hot sun needed to ripen and harden it, and this will be cut back later.

In the British Isles it is seldom the severity of the ground frost which leads to losses, but rather the variability of the climate. Of course there are many plants from hot countries which will not survive frost, or only very few degrees, and in their case it is essential to take cuttings or seed. Young plants rooted in heat, and kept in heated conditions during the first winter or two before being sent out by the nurserymen, are much more vulnerable to severe weather than those which are given little early protection. If possible get plants grown in areas where greenhouse protection is not necessary.

Abelia There are two members of this genus which are outstanding: one, *A. floribunda*, for its vivid rose-red flowers, which it carries in late spring in tubular clusters like a honeysuckle (it belongs to the same *Caprifoliaceae* family), and the other, *A. × grandiflora*, for its glossy purple leaves and rosy-pink tubular flowers which are borne over a long period in late summer. *A. floribunda* is an evergreen shrub from Mexico which, being very tender, needs a hot wall, while *A. × grandiflora* is semi-evergreen and, although it can be damaged in hard winters, generally makes a graceful and arching shrub in a mixed border, very often hanging on to some of its attractive leaves through the winter. I have planted it as part of a group with *Nandina domestica*, the tender magenta-flowered *Geranium palmatum* and *Leptospermum scoparium* 'Red Damask', in front of *Trachelospermum jasminoides* which clings to the hot wall behind. All of these are rather chancy plants, and may well disappear in the next hard winter. I intend to add *Abelia floribunda* to the wall as it

Of all the magnificent blue-flowered evergreen ceanothus, the most reliably hardy and floriferous is Ceanothus 'Cascade', *a hybrid of* C. thyrsiflorus. *In early summer the graceful arching branches are* laden with powder-blue flower panicles. It makes a perfect companion for Choisya ternata *with white scented flowers and glossy foliage and a scrambling* Clematis montana.

153

will contribute its May flowers to this group of predominantly later bloomers.

Abutilon We have successfully grown the white and pale mauve forms of *A. vitifolium*, which have vine-like leaves and large saucer-like mallow flowers in June. The shoots are grey-green and downy but inclined to discolour, so that the whole shrub – which quickly shoots up when given a sheltered wall – seldom looks perfect by the time the flowers are out. Two years ago I saw *A. ochsenii* at the Chelsea Physic Garden and was just about to order this neater plant, with smaller dark violet flowers, when I came across the new hybrid of it and *A. vitifolium* called *A. × suntense*. This is a magnificent shrub, with even darker flowers, very freely borne, which come at least four weeks earlier. Indeed it goes on flowering for so long that it is overtaken by the parent *A. vitifolium*. I see that Christopher Lloyd recommends cutting it back hard after flowering; it also needs careful staking, as it grows so fast that it tends to outgrow its root stability.

Acca *A. sellowiana*, formerly *Feijoa sellowiana*, is grown for fruit in warm climates, and in cooler climates for its ornamental foliage. Its leaves are very attractive, grey-green and shiny with felted undersides, and it will grow into a 6 m/20 ft tree in favoured gardens. The flowers are exotic, with crimson and white petals and long red stamens, but unfortunately they are not freely borne and rather hidden in the axils.

Azara The best of this evergreen genus, of which *A. dentata* (syn. *A. serrata*) and *A. lanceolata* were mentioned on page 80, is undoubtedly *A. microphylla*, with its variegated form *A. m.* 'Variegata'. This very graceful small tree superficially resembles box, but in early summer has the most fragrant vanilla-scented flowers, carried rather inconspicuously in the axils of the leaves. The variegated form is much slower and more tender, but one of the best variegated bushes for winter effect. I saw it first at Rowallane in Northern Ireland, but find it very slow here; it grows only a few inches a year and needs constant protection against the encroachment of other plants.

Berberidopsis The coral plant from Chile, *B. corallina*, needs an acid soil and deep shade. It has heart-shaped spiny leaves, attractively glaucous when young, and, if you are lucky, it will carry pendulous single crimson flowers towards the end of the summer. I have given it a bed of more or less acid soil to start its life and hope that our neutral soil will prove acceptable as its roots go down deeper.

Buddleja The hardier buddlejas have been mentioned earlier (see page 80) but not *B. crispa* (syn. *B. paniculata*). This is almost evergreen, with densely white felted leaves and stems, and in late summer pale pink to lilac flowers with an

Above *The evergreen* Abutilon vitifolium *benefits from a warm background wall. The white-flowered form A.v. Album is an attractively shaped pyramidal shrub with mallow-like flowers in early summer. There are several garden cultivars with deeper or paler mauve petals than the type, in particular A. × suntense.*

Right *The deeply toothed leaves and stems of* Buddleja crispa *are covered with silvery felt. The fragrant flowers, carried in panicles during summer, are lilac with an orange throat. This buddleja needs some wall protection in most temperate areas and should be pruned back in spring.*

orange throat. Sometimes, if it is tied back and allowed to get really hot and baked in the summer, it produces the odd flower almost right through the winter. The delicate colouring is the kind I most admire, reminding me of *Phlomis italica* and of *Dorycnium hirsutum* which, although having quite different habits, have the same pink-coloured flower combined with the very hairy greyish-white leaf. Here I have grown the *Buddleja* against a wall, from which it tends to flop forwards, and allowed a bright pink *Cistus* to flower all summer through the lower branches, much as it does through the lower part of *Rosa glauca* in another part of the garden.

Campsis Heat in early summer will encourage a mass of flowers in all varieties in this genus (often called *Bignonia* or *Tecoma*). The leaves themselves, carried very densely, are attractive and pinnate and the plant climbs by aerial shoots. The orange-scarlet flowers are tubular and borne in huge drooping panicles. There are not many pink-flowered plants which look well with this orange-scarlet shade, so it needs careful placing. Do not plant shrubs in front of it lest they cast some shade. The Asiatic species *C. grandiflora* is more exciting than the North American one *C. radicans*, which has been grown in Britain since the seventeenth century.

Carpenteria This is a monotypic evergreen genus. *C. californica*, its solitary representative, has green leaves which seldom come through the winter without some browning. It adequately compensates, however, by bearing in early summer the most beautiful saucer-like white flowers with golden anthers. It dislikes cold wind and needs a hot sunny position.

Cassinia I know only two members of this genus, *C. fulvida* and *C. leptophylla*, and much prefer the latter, which has thin grey leaves and clusters of white flowers in a flat corymb in later summer. The golden-leaved *C. fulvida* has foliage similar to an *Erica* and is also rather like *Olearia solanderi* 'Aurea' in leaf and flower. *C. leptophylla* looks attractive over a bed of the southern African *Osteospermum jucundum*. It has rather an untidy habit of growth, but since it makes little shade associates well with lower-growing flowering plants. Like the *Olearia* it comes from New Zealand and needs plenty of sun and good drainage.

Ceanothus The evergreen forms of *Ceanothus*, or Californian lilac as it is called in its native habitat, are all tender wall-loving shrubs, and some will thrive only in warmer or coastal regions. The *delilianus* hybrids, which are deciduous and have been bred from the New Jersey *C. americanus* and the Mexican *C. azureus*, are not only so much hardier that they can be given places in open mixed borders, but also less exacting in another way, in that they are happy to be pruned back into shape in the spring. Although they are useful summer-flowering shrubs, they do not have the quality of the more exciting spring ceanothus.

The earliest of these evergreens to have been brought to Europe is *C. thyrsiflorus*, which arrived in 1837 and is still one of the most popular. It makes a large bush or small tree, and has pale blue panicles of flowers in spring. Together with its prostrate form, *C. t. repens*, it is among the hardiest. Two with darker flowers are *C. papillosus* and *C. rigidus*, and the hybrid of these two, *C. 'Delight'*, is fairly tough and has long panicles of rich blue flowers in the spring. One of the best for colour and leaf interest is *C. impressus*, with its small deeply

Buddleja farreri is rather similar but flowers earlier and makes more of an upright bush. It is tender, being more or less evergreen, with large felted leaves and flowers of a darker pink. It needs to be grown with some protection, particularly from the east, as the flower buds are formed early in the year. There is a good example of it at Kew.

B. colvilei also merits a wall position, if you can spare the space, and will flower better with extra heat. However, it flowers quite freely here in a mixed shrub border, without wall protection. Its variety *B. colvilei* 'Kewensis' has darker red flowers.

B. auriculata has very fragrant creamy-white tubular flowers, which are borne all through the winter. I used to grow a *Clematis viticella* through it, which associated perfectly with the grey-green leaves, but it became too strong for the *Buddleja*.

Callistemon The Australian bottle brushes need a hot site with plenty of shelter. I have only two here, the hardiest, *C. salignus*, has pale yellow flowers (or, more precisely, coloured stamens), while *C. rigidus* has vivid bright red ones. All the callistemons have very narrow healthy-looking leaves.

veined dark green leaves and bright blue flowers which, though they come earlier than many in this spring-flowering group, seem to be unaffected by frost damage to the buds formed during the winter. It needs considerable space and a sheltered sunny wall; if it must be pruned, it should be cut back only after flowering. C. 'Cascade' is rather hardier and makes an elegant weeping shrub, most effective against a wall, but sufficiently hardy to make a free-standing specimen in a warm garden.

C. arboreus, and in particular its form raised in Cornwall, C. a. 'Trewithen Blue', makes a tree-like shrub and flowers in early summer with long panicles of deep blue, but it is decidedly more tender, with its larger softer green leaves, than the other evergreen species.

Cestrum This is a genus from Central and South America which has always had a reputation for tenderness, so much so that it is generally grown in glasshouses. However, if you are prepared, as in the case of shrubs such as *Indigofera*, to have it cut right back to the base in a cold winter, it seems to shoot again in the early spring, and then flowers a little later.

C. elegans (syn. C. purpureum) and C. 'Newellii', which may be its seedling, have ovate to lanceolate downy leaves, which are evergreen in ideal conditions. The flowers of both are pendulous and tubular and reddish-purple in colour. The time of flowering will depend on the winter conditions, but here they are usually out at the same time as the rambling white *Clematis chrysocoma sericea*, and mingle well with it. C. 'Newellii' has flowers of a brighter crimson and looks attractive with purple foliage such as that of *Cotinus coggygria* 'Foliis Purpureis', and the variagated leaves of *Weigela* 'Florida Variegata'. These plants would benefit from being tied back against a hot wall, but I prefer them twining among other shrubs. They are both easy to strike from cuttings of young soft wood.

C. parqui, which comes from Chile, has thin green leaves tapered at both ends. It can be cut down to the ground by severe weather or shoot from along the stems like ordinary deciduous shrubs. It makes a thicket-like bush, and bears lime-yellow tubular flowers, which are small but carried very freely and held erect. The fragrance is strongest in the evening and has a musky tang. In a hot summer the flowers are even more numerous, but for a shorter period in midsummer, followed by more prolific flowering later in the season. In a normal year it flowers continuously from mid- to late summer but never covers the bush to make such a dazzling spectacle as it has this year (1975). As with the other two mentioned, cuttings are easily struck and grow quickly into bushes 1.5m/5ft high by as much across.

Cleyera C. fortunei is a pleasant evergreen shrub which has very distinctive variegated shiny leathery leaves with a creamy-pink margin. The flowers are tiny and carried in the axils of the leaves in early autumn. It reminds one of another remarkable evergreen shrub, formerly included in the *Drimys* genus, *Pseudowintera colorata*, which has almost translucent young growth with similar pink tinges to the edges of the leaves. Both are really woodland plants which, while not appreciating full sun, still need a site with excellent frost-drainage. I have put the *Cleyera* against a warm wall but at the same time protected it from fierce sun by other shrubs and plants.

Corokia C. macrocarpa is more interesting than the hardier C. cotoneaster (page 84) and is a valuable foliage shrub for a sheltered spot where it can reach a height of up to 4.5-6m/15-20ft. It has oval grey leaves, with the undersurface intensely silver-white and felted. It comes from the Chatham Islands and except for the difference in leaf shape is very similar to *Olearia traversii*, which comes from the same islands. The leaves of the *Corokia* taper at both ends while those of the *Olearia*, a more erect and less bushy plant, broaden below the middle.

Correa This is another genus from the Southern Hemisphere, this time from Australia and Tasmania. The only species we grow here is C. backhouseana which has attractive small ovate leaves, with the undersides downy and buff-coloured. The stems are also covered with a buff bloom, and as the leaves are carried erect the stems and undersides are very conspicuous. In the spring it has charming drooping greenish-white flowers and is suitable for growing in a group of shrubs with a sheltered wall as a background. It seems happy and vigorous in our almost neutral soil, and apparently is not easily damaged by frosts.

Dendromecon This is a genus of only two species, closely related to the *Romneya* but having entire leaves and yellow poppy flowers. It too comes from California, is tender and cannot survive any frost. The leaves of D. rigidum are very glaucous, long and thin, and the fragrant flowers are carried on long stalks.

Desfontainea This is a monotypic genus. D. spinosa, which comes from the Andes, has shiny holly-like leaves, with pendent tubular flowers which are scarlet with inner yellow lobes. It is a woodland plant, not suitable for cold districts and happiest in moist soil, well below a neutral pH, and with good drainage, similar to that required by rhododendrons.

Eccremocarpus The only member of this evergreen twining genus that will survive winters in Britain is E. scaber, and even this may succumb to hard frosts. Since it is very easily

Illicium anisatum (syn. I. religiosum) *has fleshy aromatic evergreen leaves and bears creamy-yellow flowers in late* spring. *It is more lime-tolerant than shrubs such as azaleas and rhododendrons but prefers a deep acid loam.*

for its value as a foliage plant as it has long ribbed and toothed corrugated leaves almost greyish-green in colour. Flowering is most likely after a hot summer and the flowers are carried in a tight corymb, resembling those of a *Photinia*. It makes an excellent wall shrub here, suitable as a host plant for clematis, *Eccremocarpus*, or any twiner that is not too vigorous. The Texensis clematis hybrids look particularly attractive with their inverted red or pink pitcher-shaped flowers clambering through the strong leathery leaves of the loquat.

Eupatorium This is a large genus of plants which come from both America and Asia. The shrubby species *E. ligustrinum* (syn. *E. micranthum*) from Mexico is evergreen, its charming shiny elliptic leaves having slightly toothed edges. It will grow up to 2.4m/8ft against a warm wall, or make a rounded bush about 1.2m/4ft if grown among other shrubs. Very small white to pink flowers, gathered in a dense flat head on erect stalks, appear at the end of the summer. When the bush is in flower it resembles a distinguished *Gypsophila paniculata*, but as a foliage plant it is valuable for all seasons.

Fabiana This is another monotypic genus, but its single species, *F. imbricata*, has several different forms. The type itself is a heath-like shrub which although tender will grow to about 90-120cm/36-48ft, with a spread of nearly 1.8m/6ft. It has plumes of white tubular flowers in early summer, while *F. i. violacea* has pale mauve flowers and is more prostrate in habit. The latter is also hardier.

Hoheria This is a New Zealand genus, all the members of which flower in mid- or late summer. The two deciduous species, *H. glabrata* and *H. lyallii*, are very free flowerers, with *glabrata* probably flowering a week or so earlier than *lyallii*. The white flowers are mallow-like, with smooth juvenile foliage which becomes hairy and felty as the season proceeds. The evergreen *H. sexstylosa* and the *H. populnea* forms have smooth leaves, which in *H. sexstylosa* are quite narrow and sharply toothed, and they are attractive at every season. My favourite is *H. sexstylosa* which, although not so floriferous as the two deciduous species, has an excellent upright and tidy habit, with flowers of a creamy tinge. It is the hardiest of the evergreen species. The whole genus is easily cultivated and propagated and, even if unsuitable for cold exposed uplands, will thrive if given some protection. In one part of the garden I grow it surrounded by a sea of *Eryngium giganteum* and in another by *Atriplex halimus*, the smooth grey leaves of which make a strong contrast to the fresh green of the *Hoheria*.

Illicium This is a small evergreen genus containing both American and Asiatic species, all of which have intensely aromatic foliage. *I. anisatum* (syn. *I. religiosum*) makes quite

grown from seed, it may be as well to take seed each year, although I find here that it will germinate quite happily if left to its own devices. We never seem to be without a few of these quickgrowing plants, and I leave them to clamber at will among other more robust shrubs. The flowers are tubular, scarlet outside with a yellow inner part, while the pale green leaves are bi-pinnate and carry tendrils which coil round any possible support.

Eriobotrya *E. japonica*, the Japanese loquat, is the only one of these excellent foliage trees which it is possible to grow in Britain. In southern Europe the pear-shaped fruit ripens and is edible, but in temperate climates even the fragrant yellowish-white flowers are seldom borne. I grow the tree entirely

a large bush, with rather thick leathery leaves. The flowers are pale greenish-yellow, about 2.5cm/1in in diameter. This species from Japan is the hardiest and also the most free-flowering, but although it is obviously healthy here it makes slow progress.

Indigofera This is an attractive genus, not grown as frequently as it deserves; besides having fresh green pinnate leaves, it generally flowers from about midsummer into the autumn. The flowers are pea-shaped and carried in the axils of the leaves. All the species need full sun and respond to hot weather by quickly forming new growth and new flowering panicles. The only one I have here is *I. heterantha* (syn. *I. gerardiana*) with rosy-purple flowers. A severe winter will affect its growth but it can reach 1.8m/6ft in a season if conditions are to its liking.

Itea Unfortunately we have found only one species of this attractive evergreen shrub, *I. ilicifolia* from central China, sufficiently hardy for this garden. However I have seen *I. yunnanensis* making a striking display in a coastal district. *I. ilicifolia* has lax holly-like foliage and long fragrant racemes of greenish-yellow flowers in midsummer, while *I. yunnanensis* has less spiny leaves and whiter flowers. The catkins of both maintain their colour and fragrance over a long period. Both will grow free-standing in full sun, but prefer to have a wall to provide reflected heat and shelter. One of the best examples of *I. ilicifolia* is to be seen at Rowallane in Northern Ireland.

Jovellana This genus is sometimes included in the calceolarias and to the non-botanist the flower is very similar. The only reliably hardy species is *J. violacea* from Chile, which makes a small shrub, sometimes retaining its leaves and sometimes appearing completely deciduous. The flowers are pale violet with purple markings, and the leaves are small and attractive, with deep lobes and toothed edges.

Leptospermum This is another genus of shrubs, closely allied to the myrtles, which come from Australia, Tasmania and New Zealand. The most commonly seen are forms of the tea tree of New Zealand, which in warm gardens, or if grown against a wall, will reach a considerable height. This is *L. scoparium*, which was introduced as long ago as 1772 but for many years was considered suitable only for greenhouses. The leaves are very small, linear to oblong in shape, and filled with fragrant oil glands which give a pleasant scent

when crushed or touched. The type itself has a white flower, but there are several good forms with carmine-red flowers, such as *L. s.* 'Nichollsii', which also has bronze foliage, and *L. s.* 'Red Damask', on which the flowers are double. Given a warm border, these two thrive here and make a pleasant association with grey-leaved plants or those with large soft green leaves. They need an acid or neutral soil, good drainage and plenty of sun. *LL. cunninghamii, grandiflorum* and *lanigerum* all have silvery leaves and also seem hardier than many of the *scoparium* forms.

Lonicera Leaving aside the shrubby loniceras, some of which have been briefly mentioned on page 89, the more ordinary climbing honeysuckles of the *L. japonica* type, and the various *periclymenum* types, there are various hybrids of the American trumpet honeysuckle, *L. sempervirens*, which look splendid in full sun on a warm wall, but are less suitable for semi-shade conditions.

L. × brownii, the scarlet trumpet honeysuckle, is semi-evergreen, with long glaucous downy leaves and whorls of orange-scarlet flowers in spring and again in late summer. It is not so vigorous as some of the species which need a tree or thickets into which to clamber and so fits well into a mixture of tender sun-loving plants. It looks best in full sun since its exotic colouring would be unsuitable in a woodland site.

L. etrusca, which also prefers full sun, bears fragrant large cream to yellow flowers in midsummer. It too is semi-evergreen. I have grown it through a *Photinia davidiana* (syn. *Stranvaesia davidiana*), and also intertwined with a *Clematis* 'Marie Boisselot,' both of which will flower at the same time as the honeysuckle, while neither is too overpowering for the host plant.

Lupinus There is a small shrubby member of this genus, *L. chamissonis*, with silvery lupin-like leaves and attractive pale blue flowers, which looks well in any sunny border. It is not very vigorous and is best against a warm wall, near grey-leaved plants or those with bronze foliage. Originally from California, it is closely related to *L. albifrons*; in fact, if I had not been told mine was *L. chamissonis* I would not know the difference. It will grow to about 1.2m/4ft but may need some protection during its early years.

Mahonia The large shrubby and the creeping groundcover mahonias are included in Chapter 4, but there are some species from the south-west states of America with even more attractive blue-green or glaucous leaves, and which, although tender, are well worth growing.

M. swaseyi and *M. fremontii*, both of which need full sun, have spiny small pinnate leaflets, while a form of *M. fremontii, M. trifoliolata glauca*, has even more remarkable foliage.

Itea ilicifolia is an evergreen shrub which may reach as high as 4m/12ft in a sheltered site in sun or half-shade. The holly-like leaves are glossy green. The racemes of greenish-yellow catkin-like flowers, with narrow petals, are carried in mid- and late summer.

The clusters of pale yellow flowers, borne in the spring, are followed by red or black berries.

Melianthus M. *major* is a sub-shrub which in the past has been treated as a greenhouse plant or used for summer bedding. It was originally introduced from southern Africa in 1688, but has since been found in India. The long pinnate leaves are handsomely toothed and very glaucous, giving a sub-tropical effect. It is frequently cut down by winter frosts, but shoots again from the base, often at some distance from the original plant. In warm gardens it can grow to as much as 3m/10ft, but here it has never attained more than half that, and has never flowered. I have seen it in flower in Cornwall, with long spikes of browny-crimson, not in themselves beautiful but certainly exotic. The flowers are produced in the spring, so there is little chance of having them in an inland garden where there can be, and usually are, late frosts.

Michelia This is a genus of rather tender evergreen or semi-evergreen small trees or shrubs closely related to the magnolias. I have seen them flowering satisfactorily in Cornwall and in a garden in Italy. Among those hardy enough for Great Britain is M. *doltsopa*, which has beautiful magnolia-like long leathery leaves and fragrant creamy-green flowers borne in the axils of the leaves.

Muehlenbeckia This is a creeping or twining genus from New Zealand with dark interlacing stems and small roundish leaves. M. *axillaris*, of which there is a good example in the Chelsea Physic Garden, can make a groundcover about 30cm/12in high, while M. *complexa* makes a tangled twining mass and so, although not evergreen, is useful for growing over tree stumps. Neither species has flowers of interest.

Myrtus The two forms of the ordinary European myrtle, M. *communis* and M.*c. tarentina*, both need a sheltered spot if they are going to thrive and flower.

M. *apiculata* (now *Luma apiculata* and formerly included in the genus *Eugenia*) has cinnamon-coloured bark, which peels when the tree is still quite young to reveal a cream inner surface. Once a specimen is established, it seems quite hardy and grows quickly here into a branching shrub or small tree. It is most effective if not allowed to branch at the base, as the single stem best displays the true beauty of the bark. The white flowers are quite freely produced in late summer.

M. *bullata* (correctly *Lophomyrtus bullata*), from New Zealand, has bullate or puckered leaves which are rather more rounded than those of most myrtles and have a coppery tinge. Although quite hardy here it possibly might not survive many degrees of frost.

M. *lechleriana* is a very beautiful and early free-flowering species from Chile, the flowers scenting the whole garden in May. I saw it for the first time at Trewithen in Cornwall, where it made a sturdy hedge. I managed to buy a plant from the small nursery there, and it has come through the winter with no ill effects from our colder climate. Probably it should be given a very sheltered spot. The young leaves are copper coloured and at their best when the white flowers are in bloom. M. *ugni*, also native to Chile, is even more tender.

Nandina N. *domestica*, the solitary member of a monotypic genus, is known in Asia as the sacred bamboo and planted near dwellings for protection against evil spirits. It is an elegant evergreen shrub, growing here to about 1.2m/4ft, with double pinnate leaves which are nearly always tinged with pink. It grows, like a bamboo, with unbranched stems, and the leaves are very large, but so divided and delicate that they do not appear so unless carefully examined. We have it in a warm sheltered border, with some shade provided from overhead but with good frost drainage, and with a wall a few feet behind. It has large terminal panicles of small white flowers, which are most freely borne in a sunny position. I have found that sunlight encourages growth, but it is reputed to like shade. N.d. 'Nana Purpurea' is more compact and has a purple blush to its winter foliage.

Olearia The large and hardier olearias are described in Chapter 6. Only those which require a background wall or a very warm climate are included here. They all like a certain amount of moisture but flower best in full sun. A very wet spring followed by hot sun and drought seem to suit them perfectly, presumably approximating to the conditions of their native habitat.

O. *albida* (syn. O. *nitida*) has large undulating pale green leaves with a white undersurface and makes a conical-shaped large shrub. It is best grown against a warm wall. O. *capillaris*, on the other hand, is an erect open small shrub very closely resembling the small-leaved *Corokia*. It flowers freely with clusters of typical daisy flowers in early summer. O. *paniculata* (syn. O. *forsteri*) has bright green undulating leaves, superficially very similar to those of a *Pittosporum*, and in late autumn carries axillary flowers, which are fragrant but not showy. Like O. *albida*, if it is not in a coastal garden it prefers a sheltered wall.

O. *chathamica* and O. 'Henry Travers' from the Chatham

The South African silver-leaved Melianthus major is one of the most handsome sun-loving sub-shrubs which is proving hardy in all but the coldest districts in the British Isles. The deeply toothed pinnate leaves can be 45cm/18in long. In favoured sites the browny-crimson flowers look exotic in spring. It also makes a superb plant for an ornamental container and can be accompanied by flowering annuals.

Islands, are both very similar with long grey toothed leaves stiffly held, and exceptionally large purple daisy flowers with violet centres. The first named has marginally larger leaves and flowers earlier. They are unreliably hardy but cuttings are easily rooted, and they make attractive grey-leaved bushes.

O. phlogopappa (syn. *O. gunniana*) has much smaller grey toothed leaves and white or pink to mauve flowers. Like its various coloured forms, it is very free flowering, and in early summer the bushes are literally covered in daisy-heads. The hybrid *O. × scilloniensis* has smaller darker green leaves and white flowers, carried equally abundantly in spring. It is probably hardier, but suffers from exposure to cold wind, so in an inland garden needs a sheltered site.

O. traversii is rather frost-tender but one of the most ornamental of the olearias, with bright green leaves with silvery undersides and very rapid growth. For sheltered gardens it is one of the best evergreen foliage plants.

O. mollis, which may perhaps be a hybrid with *O. moschata* as one of the parent plants, has almost white-grey leaves and large corymbs of white daisy flowers in late spring. The leaves are slightly toothed, while those of *O. moschata* are entire and smaller but also of an intense white-grey. It is very slow growing and a cutting I took five years ago has yet to flower.

O. 'Zennorensis' can be grown in the shrub border in our garden and, therefore is described in Chapter 6.

Pittosporum *P. dallii* is probably the hardiest of this genus and suitable for quite cold inland gardens where the more tender species will not survive. It is a very elegant small shrub with very dark twigs and shoots which eventually grows to make a sprawling shape. Since the whole genus is regarded as tender, *P. dallii* is rarely grown, but there is no reason to put it in this category. Others have been mentioned on page 110 for their regular outlines and attractive foliage, but if you have a sheltered wall try *P. eugenioides* which has the most beautiful foliage of them all. The leaves are slightly undulating, 5-10cm/2-4in long, oval but tapering at both ends, and very glossy, with a prominent white leaf stalk and mid-rib. The twigs and bark are browny-red. The underside of the leaf is paler and not so interesting. The variegated form, *P. e.* 'Variegatum', is very similar except for a pronounced white margin to the edge of the leaf. I find them both perfectly hardy here, and among the most decorative of all evergreen shrubs. They also have a conical habit but make a much more open and lax bush than do the *tenuifolium* varieties.

P. tobira, which is very familiar to those who have seen it used as hedges in southern Europe, has the most fragrant flowers of the genus. Coming from China and Japan, it is drought-resistant, unlike those from New Zealand. It has bright green glossy leaves set in whorls, among which the scented flowers emerge in early summer. It is slow growing and susceptible to frost, but already flowers here while still only about 90cm/36in high. The variegated form is too tender to grow outside in the British Isles except in the warmest regions.

Punica The pomegranate, *P. granatum*, is a valuable foliage plant, and has exciting orange-red flowers as well. The fruit is seldom formed in temperate zones, so the plant is grown for ornamental purposes. The leaves are long, thin and glossy, with beautiful red young growth which turns orangey-red in the autumn. If grown in the open the whole bush can be damaged by sharp frosts, and unless planted against a south or south-west wall there will be little likelihood of it bearing flowers. The flowers are large and funnel-shaped, with crumpled petals, and the branches are so spiny that it should not be grown near a pathway.

There is a double-flowered white form, which however does not have the copper-coloured young growth, and a dwarf form, *P. granatum* 'Nana', which is hardier than the type.

Rhamnus The variegated form of *R. alaternus*, *R. a.* 'Argenteovariegata', does much better if treated as an evergreen in need of some wall protection. It is an excellent foliage plant for a tender border, giving colour and body among more important and perhaps rarer plants which may suffer damage in the winter. Its glossy leaves are marbled grey and have a cream margin. It comes from south-west Europe and has been grown in Britain since the seventeenth century – arriving just in time to be included in Parkinson (1629) – and in its hardier green form was one of the most popular of the various evergreens available at that time.

Rhaphiolepis I know only the species *R. umbellata* from Japan and the hybrid *R. × delacourii* which is a cross between it and the more tender Chinese species *R. indica*. I have never seen the latter, which is more suitable for the greenhouse or conservatory.

R. umbellata makes a dense evergreen rounded shrub, with very leathery leaves of an oval shape but tapering towards both ends. The white fragrant flowers, held erect in a terminal cluster, are quite large. A slow-growing shrub, it requires protection from other plants and likes a wall behind it but, as it will eventually reach about 2.4m/8ft in height and width, it should be planted with neighbours which can later be moved or dispensed with. I have put it in an evergreen corner with *Correa speciosa*, *Melianthus major* and *Viburnum*

Salvia involucrata, *a sub-shrub from Mexico, has cerise-crimson flower petals enclosed by pink bracts; its form S.i.'Bethellii' has longer flower spikes. The leaves* *are rich green with pinkish veining. It needs well-drained soil in full sun and, if mulched well in winter, will survive average low temperatures.*

deciduous shrub with neat dense growth, downy leaves and bright scarlet to magenta flowers. In a cold winter it can die back, and in the spring will benefit if clipped all over. It starts to flower early in summer and continues all season. The somewhat similar *S. neurepia* has more downy and less green leaves, and after a mild winter will have a long flowering period, but grows in a less compact way, and has paler scarlet flowers, slightly larger than those of *S. grahamii*. It is worth taking cuttings of both these each year.

S. guaranitica is a sub-shrub which can be cut back like an herbaceous plant, but it shoots early, with heart-shaped toothed green leaves, and bears dark blue flowers on 90cm/36in stalks from midsummer onwards. One of the best blue flowerers in the garden, it is definitely tender, although it has survived outside here now for many years. It came from South America as recently as 1925, while the typical *Salvia involucrata* came from Mexico in 1824. The best garden variety of the latter is *S. i.* 'Bethellii', which has large heart-shaped leaves about 10cm/4in long, with rounded teeth, and pink leaf stalks and ribs. The rosy-crimson flowers are surrounded by pale greenish-pink bracts. It was originally grown as *S. bethellii*, and in these days is more often seen than *S. involucrata* itself. Cuttings can easily be taken of all these salvias, which may be a wise precaution.

Senecio The invaluable *S.* 'Sunshine' and *S. monroi* are described in Chapter 4. Included here are the shrubby sun-lovers, often in nurserymen's catalogues simply called *Cineraria maritima*, with various forms of more or less lacy leaves, some whiter than others. Those of *S. bicolor cineraria* 'Ramparts' are very deeply cut, those of 'White Diamond' are less so but whiter. *S. leucostachys* (now *S. vera vera*) is much more feathery and grows less in the shape of a bush, but interweaves with the foliage of dull and darker shrubs.

S. rotundifolius (syn. *S. reinoldii*) is a truly magnificent large evergreen with thick rounded leathery leaves, shining green above and brown felted beneath. It has a reputation, like many of the plants from New Zealand, for doubtful hardiness except when near the sea, where there is little chance of hard frosts. It is remarkably resistant to salt-laden gales; at the Arnold-Forster garden at Zennor on the north coast of Cornwall I have seen splendid examples of this shrub, grown in the open, fully exposed, so that their beauty of form and foliage can be appreciated in a way that is impossible when they have to be protected by other plants. In time the shrub becomes nearly a tree and has beautiful trunks of the same fawn colour as the underneath of the leaf. So far, frost has left it unscathed here, perhaps because I have chosen positions where it is completely sheltered from cold east winds;

tinus 'Variegatum', among which I expect to have some casualties in a bad winter.

R. × *delacourii* has similar leaves but a less dense habit of growth and panicles of pink flowers. I do not have it against a wall but in full sun with plenty of protection from other plants, and at the top of a slope for frost-drainage.

Salvia Most of the hardy salvias are mentioned on page 75, but four more belong in this section. *S. grahamii* is a small but it has proved to be a favourite food of the hungry roe-deer when they come into the garden from the woods in the spring. Spraying with an animal deterrent seems to have solved this problem.

Smilax The evergreen climber S. *aspera*, which comes from southern Europe and North Africa, has odd zigzag prickly stems and very glossy green leaves, almost triangular in shape and with a prickly margin. It is more suitable for growing over a stump than formally against a wall, but it does tend to form rather a dense and prickly thicket.

Solanum These South American semi-evergreen climbers need a warm sunny position, although S. *crispum*, which has rather dull purple-blue flowers, is quite hardy and can be encouraged to clamber over other sturdy plants. It has an improved form, S. *c.* 'Glasnevin', with flowers of a brighter blue and a longer flowering season.

S. *jasminoides* 'Album' is much more tender, but can be a spectacular sight in late summer with its thin glossy green leaves liberally covered with clusters of bluish-white potato flowers with yellow stamens. Admittedly it can take up a great deal of room on scarce and precious wall space, and it is certainly not reliably frost hardy, especially when young. In fact in my old garden I lost mine during the very cold winter of 1962-3.

Sophora The deciduous Japanese pagoda tree, S. *japonica*, is the hardiest of all this genus, but the more attractive yellow-flowered species, S. *macrocarpa* and S. *tetraptera*, are evergreen and well worth growing. S. *macrocarpa* from Chile has pinnate leaves with numerous leaflets and very large flowers, with 10cm/4in hanging pods. The flowers are produced in late spring and carried in long bell-shaped yellow panicles in the axils of the leaves. The colour is rich and exotic. S. *tetraptera*, from New Zealand, is similar but carries fewer flowers in each cluster. Both can be grown as free-standing specimen trees or large shrubs in coastal gardens, but in most inland areas need the protection and heat of a south or south-west wall.

Trachelospermum This is an Asiatic genus, except for one species from the southern states of North America, and the two mentioned here are tender evergreen climbers of the self-clinging and twining type, whose extremely fragrant flowers, white with a creamy centre, are carried in midsummer. The species T. *asiaticum* (syn. T. *crocostemon*) has small oval glossy green leaves and grows neatly and tidily against a wall, making, like ivy, a sort of wall hanging or carpet. The slightly less hardy T. *jasminoides* has leaves twice as large, grows more untidily and needs initial encouragement to make it cling. It carries flowers in the axils as well as in ter-

minal panicles, while T. *asiaticum* has only terminal clusters. The leaves of both turn various shades of red and yellow in the winter. Once established they will cover considerable wall space. They flower in this garden mainly in July, but the flowering period varies a great deal depending on the site. Since they like full sun, care should be taken not to allow other plants or shrubs to grow up in front of them.

Viburnum There are several Asiatic viburnums which have very attractive evergreen leaves, and often fragrant white flowers as well. The rest of the genus have been described in Chapters 4, 6 and 7.

To take them alphabetically, V. *cinnamomifolium* makes a large and elegant bush, with glossier leaves than V. *davidii* and a more upright habit of growth, eventually reaching a height of 5.5m/18ft. The young growth is pink and translucent, and the stalks cinnamon-coloured. Together with the very different V. *harryanum*, it was brought back from China by Ernest Wilson in the early years of this century. The latter has neat almost round leaves, hairless and dark green, and flowers in late spring. Although it makes only a medium-sized rounded bush, it is one of the more unusual viburnums; no other has such a small leaf.

V. *japonicum* has large leathery almost puckered leaves of considerable beauty, and when it flowers has rounded trusses of great fragrance. It is resentful of exposure to cold spring winds, but is not listed as one of the more tender. Unfortunately in its second winter in our garden it was eaten by deer, and I have never replaced it.

V. *odoratissimum* has even larger glossy green leaves, as much as 20cm/8in long, which also colour vividly in winter, and caramel-coloured leaf-stalks. The flowers are carried after a hot summer in long conical panicles, but do not appear on young plants. A very sheltered site is necessary, and the example we have here though already about 1.2m/4ft high has not yet flowered after three years. I have seen one growing in a sheltered alley-way between greenhouses, and I have given ours a similar situation against a glass house.

Zenobia Z. *pulverulenta* is a most attractive semi-evergreen small shrub, which requires similar conditions to the andromedas and has the typical small white lily-of-the-valley flowers of that genus. It has a glaucous bloom in spring, which becomes less noticeable as the season advances. The flowers appear in midsummer. It comes from the eastern United States and was introduced to Britain in 1801. Here I grow it in a pot full of acid soil and give it some protection in winter, but it is surprising that it is not more often grown in coastal gardens. The best example I know, from which my plant was a cutting, is at Abbotsbury in Dorset.

SELECTED READING

Bean, W.J. *Trees and Shrubs Hardy in the British Isles* (vols 1-4) London (8th ed.), 1976 to 1988

Berrisford, Judith M. *Gardening on Lime* London, 1963

Chatto, Beth *The Damp Garden* London, 1982; rev. ed. 1986

Chatto, Beth *The Dry Garden* London, 1981

Clausen, Ruth Rogers and Ekstrom, Nicholas H. *Perennials for American Gardens* New York, 1989

Crane, Howard Camp *Gardening on Clay* London, 1963

Crowe, Sylvia *Garden Design* London, 1958 and 1981; New York, 1959

Fish, Margery *Gardening in the Shade* London, 1964 and 1983

Gorer, Richard *Living Tradition in the Garden* Newton Abbot, 1974

Harper, Pamela and McGourty, Frederick *Perennials, How to Select, Grow and Enjoy* Tucson, Arizona, 1985

Hellyer, Arthur *The Amateur Gardener* 4th rev.ed. London, 1972; Albuquerque, New Mexico, 1973

Hillier Nurseries *The Hillier Colour Dictionary of Trees and Shrubs* Newton Abbot, 1981

Jekyll, Gertrude *Colour Schemes for the Flower Garden* London, 1908; illust.ed. London and Boston, 1988

Jekyll, Gertrude *Wood and Garden* London, 1899

Keen, Mary *Garden Border Book* London, 1987

Fox, Robin Lane *Better Gardening* London, 1982; Boston, 1986

Lloyd, Christopher *The Mixed Border* London, 1957

Lloyd, Christopher *The Well-Chosen Garden* London and New York, 1984

Lloyd, Christopher *The Well-Tempered Garden* London, 1970; rev.ed. 1985; New York, 1985 and 1988

McGourty, Frederick *The Perennial Gardener* London and New York, 1989

Page, Russell *The Education of a Gardener* London, 1962; rev.ed. 1983; New York, 1985

Perry, Frances *Border Plants* London, 1957

Philip, Chris *The Plant Finder* London, 1987; rev. ed. 1989

Rice, Graham *Plants for Problem Places* London and Portland, Oregon, 1988

Robinson, William *The English Flower Garden* London (15th ed.), 1933

Roper, Lanning *Hardy Herbaceous Plants* London, 1961

Scott-James, Anne *The Best Plants for Your Garden* London, 1988

Thomas, Graham Stuart *Perennial Garden Plants* London, 1976; rev. ed. 1982

Verey, Rosemary *Classic Garden Design* London and Chicago, 1984

Verey, Rosemary *The Garden in Winter* London and New York, 1988

Wilder, Louise Beebe *My Garden* New York, 1932

INDEX